THE LETTERS
OF
CHARLES SORLEY

Charles H Sorley

THE LETTERS

OF

CHARLES SORLEY

WITH A CHAPTER OF BIOGRAPHY

CAMBRIDGE
AT THE UNIVERSITY PRESS
1919

CAMBRIDGE
UNIVERSITY PRESS

University Printing House, Cambridge CB2 8BS, United Kingdom

Cambridge University Press is part of the University of Cambridge.

It furthers the University's mission by disseminating knowledge in the pursuit of education, learning and research at the highest international levels of excellence.

www.cambridge.org
Information on this title: www.cambridge.org/9781107544642

First published 1919
First paperback edition 2015

A catalogue record for this publication is available from the British Library

ISBN 978-1-107-54464-2 Paperback

PREFACE

IN the spring of 1916, a few weeks after the publication of *Marlborough and Other Poems*, a letter about the book and its author reached me from an unknown correspondent. "I have had it a week," he wrote, "and it has haunted my thoughts. I have been affected with a sense of personal loss, as if he had been not a stranger but my dearest friend. But indeed his personality—the 'vivida vis animi'—shines so strongly out of every line, that I feel I have known him as one knows very few living people: and surely no one was ever better worth knowing." "I venture to beg you," the writer went on to say, "before it is too late, to give the world some fuller account of his brief life....Let us know him with his faults nothing extenuated, as his fellows knew him, with the 'rebel' side brought out—the boy who 'got not many good reports,' who was yet the same as he who stood 'with parted lips and outstretched hands.'"

Many other readers made the same request or urged the publication of a volume of *Letters from Germany and from the Army*, which had been printed privately and given to a few personal friends. At the time we were not persuaded. It seemed to us that enough had been done by publishing the poems and that, for the rest, so dear a memory need not be shared with the world.

Meanwhile, however, the poems have become more widely known; curiosity is expressed about their author; and critics form impressions of his personality. If the poems are to have a place, however small, in literature, this interest is only natural and may even be welcomed; but it ought to be well-informed, and the poems alone do not give all that is needed for a true judgment. This is one reason why the present volume is published now.

Anything in the way of a formal biography was not to be thought of. But in his familiar letters to his family and friends there is material enough, when taken along with the poems, for forming a picture of the writer. There is also in them a picture of the times, especially in Germany immediately before the war, and a criticism of life and literature, which may be found to have a value of their own.

He speaks for himself in these letters; and they have been selected so as to let him be seen as he truly was. Truth indeed—"the cry of all but the game of a few"—is hard to capture. Truth of fact needs truth of proportion also, and the two together do not always ensure truth of impression. A word written to a friend may express only the mood of the moment; set down in cold print, it appears as something permanent, irrevocable. To read it aright we must not read it alone, and we must have sympathy with the writer's mind. It is always easy to misinterpret; and the most that an editor can do is to provide the material for a correct interpretation.

This reflection has a bearing on the following letters. They extend over a period of less than four years; but in those years appreciation widened and early standards were modified. Further, in some of the letters there is a good deal of conscious exaggeration, of provocation to controversy, and even of sheer fooling. To have omitted these passages would have been to convey a defective impression of the writer's character. It would be still more misleading to take too seriously every humorous extravagance. Yet there is usually a serious meaning behind the most extreme statement. This holds of his recurring criticisms of the institutional side of religion; it holds also of what he says about the war.

The war moved him deeply, though it did not make him either bitter or unjust. He never hesitated as to his own duty in the matter, but he tried to understand the enemy's point of view as well as our own. Some of his efforts in this direction may have been mistaken; but his views were always honest and always his own. He looked on the world with clear eyes and the surface show did not deceive him. He saw that the spiritual values for which we fought could not be measured by material weapons or by material success. He saw too that the immediate effect of the war was to turn men's thoughts to material values and away from the things that are more excellent. And insight into these things underlies his occasional paradoxes.

For the most part the letters in this volume are not given in full. The following small alterations have also been made: dates have been found for many undated letters; a few names of private persons have been changed or have been replaced by a description or a blank; proper names have usually been substituted for nicknames; slight inaccuracies of quotation have been rectified; and eccentricities of spelling have not been retained. In other respects the letters are printed as they were written. A few explanations and references, where these seemed necessary, have been added in smaller type or in footnotes.

The material for the book has been selected in collaboration with my wife; and she has written the first or biographical chapter.

W. R. Sorley

Cambridge,
October, 1919

CONTENTS

CHAPTER III

SCHWERIN IN MECKLENBURG

CHAPTER IV

THE UNIVERSITY OF JENA

CHAPTER V

THE ARMY: IN TRAINING

CHAPTER VI

THE ARMY: AT THE FRONT

CHAPTER I

BIOGRAPHICAL

Charles Hamilton Sorley was born on 19th May 1895, in 44 Don Street, Old Aberdeen, and was the elder twin son of William Ritchie Sorley then professor of moral philosophy in Aberdeen University. On both sides he was of Lowland Scottish descent, his forbears having come, so far as is known, from the lands between the Tay and the Tweed. One grandfather, the Reverend William Sorley, was, as a young man, among the ministers of the Scottish Church who "came out" at the Disruption of 1843: his humour, force of character, and keenness of mind made him a man of mark in his day in the life of the border country. The other grandfather, who was known and loved by Charlie, is George Smith, C.I.E., of Edinburgh, a journalist and man of letters, much of whose life was spent in India.

A year after the boys' birth their family moved to Powis House, a fine Adams mansion standing high above the Old Town and looking over the dream-like crown of King's College Chapel to the rim of the North Sea. It is a fine windy place and a good natural nursery for children; the fields round the house were filled with beasts; and there is the exciting neighbourhood of a local railway station, which inspired the children to create imaginary kingdoms of their own "up the line," connected by a vast railway system one of whose rules was that all the officials must cross the line by the bridges only while passengers and others might do as they pleased.

At Powis the boys and their elder sister spent four happy years of normal and contented childhood, sometimes going with their beloved nurse to her home by the North Sea, where they learned to plant potatoes or ranged the windy moors in search of lapwings' eggs, coming home full of barn-door wisdom and the life-histories of every creature on the farm. In 1900, when the boys were five years old, they came to live in Cambridge, "where the low streams run," as their father was appointed Knightbridge professor in the University. Until then and for some years after they were taught at home by their mother. Their education, besides the acquisition of an angular handwriting, consisted chiefly in singing and marching games in French and English, history stories and fairy stories, reading aloud from the Bible and the *Pilgrim's Progress*, but especially in learning by heart any amount of poetry—ballads and passages of Shakespeare, Walter Scott, Macaulay, and Blake. With "Once more unto the breach, dear friends," Sir Patrick Spens, or "Tiger, tiger, burning bright" humming in their heads, it was vaguely disappointing to be set down to Mrs Hemans and Mary Howitt, when they first went to school. It is sad to have to record that well-meant efforts to interest them in natural history failed completely, nor did they ever have much inclination to collect stamps, play with bottles, or maim themselves with tools. But they were eager to write down whatever came into their heads or seemed to them worth remembering and telling about. When they were about ten, their sister had a hand in the inevitable school magazine for which she demanded contributions. Among other efforts Charlie gave her the following verses:

The Tempest

The tempest is coming,
  The sky is so dark,
The bee has stopped humming
  And down flies the lark.

The clouds are all uttering
  Strange words in the sky;
They are growling and muttering
  As if they would die.

Some forked lightning passes
  And lights up the place,
The plains and the grasses,
  A glorious space.

It is like a story
  The light in the sky:
A moment of glory
  And then it will die.

The rain is beginning,
  The sky is so dark,
The bird has stopped singing
  And down flies the lark.

The beginning of school-life, as a day-boy at the King's College Choir School, meant nothing but satisfaction and happy anticipation to Charlie. He always wanted to grow up, and this was a stage farther on. Each new experience—whether game or book or place or human being—came as an adventure to him; he always criticized eagerly, but he reaped and remembered only the best—nothing else counted. "No, I haven't got a pain, but I can't help it when I think of the future," was his explanation when he was found crying in bed, with his head far under the clothes, after he had heard that scarlet fever would separate him for six long weeks from his brother and from school. This was an almost solitary instance of complaint or depression. Whatever disappointments, apprehensions, or sense of failure he ever had afterwards, he kept to himself and met his adventures—especially the greatest of all, in August 1914—with a happy readiness and humour that gave a sense of comfort and assurance to those about him. "There goes Charlie, aye bright and brave," as our old Yorkshire hostess said at the end of a holiday. At the same time he had a quick understanding of what failure, or weakness, or limitation means for other people and his sympathy was active—even to the extent of leading him on one occasion to deplore his own easy lot: "I often feel terribly unworthy and untried in that life has given me no troubles or difficulties at home, such as alone strengthen a man," he wrote to a friend in 1915. Everybody and everything interested and had a claim on him. He knew that life had been good to him, and by instinct he gave back all he could.

In the choice of a public school Charlie was a pioneer, as his family had no previous experience or tradition to guide them. He settled the question for himself by gaining an open scholarship at Marlborough College, where he went in the autumn of 1908. The one draw-back to this adventure was the separation from his brother, who was sent to another school because even the wisest of men and schoolmasters do not seem able to refrain from making comparisons; and it is fairer for a boy to be on his own. The boys were alike in the deep love and understanding they had for each other;

but they had great independence of ideas and outlook and were—for twins—remarkably different in nature and appearance. They looked forward to being together at the University; and meanwhile there were the vacations which, in summer, were usually passed either at a Yorkshire inn where the moors approach the sea, or else in one or other of the home-places—Selkirk, Dunbar, or Aberdeen. Once we went with bicycles to France, and rode about the coast of Normandy and the land by the Seine. Charlie's comment (it was his first time abroad) was that it was the rottenest country he had ever seen and the finest holiday he had ever had. We had the habit besides of going to Marlborough every summer—not for Speech Day, which he did not recommend, but earlier when the fern and beeches are fresh in the forest "and the downs are dimpling green." Once, on an afternoon of gusty rain, when we had struggled up a steep red road and were about to cross over to the downs, we came suddenly on a field covered with great white flints. "What a lot of stones, how hopeless it looks!" said one of us. But Charlie, who generally responded readily, said not a word; he only stared at the field as if he saw something written on it[1], and then we all went on in silence.

He was thirteen when he entered Marlborough, and at first the school absorbed him completely. He had a period of hero-worship, very little qualified by criticism, for its demigods among the boys and masters; he abounded in the mysteries of its etiquette and slang; and he would pore by the hour over the blue School List, declaring that he knew by headmark most of the

[1] See *Marlborough and Other Poems*, 4th ed., p. 6 ('Stones').

boys in it—which may very well have been the case, as he had a quick memory for names and faces. His enthusiasms were always breaking forth in brilliant generalizations, which were as often cheerfully and relentlessly shelved. So at this time he was certain that there was nothing to beat the public school system: it was the finest in the world.

In January 1910 he and his friend Arthur Bethune-Baker entered one of the senior houses in college—C House, the oldest and most beautiful of the buildings, and the home of the Adderley Library, which became for him a great resource and pleasure. In the following November Arthur died at school after a few days' illness. At the time Charlie took it very quietly, but it is certain that what had been achieved in that short life became a part of him which was never forgotten or left behind.

His attitude towards the school, though essentially loyal and filial, developed in breadth and humour as he found freedom and read and thought for himself. On one of the family visits to Marlborough he asked, with subdued excitement, whether we had seen *The Widow in the Bye Street.* The reply was that we had but that it had been chained up from the youth of the flock. To which he answered, supremely scornful, "We take *The English Review* in the Sixth; and, any way, I've bought a copy and am lending it to people."

He took his share eagerly in the occupations and interests of the school, especially football and the O.T.C. But what he liked best was to tramp or run over the surrounding country. No one more enjoyed and valued his friends, or more willingly took and gave the best of company; yet when he went for long walks, or for runs in shorts and jersey, over the downs, he chose to be alone. In July 1911 he bicycled from Marlborough to Cambridge in a day; but that passion soon passed; and in the spring of 1912 he walked home, taking four days to the hundred miles or so of distance. It was stipulated that he should spend the nights in a bed under cover, and not under hedge or haystack as he proposed; but there are evidences that the condition—if there was one—was not taken too seriously by him. Part of his way lay along the bank of the canal by Hungerford; here he found the dead straight line of the tow-path so unbearable that, to keep going at all, he had to repeat aloud the thirty-fifth chapter of Isaiah, which he had just learned as an imposition. He gaily told his first teacher that it was the only portion of the Bible which he could remember by heart. In September 1913, in returning for what was to be his last term at school, he left the train at Fenny Stratford and had a three days' walk to Marlborough.

In December 1913 he gained a scholarship at University College, Oxford. In ordinary course he should have remained at Marlborough for the rest of the school-year—till July 1914. But, after some discussion with the Marlborough authorities, his father decided to give him a short time abroad as a break between the grooves of public school and university. There is no doubt that the home of his heart was the Marlborough country, and it cost him something to give up the last six months there. But he left himself in the hands of "the gods who made a pother o'er his head" and agreed to the plan with his usual happy reasonableness.

He had always kept up the habit of writing down what was in his mind. When he was a small boy this took the form of long screeds of heroic verse after the model of Scott or Macaulay. Later he indulged in stories of the "shocker" sort, which he used to tell in the dormitory at night as the works of one Jonathan Armstrong. As he grew older he became more and more reserved about his writing. Though his family knew vaguely of his connection with the school magazine, *The Marlburian*, he never saw fit to enlighten them on the subject. He would sometimes mention, however, in his letters, when he made a speech at the Debating Society, or read a paper to the Junior Literary Society—started largely on his account, when he was in the Lower Sixth, by one of the junior masters—or to the senior society, to which he was admitted on promotion to the Upper Sixth. Before he left for Germany he was asked to mark his articles and verses in *The Marlburian* for preservation among the family archives and because his mother had an idea that something was "going on." At the time he did not respond to this badgering; but some weeks later he sent a batch of verses to her. This he continued to do regularly, generally for a birthday, till June 1915 when the last lot—"Two Sonnets"—were sent from France. A few days before these arrived it was suggested to him that a slim volume should be published "for fun" and to relieve the tedium of the trenches. But he would have none of it: "for three years or the duration of the war, let be." He was equally discouraging when asked for a "gallery" letter for the private record of the daily life and doings of his battalion in France. His sense about such things was soldierly, and he disliked and dreaded anything in the way of advertisement or pose.

On the 20th January 1914 he went to Schwerin in Mecklenburg where, in the house of a lawyer and his wife, he found friends and conditions of the happiest and most entertaining kind. After he had got some hold of the language he moved at the end of April to Jena as a student of the University. There he realised a different world. Schwerin in 1914 was a place where people still said grace before meat, and meant it. In Jena they were more knowing. Both were amazingly young. Following their merciless family custom, his parents visited him in June and made with him a little tour in Thuringia, which closed with a week-end at Jena. On the Saturday night he took us through a square which was full of students—both men and women—seated at tables drinking and singing under flaring lights. Their singing was beautiful; their faces were mostly stupid and, in the case of recent duellists, revolting. The next day, as we went up towards a hill on the outskirts of the town, we met many of them again—both Korpsstudenten and Wandervögel—all in ridiculous clothes and with self-conscious looks which suggested pantomime. As we sat under the scanty shade of some scrubby trees, looking down on Jena shimmering in "the laden heat," and talking of its strange inhabitants, Charlie said dreamily, "I can't make out those fellows; they are always gassing about Goethe and Schiller; I think they're just hypocrites. But they must have some grit; for, though they do nothing at all their first two years but drink and fight and folly, yet they pull themselves together in their third year and manage to get through their exams." The following day, in the University, we were shown the fresco of the students of 1813 marching away to war.

In the end of July he reluctantly turned his steps homeward. He had planned a week's walking tour with a friend in the Moselle valley; thence he was to dash across Germany to Berlin, then join his brother at Schwerin and return with him a few days afterwards. The latter part of the programme was not carried out. On Sunday, 2nd August, he and his friend were arrested at Trier, and kept in separate cells for the rest of the day. One damning circumstance was that they had no hats, though Charlie gravely assured the officers who examined them that such was the habit of "the best people" in England. For him the long hours of that day were beguiled by the cheerful conversation of a soldier-prisoner in the next cell, who hailed him cautiously through a knot-hole in the wooden partition. They did their best for one another during the day, muttering through the hole in the wall, always mindful of the sentry in the corridor. The two tourists were released the same night, with permission and orders to leave the country. Charlie returned through Belgium, with little idea that he was making for the storm-centre. As his train passed through Liége, in the early afternoon of Monday, he roused himself from sleep to have a look at the place, but noticed nothing peculiar except the "Waterloo top-hats" of the soldiers. At Brussels and Antwerp, however, he had many difficulties till he succeeded in getting a passage on a vessel chartered by the British consul. He reached home on the evening of August 6th, still hatless and with little in his rücksack but a pair of sandals and a Jena beer-jug.

The next morning he applied to the University Board of Military Studies for a commission in the Army, and his application was transmitted to the War Office. Then followed a period of irksome delay during which he went to Oxford and made another application there. He was just about to enlist as a private, which he always said was the really heroic thing to do, when he saw his name in the *Gazette* as second lieutenant in the seventh battalion—the first of the new "service" battalions—of the Suffolk Regiment. That day he had orders to join a training camp at Churn on the Berkshire downs—"first cousins to the Wiltshire downs," as he called them. In the third week of September he joined his battalion at Shorncliffe above Folkestone. Again he was happy in his fate. He quickly realised the great history and traditions of the regiment—the "Old Dozen"—and made friends among the officers and men. We visited him for a week-end in February 1915 while he was doing a musketry course at Hythe, which he thoroughly enjoyed. During a stormy walk on The Leas he stopped suddenly and pointed across to Shorncliffe. "That's where Napoleon was beaten," he said, "at Sir John Moore's musketry school"; and then, sweeping his hand down seaward, "and that's where the Kaiser will be beaten—at Hythe."

In the end of May the battalion was sent to France at last. Charlie was then lieutenant; in August he was gazetted captain; in September there was a prospect of leave. His service during these months was chiefly in the trenches round Ploegsteert. After the opening of the Battle of Loos the battalion was moved south to take part in the offensive. In the night of 12th—13th October it took over front-line trenches in readiness for the morrow's attack; and he fell on the afternoon of the 13th, shot in the head by a sniper, as he led his company at the "hair-pin" trench near Hulluch.

CHAPTER II

MARLBOROUGH

The letters in this chapter belong to the latter half of the writer's school-days, when he was beginning to think for himself and to discover the books and causes which interested him. In the Michaelmas Term 1911 a Junior Literary Society was started, to which he read papers on Browning's Shorter Poems, and afterwards on a comparison of Burns and Scott, and on Blake. In the following term he made his maiden speech at the Debating Society, declining to "deplore the state of the Modern Drama," and later in the term he seconded a motion in favour of Home Rule before an unsympathetic house. "Next time," he wrote, "I think I shall be Conservative. It is more restful." And actually next time (4 March 1912) he was disapproving "the demands and methods of Modern Labour." The life of the school is most graphically represented in a series of letters descriptive of successive Field Days. Of these only one is given, and it shows that other things than tactics had then found a place in his mind. But an account of an O.T.C. "outing" to Devizes for an oral examination is given in full.

As all the letters in this chapter were written to his father and mother, the addresses are omitted.

10 *December* 1911

On Tuesday we went to Devizes Barracks for the oral examination. There were thirty of us and two brakes to take us—the drive is twelve miles. We started off at nine o'clock in uniform and O.T.C. greatcoats (most comfortable things), with Sergt-Major Barnes (wot we didn't tip) and not (thank Heaven!) the Major to look after us. I got a pew next Barnes and I was sure of an interesting drive. We left the Bath Road at Beckhampton, near Avebury, about six miles from Marlborough, and the scenery, commonplace up till then, opened out and we were soon rolling over the wildest expanse of down I have ever seen. Then Sergt-Major found his true form. Two miles past Beckhampton he asked us to look round. Was there any sign of human habitation in sight? The day was misty and we could see nothing but downs and the road. On this spot, he told us, on this road, about 100 years ago, the Royal Mail had been attacked by a gang of highwaymen. They had killed the driver, made a thorough search of the mail-sacks, taken all that was valuable, and proceeded in the direction of Beckhampton. On the way they met a labourer of Devizes who had been to Beckhampton for some work and—presumably successful on his errand—was returning intoxicated. Him they stunned at a blow and carried back to the wrecks of the mail-cart and the dead driver. They put a pistol in his hand, and laid him unconscious beside the driver's corpse: and they scattered over the country. Next day there were no letters in the West of England, and early goers along the Devizes road had brought information of a wrecked mail-coach, clear signs of a scuffle, stunned horses, a driver shot through the head, and his murderer beside him, stunned, with the fatal pistol. The evidence seemed conclusive—and the wretched labourer was condemned to death.

At this moment a tall and dark farmhouse loomed into sight: "That," said Sergt-Major, "was once Devizes gaol, on that small hillock to the right were once the gallows." Then he told us to look straight ahead. In front lay miles and miles, as it seemed, of downs: but right at the edge, on the very horizon, a statue of a man on a horse facing towards us. "It was on a misty December morning like this," he went on, "when the man was had out to be hung: the usual crowd of people had assembled: and he was led up to the gallows. He was already standing there looking westwards, when suddenly he lifted up his voice and said, 'I was born and have lived forty years in these parts, and have always seen the statue of one man on horseback; look westward, for to-day there are two.' The crowd, the priest, the sheriff and the hangman looked to the west: there were two men on horseback facing towards them: then the mist thickened and the sight was blotted out. A short consultation followed; they decided the thing was a delusion: the wretch was strung up on the gallows: the crowd dispersed, and his corpse was left hanging in the mist.

"Half an hour later from a direction due westward, a breathless horseman arrived through the mist—now thickened to a fog—at Devizes gaol. In his hand he held a reprieve for Walter Leader, labourer of Devizes, wrongfully convicted of the murder of Henry Castles, driver of the Royal Mail. There had been a quarrel in the gang of highwaymen, one had turned king's evidence at Bath, and a rider had been sent post-haste to Devizes over the downs with the news. They took the body down from the gallows, and under the only tree for two miles round by the side of the main road they buried him. And," concluded Sergt-Major, "look to your lefts, gentlemen, please; there is his grave." We looked to our left. There was one of those crooked trees —the kind we used to say were witches—by the side of the road breaking the monotony; underneath was a mound, six feet long, and a cross at the foot and the head.

Devizes Barracks are up on a hill, a mile this side of

Devizes. Apparently we were late, so we dismounted as quickly as possible. The examination is divided into three parts—Company Drill, Tactical and Musketry; for each part the full is 100, and to pass one must get at least 50 in each subject and at least 180 in the whole. We were divided into three groups so that all three portions could proceed simultaneously. My lot was Musketry first, of which I was glad as lack of time has forced me to take it practically unseen. There was a horrible dark little rabbit-hutch, concealing a gawky subaltern with a rifle. We went there one after another alone, and an air of sanctity hung over the whole proceeding. I entered with fear and trembling. Twenty questions I was asked, and I looked sheepish and I said "Don't know" to each one. Then he said, "Is there anything you do know?" and I gave him the two pieces of knowledge I had come armed with—the weight of a rifle and episodes in the life of a bullet from the time it leaves the breech till it hits its man. Then I saluted really smartly, and the gentleman gave me 60 out of a hundred. Company Drill came next which merely consisted in drilling a Company (as you might think) of most alarmingly smart regulars. For this I got 70 (every one got 70)—and then I went off to Tactical. Tactical was equally a farce. I was told to send out an advance-guard, lost my head, sent out a flank-guard, scored 70 per cent. I only pray that the examiners in the written exam. are as lenient.

I will not begin dilating on the lunch, first because it would show how greedy I am and secondly because I would never stop. I felt it doing me good all the way home.

After lunch we went over the barracks. I had thought that a Tommy's life was one of comparative hardship. But at Devizes I was disillusioned. They are fed twice as well as we are at Marlborough—bacon every morning for breakfast, and eggs for tea and as much butter and jam as they like. Sergeant B. was speechless with indignation at the pampering they now get. When he was in the same barracks 20 years ago, he had existed for weeks on end on "skilly," *i.e.*, dry bread soaked with tea, for these two meals: if they wanted even butter they had to buy it for themselves; and now butter, jam, bacon and eggs at the State's expense. Their dormitories are just like ours, only the beds fold up and they have to do their own dirty work. Though the mess-rooms smell of dirty plates, and the dormitories of beds that are never aired, they have two most magnificent billiard-rooms with full-sized tables, a well-filled library and reading-room, and a very up-to-date gymnasium, all, of course, since Sergt-Major's time and all very extravagant. They have two soccer grounds—one quite level—and a bathing place in the canal. So I should not think they have much to complain of.

They were very interesting to watch—those Wiltshire Tommies: not one of them, I should say, above 5 ft. 8 in height, and precious few of them less than 40 round the chest: short, thick, sturdy fellows, fair-haired for the most part and red-faced and, when once parade was over, very merry but very shy.

We left the barracks about 2.30: only three people had been ploughed—they must have been bad. It was a very fine afternoon and a good drive home. I only wish they had not been so kind in marking me so that I might have tried again in the summer. I quite envy the three failures.

17 *March* 1912

Confirmation was this morning. The service, whether thanks to the new master or the new bishop I do not know, has been considerably shortened, simplified and improved. The bishop spoke twice to us—once an address to the candidates, standing from the lesson-desk, and after the actual confirmation a regular sermon, and I do not know which was the best. He seems a wonderfully sympathetic person, and what he said could not have been more sensible or fitting.

Mrs A. who was down for her son's confirmation asked D. and myself out to lunch this afternoon. She had seen you lately, she told me, but made no allusions to you, as she usually does, either as a beauty or a buffoon. She was exceedingly nice and spirited, and from what she said, I am really afraid it will not be long before she has bought a hammer, smashed a window and marched victoriously to prison.

2 *June* 1912

This evening I read my paper on Blake to the Lit. Soc.—rather a hurried compilation guaranteed not to extend beyond twenty minutes. But, in the short time at my disposal to get up as much of Blake as is in Rossetti's Selections and write a paper on him, I have become very keen indeed upon him. I think some of his later poems that I have never come across before, such as *The Mental Traveller* and *Uriel* and the short extracts from the Prophetic Books in verse upon the building of Jerusalem in England, are quite the finest things I have ever read. I borrowed from one of the ushers that copy of selections that Kenneth has got in a luminous purple binding, and I think that Raleigh's introduction to it does nothing approaching justice to him. And I can't make out why all English anthologies only give pieces from his slightly ingle-neuk earlier works (if they give any extracts from Blake at all) instead of his much more powerful later ravings. I wish you would read that *Mental Traveller* (it is in Raleigh's selection) if you have not read it before, for it seems to me quite the finest allegory there could possibly be. But it needs to be read considerably more than once.

1 *July* 1912

I am late in writing this letter because I borrowed from one of the ushers a poem by Masefield called *The Everlasting Mercy*. It is about the length of *The Widow in the Bye Street*, and just as engrossing and gripping, but the story is much less pessimistic, and there are bits of poetry in it of a far finer kind than any in the *Widow*. The first seventy pages are just like *The Widow in the Bye Street*, with just as much power and grip and sordidness; but the last twenty pages are poetry of an entirely different range, containing outbursts which are about as lofty and about as pure poetry as anything I have ever read. The whole is a story of the reformation of a criminal, and is the only story on that hackneyed theme that I have ever found in the least convincing. And though there are obvious faults in the poem, it is wonderfully convincing, absorbing and inspiring; and if Boots, the Union, or your purse can rise to it, I advise you immediately to beg, borrow or buy *The Everlasting Mercy* by John Masefield. It takes about an hour to read—unless you find, as I did, that it is bed time already and that you are reading it for the fifth time on end, and that prep., letters and everything have been thrown to the wind.

The above letter is the first of many discussing and replying to criticisms upon Mr Masefield's poems, which at that time absorbed him. The other letters are omitted, as his enthusiasm is fully expressed in the paper on pp. 24 ff.

7 *July* 1912

On Thursday afternoon a party from the Mission at Tottenham came down to Marlborough and I was one of those who—being not engaged in cricket—had to take them round. We showed them over College, took them up to the field, gave them tea at the Master's, and played croquet or bowls with them from 2.30—6.30. Some were quite respectable—almost mistakable for gentlemen till they opened their mouths—others were about as poor as they could be. Some were completely mummified and dazed, as if being led about in another world, but most were exceptionally lively and interesting—and oh! their intelligence! I took a couple of them up to the Museum, and they turned out to be disappointed Darwins. The amount I learned from them was simply stupendous. John (now try and think who John is) simply isn't in it. They had twenty thousand humorous stories about the doings of toads and bugs; there wasn't a shell for which they couldn't give the Latin name. They were simply brimful of information and delighted to find someone to whom they could impart it. Others were earnest devotees of the Mission and told me with joy the amount of the collections for the last—how many ?—years. And one was "very fond of pretty poetry." And one was very anxious to study "you young lads." And one had a sister in the service of the Duke of Marlborough, whom he fondly believed reigned over this part of the world. And a few—poor fellows—in clothes as old as themselves, would not talk a word, but they ate heartily and, I think, enjoyed themselves. But one and all considered that everything at Marlborough was of the best and finest and that Marlborough was a name and a place second only to Heaven; and after all that is the perfect state of mind. The day was mercifully fine, and they were undoubtedly very grateful, and I do not think they regretted the loss of a day's pay and—in many cases, I think—the price of a new and startling suit of "hand-me-downs."

14 *July* 1912

The Field Day was on Thursday at Clifton and was a huge success. We had only Blundell's on our side, and had Clifton, Cheltenham and a host of little pinchbeck public schools against us. Our main object, though I didn't study the scheme very thoroughly, was to attack the Clifton Suspension Bridge from the west by drawing the enemy away up north. We had to start very early—by 7.20 we were in the train—and arrived at Flax Bourton, a crocked old village about seven miles west of Bristol, at about ten. We got started in an unusually short time and reached the rendez-vous at about eleven, after a tiring march uphill along a dusty road in which we must have ascended a good 300 feet. Operations began at 11.15; our company was the advance guard, and after marching a mile or so along the Bristol Road, we struck up north across some open country to deceive the enemy of our intentions and make them also move northwards, taking particular care not to capture any of their scouts we saw. We moved at our leisure across a very high plateau of cornfields, and I am glad it was at our leisure, for it was a very strange coincidence for me that the field-day was just at that time and place. For right at the top of the plateau there was the finest view I have ever seen. Down on our right were Clifton and Bristol lying in the Avon valley. And full in face was a broad expanse of water "where Severn's stream goes out to sea," and black in the distance against the horizon was a smoky cloud that can only have been Cardiff. On the field to our left at the very top of the hill was Farmer Callow ploughing (what he was doing ploughing at this time of year I cannot tell), and away to the north-east was a spire shining against the sun. And then I knew why

> The sea with all her ships and sails,
> And that great smoky port in Wales,
> And Gloucester tower bright i' the sun
> All know that patient wandering one.

You recognise the quotation?

And then for two hours on end we ran. We scattered all over the country and went in all the wrong directions. We annihilated pinchbeck little public schools, 30 strong, all over the place. But we could not find their main guard Clifton, and seemed to get no nearer the Suspension Bridge. At last we managed to rally, we managed to find Clifton sulking in a hollow, we managed to drive them back a mile in ten minutes, but the Suspension Bridge was still secure when Cease Fire sounded at two.

And now I have got a card up my sleeve still to play. "I've been to church." I have been moving in dizzy circles. Last night (Saturday) I was having dinner at the Lodge, and next door to me on my left hand was—the Bishop of London.

Taking it altogether—and I talked a good deal to him—I could not imagine a nicer man. He really is simply perfect, and now I understand why all those men who came down from Tottenham the other day spoke of him in the way they did. He is, of course you know, an O.M. to add to his other virtues. He has none of that clerical self-consciousness or other-worldliness you expect in bishops. He was just about as delightful as you could hope. He preached this morning—very well indeed.

And to-morrow we take our plunge into the valley of the shadow of the Certificate. It is still a month before we meet again on the Delectable Mountains of Dunbar.

13 *October* 1912

I hope you will like *Dauber*. I have read it several more times, and it certainly shows great improvement in expression and handling of that rather difficult metre. I think in many ways it is the best of the three—there are no bad bits in it. But it needs time, and is never furiously exciting. I should not wonder if Kenneth liked it. As to your two requests about my paper on John, both are, I am afraid, impossible to grant. For first, the Literary Society is an entirely private affair, and no accounts of its doings ever appear in *The*

Marlburian. And secondly, papers read to the Literary Society immediately become the property of the Society. They are locked away in a drawer and never see the light of day again. This is very sad but so it is.

The paper "locked away in a drawer" may now be allowed to "see the light of day."

JOHN MASEFIELD

AND THE XXTH CENTURY RENAISSANCE[1]

The Everlasting Mercy, *October* 1911
The Widow in the Bye Street, *February* 1912
Dauber, *October* 1912

With most people there is something that they ought not to be allowed to talk about: with Cato it was Carthage, with Mary it was Calais, with Mr Dick it was King Charles's head, and with me it is John Masefield. And yet that is precisely the reason why I am going to talk about him to-night. My admiration for him is so unreasoned and intense that it would not be satisfied until it had written a paper on him, and is still more dissatisfied now that it has. Indeed, to quote his own words in one of his shorter poems,

I cannot tell that wonder, nor make known
Magic that once thrilled through me to the bone.
But all men praise some beauty, tell some tale,
Vent some high mood which makes the rest seem pale,
Pour their heart's blood to nourish one green leaf,
Follow some Helen for her gift of grief,
And fail in what they mean, whate'er they do.

My magic, my thrilling beauty, my Helen, my green leaf is this trilogy of Masefield. Hence I should not

[1] Read Sunday evening, 3 November 1912.

write on them, seeing I am doomed to "fail in what I mean, whate'er I do": but comforted by his words that "the only glory is failure. All Artists fail," I take in hand the forbidden task.

Now various critics have told me two reasons why Masefield is not a great poet: first, that he does not express the spirit of the age, as a great poet must: the psychological impossibility of his poems is discordant with this age of science; and secondly, the majority of his readers would be struck by a first reading but would be content that that should be the last: his pleasure and power are ephemeral. Let me deal with these in turn.

First, that he does not express the spirit of the age. Beyond any question this spirit of the age is to be found in the upheaval of the masses of the population. We all know about what happened to men's minds in the sixteenth century: it was called the Renaissance. The chief thing that strikes me about this Re-naissance is this: that it was a most tiny and undersized Renaissance. The knight became the knight of the pen as of the sword: the noble deserted Diana for the Muses: the courtier turned poet and the gentleman man of letters: but the tiller of the soil remained the same. The joy that had lifted the soul of his master to infinitely higher heights, the joy of the discovery of the magic of word and thought for purposes both receptive and constructive (they say this is the greatest of joys), that joy was deliberately denied to him. Two centuries elapsed, and the tiller of the soil became the worker in the city: and that class, self-named the Upper Class, had grown so accustomed to the treasures of literature, aesthetic or emotional, that they took them as the everyday blessings of life, nor tried to imagine what life could mean without them: forgetting to think that thousands of their fellow-creatures, with a capacity for enjoying these blessings at least as great and unassuageable as their own, went stunted, pinched and starved for want of what was to their neighbours the necessary food of the soul. The love, that is a demand, of the noble expression of noble thoughts, the discovery of the path of approach to God by the road of great men's great words, which was born in the few so many years ago amidst joy and gladness and ringing of bells, is now being born in the many, the masses, with tears and sweat and dire unrest—the earnest of a fuller and more profitable life. Surely the body of the people is in the birth-throes; and that which is being born is the knowledge of the beauty and strength of word and thought: and this is the spirit of this restless age. Something is calling the poor man to the better pleasures of life; and Masefield is the herald of this spirit, the echo of this trumpet call.

The wet was pelting on the pane
And something broke inside my brain.

* * * * *

I heard her clang the Lion door,
I marked a drink-drop roll to floor;
It took up scraps of sawdust, furry,
And crinkled on, a half inch, blurry;
A drop from my last glass of gin;
And someone waiting to come in.

* * * * *

I know the very words I said,
They bayed like bloodhounds in my head.
"The water's going out to sea
And there's a great moon calling me;

> But there's a great sun calls the moon,
> And all God's bells will carol soon
> For joy and glory and delight
> Of someone coming home to-night."

This is the very spirit of Re-naissance, the joy, the wonder, the compulsion of it all. A new day is breaking for these men, and Masefield is the prophet of that dawn.

> O glory of the lighted soul.
> The dawn came up on Bradlow Knoll,
> The dawn with glittering on the grasses,
> The dawn which pass and never passes.
> "It's dawn," I said, "and chimney's smoking,
> And all the blessed fields are soaking.
> It's dawn, and there's an engine shunting;
> And hounds, for huntsman's going hunting.
> It's dawn, and I must wander north
> Along the road Christ led me forth."

For *The Everlasting Mercy*, the story of the re-naissance of faith in an individual, may be taken as symbolical of the wide re-naissance in all the masses of the country. That is why it is such a very great poem, though it may be twenty years or more before men realize that it is one of the greatest poems ever written. It is the chronicle of the Re-naissance of the poor and worthy of its subject. And yet, more than one critic has expressed himself displeased because the tale of this conversion or re-naissance in this very bad young rustic is what they call "psychologically impossible." Just so. That is the point of the whole poem—that it is psychologically impossible. The conversion of St Paul was psychologically impossible too: I suppose they therefore do not care to read about it. With men there are one or two things that are still impossible. With

God all things are possible. And it does mankind no harm to be occasionally reminded of this. For if in this age of science and wise men, this age which has reached such a pitch of presumption that it attempts to clap an explanation on to everything and cannot away with what is too noble or spiritual for such explanation, if in this efficient analytical age a poet tells the story of the power of good in a man without providing a public vivisection of that man's soul for any passing theorist to reduce to rule of three, it is earthly, sensual, and typical of the age to say "we can't explain this: throw it over; and the next, please."

> I did not think, I did not strive,
> The deep peace burnt my me alive;
> The bolted door had broken in,
> I knew that I had done with sin.
> I knew that Christ had given me birth
> To brother all the souls on earth,
> And every bird and every beast
> Should share the crumbs broke at the feast.

A little less of that thought and strife, a little more of this knowledge and faith, and perhaps men would easier see the message and the truth of *The Everlasting Mercy*.

And second—that they are ephemeral. When a person says that a poem is ephemeral, he means one of two things: either that the world will forget it a week after it has read it: or that he will forget it a week after he has read it. And when a person says that John Masefield's poems are ephemeral, I strongly suspect him of using the second and personal sense of the word. It is a very common sort of joke, you know, to say that English poetry has died a natural death with the birth of the twentieth century. But really it is not that there is a dearth of poets (there are many of them, one very great one, called Masefield), but a dearth of ears to hear. For modern life, that vast and complex structure, has at once demanded that its poetry should be vast and complex (to give its proper spirit) and its audience curt and superficial (because the race is run so fast). Therefore when someone tells me that Masefield's poems are ephemeral he merely means that he, the person in question, will forget them before the week's out; or in other words he is merely informing me that he is superficial and forgetful and his mind is not worthy of so great a poem.

For this is my point. The latter two poems, *The Widow in the Bye Street* and *Dauber*, are stories of almost unmingled sadness and bitterness. But a very bad habit has grown up among English authors, who tell a tale, of doing the moralizing and sentiment themselves, instead of leaving it to the reader: and unfortunately the reader likes this, especially the hurried modern reader, for it saves him time. Both poems are very bitter: but Masefield is never bitter with them: there is no scrap of sentiment in either of his poems; nor of that gratuitous profanity which is called bitterness and ensures a sale. To the superficial they are bitter stories without the gems of bitter sarcasms (directed against God) or the lace of putrid sentimentalism (educing the effeminate in man) which rotters like Tennyson and Swinburne have taught his soul to love: the moral is not cut and dried, there are no trite blasphemies for him to remember: so he says it is ephemeral and puts it away. But to those who have ears to hear and who (what is more) read the poem more than once and with their brains working, there is a wonderful under-current of suggestion that runs throughout that cannot escape them. The Widow in the Bye Street is a woman of great goodness: goodness that serves to make her son a murderer and herself a lunatic. Let us read three of the closing stanzas of the poem and try and trace the suggestion of hope in that apparent sadness, which runs through them.

And sometimes she will walk the cindery mile,
Singing, as she and Jimmy used to do,
Singing "The parson's dog lep over a stile,"
Along the path where water lilies grew.
The stars are placid on the evening's blue,
Burning like eyes so calm, so unafraid,
On all that God has given and man has made.

* * * * * * *

And in the sunny dawns of hot Julys,
The labourers going to meadow see her there.
Rubbing the sleep out of their heavy eyes,
They lean upon the parapet to stare;
They see her plaiting basil in her hair,
Basil, the dark red wound-wort, cops of clover,
The blue self-heal and golden Jacks of Dover.

Dully they watch her, then they turn to go
To that high Shropshire upland of late hay;
Her singing lingers with them as they mow,
And many times they try it, now grave, now gay,
Till, with full throat, over the hills away,
They lift it clear; oh, very clear it towers
Mixed with the swish of many falling flowers.

It is not enough to read these lines once. The modern red-hot, hasty reader cannot appreciate such lines. They must be read more than once: pondered over. And then it is seen what depths of hope they suggest. This goodness, the goodness of the widow, which is seemingly so barren, so dry of fruit, this goodness he shews us with a marvellous delicacy in these stanzas, must yet go forth a great unnoticed influence among men and women who wake and sin and die:

> Oh, very clear it towers
> Mixed with the swish of many falling flowers.

And when the Dauber dies in that other poem of his and his painting genius perishes unused, does he sentimentalize or grow bitter over this? This is how he describes the death.

> He said, "It will go on."
> Not knowing his meaning rightly, but he spoke
> With the intenseness of a fading soul
> Whose share of Nature's fire turns to smoke,
> Whose hand on Nature's wheel loses control.
> The eager faces glowered red like coal.
> They glowed, the great storm glowed, the sails, the mast.
> "It will go on," he cried aloud, and passed.

And, describing the tropical scene, when the ship had reached port and the body had been buried, he finishes with those lines of infinite suggestion upon which it would never be a waste of time to meditate.

> And all day long, where only the eagle goes,
> Stones, loosened by the sun, fall; the stones falling
> Fill empty gorge on gorge with echoes calling.

Perhaps you do not feel their whole suggestion, for you have only heard them once. But, believe me, there is more teaching conveyed in such lines as these than in all the philosophies of Swinburne or Browning or Meredith. Only you must bring to it a mind prepared to give as well as to take—a mind that is ready for spiritual as well as intellectual concentration, and it shall in no wise lose its reward.

Masefield has founded a new school of poetry and

given a strange example to future poets; and this is wherein his greatness and originality lies: that he is a man of action not imagination. For he has one of the fundamental qualities of a great poet—a thorough enjoyment of life. He has it in a more pre-eminent degree than even Browning, perhaps the stock instance of a poet who was great because he liked life. Everyone has read the latter's lines about "the wild joys of living, the leaping from rock up to rock." These are splendid lines: but one somehow does not feel that Browning ever leapt from rock up to rock himself. He saw other people doing it, doubtless, and thought it fine. But I don't think he did it himself ever. Turn from that to these lines from *The Everlasting Mercy*:

The men who don't know to the root
The joy of being swift of foot,
Have never known divine and fresh
The glory of the gift of flesh,
Nor felt the feet exult, nor gone
Along a dim road, on and on,
Knowing again the bursting glows,
The mating hare in April knows,
Who tingles to the pads with mirth
At being the swiftest thing on earth.

We cannot doubt, as we read these lines, that Mr Masefield is a runner. For, being a writer of whom it can be said more truly than of any other modern writer

πολλῶν δ' ἀνθρώπων ἴδεν ἄστεα καὶ νόον ἔγνω,

he draws the pictures of situations and characters with a wonderful vivid and truthful touch. He takes you right into the slums of a nasty little Shropshire town: he introduces you to people who are ignorant, narrow and stupid; and yet by the end of the poem he has brought you into sympathy with these surroundings and admiration for these characters. Especially is this the case with the Widow in the Bye Street: you see her first and despise her with the well-bred pity of a gentleman: you see more of her, admire her with the humble thankfulness of a reader of John Masefield. "I know," says she in her first interview with her son about his attentions to the worthless woman,

> I know a woman's portion when she loves,
> It's hers to give, my darling, not to take;
> It isn't lockets, dear, nor pairs of gloves,
> It isn't marriage bells nor wedding cake,
> It's up and cook, although the belly ache;
> And bear the child, and up and work again,
> And count a sick man's grumble worth the pain.

Let the modern woman study that!

For Masefield writes that he knows and testifies that he has seen. Throughout his poems there are lines and phrases so instinct with life, that they betoken a man who writes of what he has experienced, not of what he thinks he can imagine: who has braved the storm, who has walked in the hells, who has seen the reality of life: who does not, like Tennyson, shut off the world he has to write about, attempting to imagine shipwrecks from the sofa or battles in his bed. Compare for instance *Enoch Arden* and *Dauber*. One is a dream: the other, life.

One of the great lessons that John Masefield has taught to the world is the possibilities of doggerel. But it must not be imagined that it is through necessity that he writes in slang. Rather, it is by preference, for it is one of the man's great missions to show the hollowness of nobility of style. But he occasionally shows us that he can reach the highest flights of poetry (as the word is now conceived), but he has chosen the better part and prefers the language of the common man. Yet that it is by preference he does this, the nobility of the following stanzas must show.

> She turned, and left the inn, and took the path.
> And "Brother Life, you lose," said Brother Death,
> Even as the Lord of all appointed hath
> In this great miracle of blood and breath.
> He doeth all things well, as the book saith,
> He bids the changing stars fulfil their turn,
> His hand is on us when we least discern.

Or this,

> All the tides triumph when the white moon fills.
> Down in the race the toppling waters shout,
> The breakers shake the bases of the hills,
> There is a thundering where the streams go out,
> And the wise shipman puts his ship about,
> Seeing the gathering of these waters wan:
> But what when love makes high tide in a man?

Thus he has at his command the nobility of Milton, the word-painting of Tennyson. And he chooses the lingo of the Shropshire slums. This is an example worth thinking about.

There is one feature of Masefield's style which has laid him open to much criticism and deprived him of many admirers—his outspokenness. One of the worst traits of modern literature, as of modern conversation, is its inability to call a spade a spade. If there are certain things in life that we do not like to mention in the drawing-room, and all these things have honest Saxon words to express their meaning, is it not the height of inconsistency, indecency and self-hypocrisy to use a phrase or sentence for such things, to let the bad part of you dwell on the subject for an unnecessary length of letters, while the good part congratulates itself on its extraordinary self-respect in hedging the honest word? This is the outcome of guiltiness of conscience, and is gloating and morbid and the reverse of decent. I will quote some of Masefield's own words (used in a different context) that incidentally show the harm of this semi-self-deception and the good of telling the truth outright, however ugly it may be.

> The Dauber watched it come and watched it go.
> He had had revelation of the lies
> Cloaking the truth men never choose to know.
> He could bear witness now, and cleanse their eyes.
> He had beheld in suffering, he was wise.

Half of life's evils arise from this false shame. But John Masefield is honest and clean and fearless and has none of the gloating guiltiness that cannot call filth filth. Such outspokenness can only have a purging influence for good. "He shall bear witness now, and cleanse our eyes."

So you see what I think of John Masefield. When I say that he has the rapidity, simplicity, nobility of Homer, with the power of drawing character, the dramatic truth to life of Shakespeare, along with a moral and emotional strength and elevation which is all his own, and therefore I am prepared to put him above the level of these two great men—I do not expect you to agree with me. The appreciation of an author's work is so much a question of personal prejudice—you like him because you do, you can give no reasons—that I will not undertake the futile task of attempting to convert anyone to such an appreciation of Masefield. So, letting alone the genius of the man, I will try to display the possibilities of his cause. I do not think there can be any doubt about this: he has brought poetry down to the level of low life and in so doing has exalted it to the heaven which there exists ignored. The most awfully sad thing in history is, I think, that poetry up till now has been mainly by and for and about the Upper Classes. There has been a most horribly mistaken idea that poetry and the praise of God must be written in high-falutin' language. It can be written in any kind of language. If it is genuine and wells up irresistibly, then it is great, be the wording never so meagre. If it is sham or a mere religious recreation, it is a staring profanity, be the wording never so fine and sonorous. All poetry is primarily praise, praise of God or God's works in some form or another. And praise only needs verbosity to cover insincerity. Is there anything finer, purer or sincerer in the English language than this in which there is not a word that the lowest farm-hand might not use?

"Don't think of that, but think," the mother said,
"Of men going on long after we are dead.
Red helpless little things will come to birth,
And hear the whistles going down the line,
And grow up strong and go about the earth,
And have much happier times than yours and mine;
And some day one of them will get a sign,
And talk to folk, and put an end to sin,
And then God's blessed kingdom will begin.
God dropped a spark down into everyone,
And if we find and fan it to a blaze
It'll spring up and glow like—like the sun,
And light the wandering out of stony ways.
God warms His hands at man's heart when he prays,
The light of prayer is spreading heart to heart;
It'll light all where now it lights a part.

* * * * * *

And when thy death comes, Master, let us bear it
As of Thy will, however hard to go.
Thy Cross is infinite for us to share it,
Thy help is infinite for us to know.
And when the long trumpets of the Judgment blow
May our poor souls be glad and meet agen,
And rest in Thee. Say 'Amen,' Jim." "Amen."

Or than this from *The Everlasting Mercy*, when the new-converted sees the plougher ploughing his field at dawn?

O wet red swathe of earth laid bare,
O truth, O strength, O gleaming share,
O patient eyes that watch the goal,
O ploughman of the sinner's soul.
O Jesus, drive the coulter deep
To plough my living man from sleep.

* * * * * *

The share will jar on many a stone,
Thou wilt not let me stand alone;
And I shall feel (thou wilt not fail),
Thy hand on mine upon the hale.

Or the trumpet-call of the twentieth-century Renaissance?

"It's dawn," I said, "and chimney's smoking,
And all the blessed fields are soaking.
It's dawn, and there's an engine shunting;
And hounds, for huntsman's going hunting.
It's dawn, and I must wander north
Along the road Christ led me forth."

The sower, who reaps not, has found a voice at last—a harsh rough voice, compelling, strong, triumphant. Let us, the reapers where we have not sown, give ear to it. Are they not much better than we? The voice of our poets and men of letters is finely trained and sweet to hear; it teems with sharp saws and rich sentiment: it is a marvel of delicate technique: it pleases, it flatters, it charms, it soothes: it is a living lie. The voice of John Masefield rings rough and ill trained: it tells a story, it leaves the thinking to the reader, it gives him no dessert of sentiment, cut, dried—and ready made to go to sleep on: it jars, it grates, it makes him wonder; it is full of hope and faith and power and strife and God. Till Mr Masefield came on earth, the poetry of the world had been written by the men who lounged, who looked on. It is sin in a man to write of the world before he has known the world, and the failing of every poet up till now has been that he has written of what he loved to imagine but dared not to experience. But Masefield writes that he knows and testifies that he has seen; with him expression is the fruit of action, the sweat of a body that has passed through the fire.

We stand by the watershed of English poetry; for the vastness and wonder of modern life has demanded that men should know what they write about. Behind us are the poets of imagination; before us are the poets of fact. For Masefield as a poet may be bad or good: I think him good, but you may think him bad: but, good or bad, he has got this quality which no one can deny and few belittle. He is the first of a multitude of coming poets (so I trust and pray) who are men of action before they are men of speech and men of speech because they are men of action. Those whom, because they do not live in our narrow painted groove, we call the Lower Classes, it is they who truly know what life is: so to them let us look for the true expression of life. One has already arisen, and his name is Masefield. We await the coming of others in his train.

24 *November* 1912

I am quite befoozled. I have just finished my weekly hour's course of Walter Pater. That creature has been foisted on me by Gidney and I have to read an essay of his every week. This is only the second week so I really ought not to give an opinion, but I think he is the dullest and most stilted author I have ever read. I have to read him as a kind of punishment, I am not quite sure what for. I think it is because I do not write essays in the Oxford manner, as Gidney loves. So I have to beat out an hour every Sunday with this brute's *Appreciations*. It is a bore because otherwise I have found I have learnt more by giving up maths. than in the whole time I did them, as instead of maths. I do English with Gidney and (except when he is obsessed by Pater) he is a very inspiring teacher. I have also, through Gidney, made the acquaintance of Emerson's *Essays* which we are doing with him in form. I couldn't stand them at first, but now I like them immensely. I think he is the finest and most suggestive essayist I have ever read, though I have read very few. I think Gidney would be an ideal teacher of English, if only he wasn't an Oxford man.

I don't know that there's any news this week. If there is, that happy hour with Pater has made me forget it all.

I hope this morning's collect[1] had the proper effect and the great work has begun. Remember my dislike of currants is of the same quality as my fainting at the sight of blood. So please don't construct a companion

[1] "Stir up, we beseech Thee," Collect for the five-and-twentieth Sunday after Trinity.

fig-pudding for Charlie, that sits and looks bulbous like a poor relation. Rending ladders and talking about food! I am sorry, but Walter Pater has befoozled me.

1 *December* 1912

With the longer evenings and shorter games, I have been getting through a lot of reading lately. At a meeting of the Literary Society on Wednesday, a paper was read on J. M. Synge, and since then I have read three of his plays, *The Playboy of the Western World*, *The Shadow of the Glen* and *Riders to the Sea*. The first, so far as I can make out, is supposed to be the finest drama of modern times with subtle tragic irony etc., etc. (as the reader of the paper said); but I could only see in it a really exceptionally good farce. I think those English people take him too seriously. The only one I was really struck with was *Riders to the Sea*. I mean to buy that as it costs only a shilling. I think he's pleasantly suggestive without being anything wonderful. He was apparently a great friend of Masefield's. With that gentleman I am still extending my acquaintance. The latest acquisition to my library is his *Tragedy of Nan*. I think it's a marvellous play to read; and I should imagine even better on the stage. He's much stronger than Synge, and his language is just as poetical, though he hasn't got half as easy material in his Shropshire labourer as Synge has in his Irish peasants. I shall bring back *Nan* with me and I hope you will like it. Though on the whole I prefer his poetry, I think he is more in his element with prose. However, I see in the *Westminster* that Edmund Gosse, in presenting him with this silly little cheque, told him that "he was henceforward responsible for maintaining the position of English poetry."

Gidney, who likes to see that I do not read only such as Masefield, lent me Frederick Myers' English poem *St Paul* the other day. I like it better than most of Browning's *Dramatic Lyrics*, though it might be shortened. Gidney is very keen on Myers and introduced me to his *Essays* about a year ago. Though he just fails to be inspiring, I think he is fine reading.

I am glad *Oedipus* was liked. But I am sure *The Tragedy of Nan* is finer, though it isn't really a tragedy, as nothing that Masefield writes could be a tragedy.

27 *January* 1913

I have been having an exciting time talking to various ushers all to-day about various things. I wanted (and still want) to give up Classics, but they were very patient and talked me round. I find Classics more and more boring every day; but Dyson (the Music Master) after a long talk showed me that it was far best to keep it on and go up to the University (which I have never wanted to do, in secret), and that was the only way to get a kind of Alexander-Paterson post, which is the career I have always wanted. I had a mad idea, precipitated by a row with Atkey at the beginning of the term, of chucking Classics, leaving and becoming an Elementary Schoolmaster—with an utter ignorance of how to do so. Dyson (who knows a lot about it having done that kind of work himself) pointed [out] that that would defeat its own end, and that the only way to get that kind of career I wish was to keep on with Classics and go up to the Varsity—merely as a means to an end.

After taking my degree (I would not in that case need to stay four years), it would be easy to get a post at a night-school or working-man's college : but that was the only way to get at that kind of career. While up at Oxford, he showed me, I could make a beginning by working at Oxford House, and, after I had got a scholarship, there would be no pressing need to continue those detestable Classics in the detestably serious spirit demanded. I could spend a lot of time in social work and make a beginning then.

This is no new idea of mine—to become an instructor in a Working Man's College or something of that sort. Why I didn't tell you before I don't know. But until to-day it was only a hazy dream—I had no idea of how or when to do it. But now that Dyson has given me facts, it seems much nearer than before. And it will mean staying on here, as in any case, and going up for a scholarship at Oxford, just as if I had been going in for the Indian Civil Service. I did not foresee that, and thought I should have to leave and go straight into it, which would have been more satisfactory, but is, as Dyson showed, utterly impracticable. I feel much more easy now, except that I doubt that it is really good my staying on here at any rate after I go up for a scholarship. When one reaches the top of a public school, one has such unbounded opportunities of getting unbearably conceited that I don't see how anyone survives the change that must come when the tin god is swept off his little kingdom and becomes an unimportant mortal again. And besides I am sure it is far too enjoyable, and one is awfully tempted to pose all the time and be theatrical. But still, till the end of this year, I suppose

I had better stay on, *i.e.*, till scholarship time. Of course I want to awfully—that is the chief reason against it. The next four years have got to be bridged over somehow, and I had better bridge them in the conventional and, I suppose, the best way till I am able to enter the career I have always wanted since I read *Across the Bridges* in the courtyard of the Unicorn Inn[1].

I ought to have explained all this before. But somehow—you'll understand—one hates talking (I know it's only silly shy self-consciousness) about anything one really feels. These things go much better into ink. But I hope you agree that the best thing is to go in for a schol. which can take me up to Oxford (Dyson says Oxford offers much more opportunities that way: he is unbiassed having been at neither), and, after taking my degree, he says there will be no difficulty in obtaining the kind of post I want. There are objections to this. A year more of downright hard Classics is not a pleasant prospect. And a year more of being a little tin god is alarmingly and disastrously alluring. But Dyson assures me it is the best and only way—though four years is a long time to wait. But if ever I forget the kindness of Dyson, I ought to be knocked down!

So now I feel clearer. What I have wanted in secret has become realisable and without any change in my routine at present. I hope you are not angry that I did not tell you before that the idea of India was always a bit of a bogey to me: I shouldn't suit the life at all.

[1] At Bowes, Yorks, August 1911. In the preceding term, Mr Paterson, the author of *Across the Bridges*, had given a lecture at Marlborough of which C. H. S. wrote, "It was a magnificent lecture; I have never heard a better: he was humorous and practical and had no nonsense or cant or missionary canvassing about him" (16 July 1911).

2 *March* 1913

The general lightness of the atmosphere reminds one of the last chapter of the first book of *Eliza*. And that is one of the pleasantest chapters in fiction.

I hope Cornwall will be a success. As you flash through Savernake on the 10th (presuming you are going by that terror called the Cornish Riviera Express that passes through Savernake at 75 miles an hour) keep your eyes open on the left—between Hungerford and Savernake, that is. That is the part of the world where at present I spend my Sundays. In the winter the downs, in the summer the forest, but the Kennet and Avon canal, that runs alongside the railway from Hungerford to Savernake, in spring is worth ten of these. So catch a glimpse of it, if the day is fine. As you're passing Savernake, I shall be four and a half miles east either quaking with [the] awful desertion that comes of having eaten nothing since breakfast and the prospect of having shortly to compress all the dormant energy and training of the last two weeks into the next two minutes ; or racing round the half-mile course (a peculiarly venomous race, the half-mile—neither one thing nor another—going your hardest the whole way), or hiccupping a little and wondering how three other people in my heat can possibly have been better than me. For, the shadow of the Booth Prize departed, the shadow of the Sports is coming on.

We have just had a miniature "joy-day," on Thursday, when a few of us re-formed the Marlborough College Dramatic Society which has not existed since Laurence Irving left. Two of the younger masters, men of "Belial" and late members—we like to think prominent members—of the O.U.D.S., form the necessary background of Common Room. The Master, without throwing any cold water, was not very encouraging and stipulated that the society must be called the Shakespeare Society, as he considers the word "dramatic" is disturbing. This term, of course, we will do nothing ambitious, merely meet and read Shakespeare and then a modern dramatist turn about (I don't mean we begin one when we're half-way through the other), but next term we hope to do something startling—to act before the whole school, though the question "What?" is at present difficult to solve. Still it is a great thing to have got this going, and even if it leads to nothing public, it will at least mean a thorough knowledge of Shakespeare. I am very glad of it personally because it is one of the things I don't talk about that I can't read Shakespeare to myself; but it is a different thing for a "group" to read it aloud, as we used to do—only it was apt to end in tears. So we are excited and pleased to have something new to think about.

I have newly squandered 3*s*. 6*d*. on another new toy. It is called *Georgian Poetry* and is an anthology of the best poetry—short poetry, of course—of the last two years. There is a little in it that is bad, and the vast majority is quite inconsequent. But there are two poets with strange names—Lascelles Abercrombie and Walter de la Mare—whom I am very glad indeed to have met: very striking both of them. Then there is a man Wilfrid Wilson Gibson whom I have come across before in the *English Review*, and he is the poet of the tramp and the vagabond, and he can write. There is also our "local poet," your friend without a shirt, whose sex caused us such trouble that day on the river—and I think he is undoubtedly a poet, though a slight and lyrical one. I think the lines

> Say, do the elm-clumps greatly stand
> Still guardians of that holy land?

are as true a description of the fens as there is. But, as you would expect—since the fens seem to be the only thing he has any experience of—he is nearly perfect when he keeps to them, but quite shadowy on anything else. And I'm blest if the truest poem in the book isn't by—Chesterton! It is certainly a surprising book, and I am glad to have it. I will bring it back with me when I return.

16 *March* 1913

On Monday and Tuesday it rained, being the Sports. Faithful to the athletic traditions of our family, I was spared getting a pew in either of the events I had attempted. So that's all right.

Thursday was Field Day—much more the kind of thing. The day was wonderfully fine, and, in spite of it being on Salisbury Plain, the scheme most enjoyable...

In the evening was the annual "Corps Brew" and heartiness. My part was to propose the visitors. I left out three of them, but nearly balanced it by putting in two who weren't there. I think our Corps Brews are the most perfect type of a Mutual Admiration Evening. We go away thinking each of us personally is the smartest member of the smartest corps in the world. But this time a very fortunate incident occurred on the way home. The band were so puffed up by the nice things that had been said about them, that they were making a great deal more noise than was right at 10 p.m. The result was that the first horse we met bolted. We were marching on the left of the road and the horse was on the right, and you know how broad the High Street is. There was no danger; even the horse was not very frightened. But College Corps were! In a second we were all on the pavement, making for the wall; and we had been marching at attention under military discipline. I have never seen anything so disgraceful; but it just reminded us that we weren't all Wellingtons yet. I think this should be arranged to happen after every Corps Brew. The humorous horse, when he saw us beginning to venture back into line again, settled down into a trot; and we marched back to bed trying hard to pretend it was a dream.

The Dramatic Society is very flourishing. We have read *Richard III* and Ibsen's *An Enemy of the People.*

11 *May* 1913

As being a kind of useful wind-bag, fond of the sound of his own voice, I have been trysted to read an "emergency" paper to the Lit. Soc. next week. I think I shall write on the *Shropshire Lad.* So I am rather rushed.

The paper was duly read to the Literary Society in the following week, and the manuscript has been recovered in the same way as that on Mr Masefield's poems. It is even more fully illustrated by quotations; and these quotations are so numerous that only references to them have been given in the paper.

A SHROPSHIRE LAD[1]

I am writing this paper under the impression that to the majority of my hearers A. E. Housman, as a poet, is not familiar. It must have been some German who first remarked that the best critic of Shakespeare is Shakespeare; from which we may deduce that the most competent critic of the Shropshire Lad is probably the Shropshire Lad himself. Consequently I do not feel many misgivings in making this paper little more than an annotated edition of selections from his works. And further, since I am presenting him to-night, as a dealer accustomed to puffing objects and possessions of real price might once in a way exhibit a curio without much comment, since the value of that curio depends very much on its defects: I shall avoid the rôle of either champion or iconoclast; nor burden you with any very startling exaggeration of his talents.

Mr Lascelles Abercrombie, in a very brilliant book on Thomas Hardy which I have not read, has tried to define the poet as one who, having searched and reached a final idea or philosophy of the universe without him: having looked also, and found the essential distinctive kernel of the personality within him: can express the results of this successful search in words most suitable and most fair. The inadequacy of this definition may be measured by the fact that, according to it, the perfect poet would be Mr A. E. Housman. He has come to a conclusion about the universe: he has found the essence of his own personality: and of these his expression is (to use purely two misused words) compleat and perfect. Let us see.

[1] Read Thursday evening, 15 May 1913.

First, to show that as a language-maker alone, apart from what he expresses, he is second to none of his contemporaries and can sit beside almost any other English poet, except Shakespeare: I would read the following extracts.

IV ("Réveille"), stanzas 1, 2;
XXVIII ("Welsh Marches"), stanzas 1, 2.

Now for his expression of his idea of the universe—the first postulate of Mr Abercrombie—not only is it plain; it could not possibly be more plainly presented.

VII ("When smoke stood up from Ludlow");
XXVI ("Along the field as we came by");
XLVIII ("Be still, my soul").

And here I would add a note. The fact that rest is to be the end of Housman's existence prevents him, once for all, from being a great poet. None the less he stands high among the ungreat. He does not therefore advise sensuality as long as life lasts, like that dewy rhetorician FitzGerald. And he looks forward and would welcome rest: but not the smooth accessible unearned rest that the average hymnast likes to paint: not the charming semi-conscious post-prandial rest of Mr W. B. Yeats: not even the more ideal but somewhat stagnant-smelling rest, Rossetti's "Sunk stream, long unmet"—but a cold hard deathy rest, welcomed not for itself, because it has no pleasure to offer at all, but welcomed as less than the other evil, the evil of existence in an ailing earth.

But this somewhat self-satisfied dislike of life breeds no dislike of his fellow-partners in it. Indeed, one of the qualities in his nature that he brings into strong relief is a strong almost defiant love of man *quâ* man:

of his fellow-creatures, for being creatures. He has given it a perfect expression; as in these:

IX ("On moonlit heath");
XXII ("The street sounds to the soldiers' tread").

The quotations I have given you thus far may have produced a somewhat false impression to the effect that Housman is not much more than a peevish and perverse dyspeptic. This is not so at all. His idea of the universe and himself, and his expression of it, without any modification or inconsistency, can, if turned upon other sides of life, come very near nobility indeed. These following are as fine as anything I know.

I ("1887");
XXXV ("On the idle hill of summer").

I do not know much about the Greeks: perhaps something less than I ought to: but it has struck me that Housman would have pleased them very much. His perfect restraint and refinement of obloquy or irony: no less than his limited and reasonable conclusions about the universe: would have charmed many lesser Greek philosophers with the charm that is produced by reflecting "That's exactly what I think too: and if I had had to express it, I should have expressed it in precisely the same way."

XII ("When I watch the living meet").

Not only the perfect dual grammatical antitheses of the first two stanzas: but the root idea and thought of the poem culminating in a restrained regret that sensual pleasures are not practised after death, which makes the philosopher superior to their indulgence on earth—Greek, typically Greek. This side of his nature is startlingly stoical: as also is his cold refusal to take any pleasure in life except the grim but, I should think, fairly satisfying pleasure of knowing that "high heaven and earth ail from their prime foundation" and pitying the ignorance of others on this subject. For this is the only thing he allows to give him pleasure, this, and Shropshire.

Shropshire. For Shropshire is the root of the inspiration of the man. And let us turn aside for a moment to consider a remarkable feature of his poetry—its earthiness. Every century or so poets have been returning to the earth, and with their return poetry becomes alive and true once more. Such a return was made at the end of the eighteenth century. And, as is inevitable with any noble movement in this country, it became before long vulgarized. Tennyson vulgarized it. A paltry poet in general, Tennyson is most preeminently paltry and superficial when he sings about nature and earth. He was not long in hedging her in with the shapely corsets of alliterative verbiage. Meredith was the first to break through this barrier and discover her again in her truth. England, however, was so busy reading Tennyson that they thought Meredith a clever novelist but too smart for them; and no poet at all. In our own days another poet has returned in truth to the earth—of course I am talking of Masefield. His return was purely emotional, and probably less interesting than the purely intellectual return of Meredith. Both men set out in exactly the opposite direction, but, being true poets, are making for exactly the same end. But what I wish to make clear here is that, in a much more limited and local way, Housman expresses the same root ideas, limited and localized, as they. All through the closing years of last century there has been a grand but silent revolution against the essential falseness and shallowness of the mid-Victorian court-poets. But all true poets (that is, poets who insist on truth) have been consciously or unconsciously in revolt: and Housman, whose fine hall-mark is his cold bare truth, is not the least of those (in the words of Earth's greatest seer) "who read aright Her meaning and devoutly serve[1]." This is how he read her:

XXXI ("On Wenlock Edge");
LV ("Westward on the high-hilled plains").

Such is the man. And if I were asked to put in one sentence his essential features, I should say they were primitive impulses and emotions, purged and civilized, as it were, but never essentially altered or improved, by a restrained and balanced intellect. And I should add that it was wonderful how restrained and balanced that intellect was, so that it is content with nothing but cold truth: that truth of his with its obstinate magnificent rejection of ideals, that so consistently chooses the evil and refuses the good as to make the evil something grand as well (so that we might well call him "the hero that the grand refusal made"): and his fine artistic truth, which makes his portrait of himself so unflattering and admirable. And though his rejection of ideals bars the road to the stars and there is nothing noble, no onward motion in his poetry, there is much in it that is good to read. This compound of civilized instinct with primitive emotions has made him at his best reach the highest point of primitive virtue ("Woman

[1] G. Meredith, *Poetical Works*, p. 321 ('Hard Weather').

bore me, I will rise"); and at his worst he never sinks below the demands of civilized morality. And if there is nothing ennobling in him, there is nothing that can lower man: if he has rejected ideals, he has purged and corrected reality. He lacks the attractive virtues of high striving and endeavour, but he keeps the somewhat duller virtues of temperance, patience and truth. He has no faith: but he has certainly no fear. And whatever else he is or is not, he is always himself. Perhaps no other English poet has been less influenced by the thoughts and words of the speakers of his or indeed of any other time. One thing and one only mated with his personality has produced his poetry, and that one thing is Shropshire. For Shropshire is the only true begetter of his poems. It has been the fitting flame to set alight his impotent irascible independent egotism. It is not certain whether anyone is the better from the *Shropshire Lad* ever having been written. But it is certain that it never would have been written, had the writer not been unavoidably controlled to write it.... But why do we go on admiring him thus? He does not want our admiration!

XXI ("Bredon Hill").

30 *June* 1913

By now the festivities are fairly over and we have fallen back on work. The Inspection of the O.T.C. was on Monday, and a very respectable person inspected us. He was not an O.M., so we got less superlatives than usual, and afterwards he made us an exceedingly sensible speech about the General Reserve. He had a charming Yorkshire accent, which greatly bamboozled his audience when he seemed to say that "after the Boer war it was found that the British Army had four too few officers, four too few." It reminded me of Ada and the three jolly sailor-boys looking for war.

Friday was the day of reckoning. For the first time in my career it was a fine day. The Prize-giving part went well. The concert in the evening was marked by a splendid new song called *The Scotch Marlburian* by the greatest living poet in his way, an old assistant-master here called Johnny Bain, a Scotchman of course. He refuses to publish anything, but can write wonderful verse in seven languages. The tune was a Scotch air adapted by that Dyson I would not let you see, and the whole thing went off admirably. I am sending the words to see if you like them as much as I do.

Yesterday after Chapel, the weather being perfect, I went the best walk I have ever had. I went out along the downs almost to Swindon, but turned off into a village known as Liddington, and made a life-long friend of the publican, whose heart is in his back garden, so that I left Liddington laden with bouquets which it was no child's work carrying in the heat of the day. I then scaled Liddington Castle which is no more a castle than I am, but a big hill with a fine Roman camp on the top, and a view all down the Vale of the White Horse to the north, and the Kennet valley to the south. I sat down there for about an hour reading *Wild Life in a Southern County* with which I had come armed—the most appropriate place in the world to read it from, as it was on Liddington Castle that Richard Jefferies wrote it and many others of his books, and as it is Jefferies' description of how he saw the country from there. Jefferies, I suppose you know, was a Wiltshire man, and was brought up at Coate, now a suburb of Swindon, not ten miles north of Marlborough. Indeed there are to be found horrible critics with a passion for labelling everything, who refer to the country between Swindon and Marlborough as the Richard-Jefferies land. I then walked along a hog's back to Aldbourne where I had tea and returned in the evening across the Aldbourne downs.

6 *July* 1913

The Master has lent me a Journal of English Studies or something containing a lengthy and laudatory review of the poems of that Irishman James Stephens whose Thread or Cloth or something of Gold was lying about the drawing-room last holidays. The authoress of the review regards him as a second Milton and the greatest living poet. And though this is a bit much, the extracts she quoted are some of them striking. You may have read a rather forced thing by him about Eden in the *Georgian Poetry* book. But some of his things are much better than that; *e.g.*, [the one beginning]: "On a rusty iron throne."

He is apparently only a beginner too. Mrs Henry may come across him. He lives in Dublin and I should not say he was in Society there.

Gidney, in a fit of great kindness and rather conventional Bohemianism, is taking the Lit. Soc. out next Saturday to a rustic spot near by where he will feed us under an oak and celebrate the Borrow Centenary by reading us himself a paper on Borrow. The result is I am getting up Borrow for the occasion and am at present knee-deep in *Lavengro*. I like it immensely but just in the same way as you like *L'Île Inconnue*. I hardly hope to have finished it this year. Like the Bass Rock[1] it is very good, but always remains on the table.

21 *September* 1913

As you ask the question, I think the Greats course seems wiser and safer than Economics at Cambridge—safer, that is, in case my opinions about a profession change in the meantime; and from what you say, I should think ultimately more useful.

The walk, thank you, was most successful after the first day. After ten miles of tow-path, interesting at first from the number of gaudy barges with spitting men that passed up the canal with loads of sand, but after a little very irritating, I struck west for the Icknield Way and spent the rest of the day making bad shots at short cuts till in the end I was glad to get to Princes Risboro, almost entirely by the road. But the next two days were much better. I struck the Icknield Way, and, except for a few miles in the Thames valley, was on grass for the rest of the way. My progress at first was very slow owing to the abundance of brambles by the side of it; but, after crossing the Thames and leaving Bucks for Berks where vegetation gave place to downs, I got on much faster and soon came into a land well-known to me from memories of past field-days. About this time the sky grew very black behind me and I raced the rain to East Ilsley and arrived a few minutes in front of it.

The last day was the best of all. Almost all the time I was seven or eight hundred feet up, for I was walking

[1] A famous cake.

on the ridge that forms the southern wall of the White Horse Vale, and all the time had a fine panorama to my right. The early morning was thick with mist, but cleared up wonderfully later on. There was a track all the way, sufficiently visible to follow, and I kept it till the ridge breaks off due south of Swindon. Then I turned at right angles on to the top of that other ridge that runs by east of the road from Swindon to Marlborough, and separates Wilts and Berks, and on its back I threaded my way back to College. When once I had arrived there, it rained for the rest of the night. So altogether I was in very good luck.

7 December 1913

I returned here yesterday morning hand in hand with De Saumarez who is spending the week-end here. I am awaiting Wednesday's news[1] with perfect composure meanwhile—not because my verses, whose since discovered howlers have been haunting me ever since, can have done much to redeem the rest of my work—but because where ignorance is bliss, it's no use worrying. I have made arrangements for the result to be telegraphed here and to Cambridge.

Masefield's new poem in the *English Review* which I read on the way back here is rather uninteresting. It is quite short and has some fine passages of description; and, which is a blessing after the daffodils, never in the least sentimental, only rather dull and so nautical that it's difficult to understand. Besides that, the story has absolutely no point: that is to say, I've missed it.

[1] The result of the scholarship examination.

12 *December* 1913

I suppose you would be angry if I concealed the fact that I have got a "forty" cap which, being interpreted, is about the same as a second XV. In case you wonder, I did not get it till *after* I had got my schol. at Univ. Of course it isn't a sufficiently "nutty" thing to have to influence their decisions really.

C. H. S. wrote so often about Marlborough and its ways that the question may be asked what Marlborough thought of him. As an answer to this question the following statements are inserted here. They were not written at the time he left school, so that they may be coloured more or less by subsequent events; but neither were they written at the request of any of his family.

Dr Wynne Willson, Dean of Bristol and formerly Master of Marlborough College, wrote as follows:

"Charles Sorley was a boy at Marlborough College, and for two years (1911—1913) under me as Headmaster.

"When I went there he had reached the Lower Sixth Classical. His personality struck me at once. His fine face and splendid head bore the stamp of intellect and individuality. My first impression of him was that he was a rebel against a new regime. And I am not sure that my impression was not correct. With all his keen radical theories and sympathies, which he held in common with most clever boys, he was—a frequently occurring paradox—doggedly conservative in all that affected his own environment. He had a passionate love for Marlborough as he found it, a love which was not inconsistent with a mordant power of criticism. This love and this criticism alike are displayed in his poems and letters.

"Certainly Sorley was in a sense a rebel, but a very lovable rebel. A spirit of revolt is the prelude to renaissance, as history bears witness. He was a rebel against mere convention, and in one of his letters to me he admits his spirit of rebellion. This spirit displayed itself in his attitude towards his work and study and reading. He had the makings of a good pure classical scholar, but he revolted against the routine of classical education and vowed that he would not read for 'Mods' at Oxford. In the VIth we were reading Martial one term. Something in this writer (probably his subservience and smug deference) stirred the boy's wrath. Nothing would induce him to work at the author. In fact Latin literature as a whole failed to appeal to him, whilst he found satisfaction for his soul in the greater passion and idealism of Greek. It was certainly a tough struggle to induce Charles to work at anything that did not seem to him to come straight from the soul. But we came to some kind of working agreement. He did a modicum at work he disliked, and threw himself heart and soul into anything that touched humanity and reality.

"He was a voracious reader of English literature, but was fastidious. Tennyson and Browning he could not away with. He thought they were imbued with Victorian artificiality and smugness. He was an ardent admirer of authors like Richard Jefferies and John Masefield. He felt that they expressed the popular mind. In his study he kept a list of converts to the latter writer. I remember one day when I was ill in bed he sent me to read one volume of his poems in the morning, and when I wrote him a note of appreciation, sent me another in the afternoon. Another name for his list! He wrote a very remarkable paper on his works.

"In debates his ardour of spirit found free scope, and his speeches gave promise of great power in maturity.

"Religion, the attitude of the soul to God, played a great part in his life, as his poems show, and I can see him now joining lustily in such hymns as he felt rang true, and listening intently to any sermon that stirred his thought and feeling. But in this sphere again he was a rebel: for there more perhaps than elsewhere a spirit of convention enters. In our hymn-book we had one or two Latin hymns. These he stoutly refused to sing as he felt the use of an ancient tongue to be an affectation, savouring of unreality. His appreciation of thoughtful sermons was generous; his criticism at dinner in hall of what was conventional and commonplace often needed checking.

"His table talk was brilliant, if at times wild. It was a daily refreshment to sit opposite to the boy at 'Hall' and hear him talk. He was never dull or depressed. In fact a bubbling joy in life was one of his greatest charms. He seemed to revel in all its phases. One of the chief characteristics of his poems is his love of rain.

"One morning after repeated failures on his part to produce sufficient signs of preparation in his work, I told him in Form to write out the translation of the lesson. That day was glorious and after dinner I sent for him. I knew the boy's passionate love of open air and I could not bear to think of him spending the hours of sunshine in doing an imposition. I told him so. 'But, oh! Sir,' he said, 'that isn't fair: you know, I never did a stroke of work at it.' He was so charmingly frank and honest. However he did not do the imposition and for a time prepared his work better. One Sunday evening during chapel service his house-master was in his room, when suddenly Sorley entered. He had come to say that he had 'cut chapel' and to receive the normal penalty. 'I suppose,' said the master (a keen friend and adviser of the boy) 'you mistook the time.' 'No, Sir, I was on the downs and it was so jolly that I decided not to come back.' Some debate ensued between them, the boy insisting on the penalty and the master refusing to inflict it. As Sorley left the room he said, 'It's very unsatisfactory, Sir; you see, I shan't be able to do it again!'

"It is very difficult to convey any idea of Sorley's vivid personality, but, old and young, all were held captive by it. All life to him was an adventure full of delight. He revelled in big horizons, natural or social: he loved alike the boundless sweep of the Marlborough downs and the wide problems of human life.

"He left school at Christmas 1913 and went to Germany. There he met with great kindness and was full of pleasure at his new environment. He used to dash off long letters to me, full of the most delightful humour. These letters are perhaps almost more expressive of his personality than his verse. He escaped from Germany at the time of declaration of war and hastened to serve. And in this new phase of life he found new delight, especially in his intercourse with his men whose great qualities he saw. And then he went to France and died.

"What would have been the career of such a boy? Whenever his house-master came to see me on business, that being disposed of, we always found ourselves discussing Charles Sorley and his future, was it to be literary, or social, or political? Well,

God knows! But anyhow he would have been a great and a true man, who would have served his generation and made a big name."

Mr A. R. Gidney, his house-master, wrote as follows:

"Charles Sorley was killed on the afternoon of Oct. 13, while leading his company to the attack, after his Company Commander had been wounded. A bullet struck him on the side of the head, and death came in a moment. He would have sought no other end. Death had been in his thoughts: he had faced it unafraid, and with hope, as the promise of an intenser life:

> And your bright Promise, withered long and sped,
> Is touched, stirs, rises, opens and grows sweet
> And blossoms and is you when you are dead.

"For it was life that he loved. He was gifted beyond the ordinary with an exuberant vigour of mind and body. Scholar of University, XL Cap, enthusiastic Captain of House 2nd Cricket XI, House Prefect, lover of Masefield, and of all poetry that throbbed with his own joy of life—how powerfully he impressed on us here the fascination of a noble and joyous vitality! He seemed to have some unique privilege of life, *εὐφυὴς καὶ ἔνθερμος*. Marlborough he loved with a deep and growing love; and not the school only, but the downs, in rain, wind, and sun—Barbury, and Four Miler, and Liddington, the swift skies, and windy spaces, the old turf on which he ran for miles, with all its memories and traces of a bygone people. For shams and pretences, real or fancied, he had a refreshing and outspoken scorn. That was why he loved Masefield. 'Throughout his poems there are lines so instinct with life that they betoken a man who writes of what he has experienced, not of what he thinks he can imagine; who has braved the storm, who has walked in the hells, who has seen the reality of life; who does not, like Tennyson, shut off the world he has to write about, attempting to imagine shipwrecks from the sofa and battles in his bed.' So he loved Masefield, read him, wrote of him, made us read him and like him. One who heard him will not forget the intonations, rhythmical and insistent, with which he almost chanted 'Dauber' or 'Daffodil Fields'—as he read the lessons in Chapel, or Richard Jefferies, or anything else that moved him. And below all this, seldom shown and never paraded, lay the most uplifting idealism. In the stirring of the masses he found the spirit of the age. 'The love that is a demand for the noble expression of noble thoughts, the discovery of the path of approach to God by the road of great men's great words, which was born in the few, so many years ago, amid joy and gladness and ringing of bells, is now being born in the many, with tears and sweat and dire unrest.' To this, inarticulate and groping blindly after better things, to this he would give a new voice. 'The most awfully sad thing in history is, I think, that poetry up till now has been mainly by and for and about the Upper Classes.' He would give himself to social service. In his last year here, with the love of Marlborough and the downs strong upon him, he wished to leave and work in a London slum. In the service of an ideal it never occurred to him to count the cost. Yet with such zest did he live the Marlborough life—work, brew, discuss, play, and throw himself into the activities of School and House—that many scarcely realised his finer gifts. Doing most that other boys did, he seemed to have little time for anything else, and was so much one of them that they hardly suspected what he was besides. All this time he was thinking, alive with ideas and longings, and writing poems."

The above is taken, with a few minor alterations made by the writer, from an article in *The Marlburian* of 24 November 1915. To this Mr Gidney afterwards added the following "further impressions":

"I think there has been a tendency—an inevitable one—to regard Charles Sorley too much as a literary boy. I don't think he would have given his life to literature, if he had lived. No doubt, he studied artistic form; but he did not live for poetry; he wrote poetry because he was vitally alive, and this vital force welled up into expression in that way. I can't imagine him sitting down in his study to compose poems: he may have shaped them there, but in their essence they came to him in the deep intensity of his way of life—many, perhaps, actually as he ran or walked on the downs in rain, wind, or sun. That, I think, is why the mystical element is so strong in them, some of which his lovers have caught from him, *e.g.*, I. d'A. S. Stitt. Some of his poems are less suggestive than others, but I don't think it is the mere face of nature that he sees in any of them. The more I think of Sorley and his poetry, the more I seem to find at the heart of each a spiritual force with its roots right away from this surface world. In his poetry there is a complete absence of the lusciousness common to youthful verse—not a shadow of the sensual anywhere. Well, that is how his personality struck me. Its quality seemed to be the quality of light itself—warmth, glow, brightness, purity above all. He enjoyed life immensely, but was the least self-indulgent of boys; not that he was austere or ascetic, as he had no need for such disciplines; he seemed to live with an extraordinary thrust of life, with an élan vital harmonising itself sanely and naturally in a due temperance of body and spirit.

"That is why we never regarded him as in any way eccentric, or distinctively rebellious; his life was not a protest, but a burning positive thing of his own. Perhaps, too, that accounts for his humility, a quality which his vitality did not always show on the surface—the humility which a really seeking spirit feels in the presence of that which it finds. I can see his face now, alive with it. It was part of his reasonableness. After the chapel incident to which the Dean refers, when he came to say good night before going to bed, we had a long talk on the philosophy of punishment, and I remember how he took to the less penal view I put before him. It was part of his loyalty and efficiency. He was Head of my house, and I don't want a better one. He took a tremendous interest in it. I realised this at the house supper in the Town Hall when my predecessor was moving to another house. Sorley got up and recited a long string of clever, kindly doggerel, touching off the characteristics of leading boys in the house. Of course, he was always in a way detached: in the life here, yet not wholly of it, always ready to discuss and criticize. But he could never be a mere critic: the positive need to live was far too strong. There were in him, too, the qualities of pity and sympathy. He burned to help. Once, while running on the downs, he lay down and slept under a bush, in his shorts and house jersey, and awoke to find himself surrounded by the local W.E.A. At once he entered into the spirit of the thing, with a characteristic courtesy and lack of self-consciousness. It was always like this. Whatever he did of his natural inclination, he did with such whole-hearted force that those who saw him only in certain phases of life never realised his other activities. I don't suppose most boys in his house regarded him as a poet, distinctively so called; but every boy who came much into contact with him regarded him as the greatest personality he had come across. Marlburians of very different types have all told me the same thing."

In the same number of *The Marlburian* appeared the following verses over the signature "J. B.":

Sweet, singing Voice from oversea,
Lover of Marlborough and her Downs,
Sure now thy Spirit, wandering free,
Is hovering near the Town of Towns,
There where the bents and grasses wave,
And winds roar round the Hoary Post—
No wormy earth, no gloomy grave
Shall hold thy homing, eager ghost.
From some bright corner of the sky
O hearest thou the praise we give?
Who knows? To live may be to die;
To die (who knows?) may be to live.
More than the most was thine to spend
For Mother England, Freedom, Truth;
Gladly thou gav'st, dear poet friend,
The splendid promise of thy youth.

CHAPTER III

SCHWERIN IN MECKLENBURG

To Professor and Mrs Sorley

Schwerin, 22 *January* 1914

...At Bentheim I got out and opened the old Gladstone which was then graciously permitted to enter Germany. But the black box was nowhere to be seen. Dictionary in hand, I explained to some really foul men in fluent racy and idiomatic German the true nature of the case. They only talked to each other in quite unintelligible German till I went back sadly to the train and left them in their ignorance. Shortly afterwards I had a considerable Mittagsessen and, managing to consume a glass of beer, went back to my centrally heated carriage contented. There, instead of intelligently watching the scenery, I fell asleep till the person opposite me, an Englishman, awakened me to look at the Elbe, which we were just then crossing, making its way laden with ice-blocks to the sea. The ice-blocks were snow-capped, so the river looked horribly diseased. After passing by the market which was black with people, and passing through what I hope for the sake of the Hamburgians are the Hamburg slums, we reached the Hamburg Hauptbahnhof.

I was done with Germans. But seeing a man with "Interpreter" on his cap and "Thomas Cook" all over his clothes, I fell into his arms and told him the whole truth about the box. He was a man of remarkable intelligence, and after wonderful conversations with the station officials he told me I would find my box at Schwerin next day and the Zollrevision would be there. He told me that a fast train left for Hagenow in an hour's time, and set me on the platform and put my suit-case etc. in a wonderful cloak-room for a penny, took my ticket for me, and obviously considering me feeble-minded told me not to leave the station, though the train did not leave for an hour, in case I might get lost. I was so impressed that I gave him one and six, and left the station at once.

I somehow missed the one-armed waiter, but with my infallible intelligence noticed that at Hamburg the tram-cars go two and two together, that is, each tram has an old done tram yoked on behind it, which holds passengers but cannot move by itself. This knowledge may one day prove useful. I noticed nothing else about Hamburg except that I passed four cinemas in as many hundred yards. I then returned to the Bahnhof and caught the fast train to Berlin.

I did not register the Gladstone bag, but took it in the carriage with me along with the suit-case and rug, to say nothing of the umbrella. The sight of the passenger with the "so viel Gepäck" amused the man who gave me tickets for my seat at intervals enormously: so much so that he brought another official to see me and they both made jokes (which I did not understand) and I laughed enormously and said "ah ja" in the intervals of laughter, and they returned to know where I was going to and told me (having by now discovered that the so viel Gepäck in the carriage was merely a proof of feeble-mindedness)—told me very slowly that Schwerin was a very beautiful place but man must change at Hagenow to get there. I knew this already, but I feigned delight at the knowledge, told them I was not English but Scotch, and they shrieked with delight at Hagenow to see the Schottländer with the three Gepäckstücke. At Hagenow there is a subway to the platform for Schwerin. This in England would be nothing epoch-making, but it fills all true-born Hagenovians—ay, and all the neighbourhood of Hagenow—with pride. They had explained to me all about it by dumb show (indeed my conversation with them throughout resembled a game of dumb-crambo), so I took it at once. It was quite dark when I boarded (this is the correct word) the train to Schwerin, so I could not see the surroundings, which was lucky, as travelling in Germany seemed like travelling in *Alice through the Looking Glass*—the train goes at a tremendous pace, but to right and left the scenery remains the same. On arrival at Schwerin, I took a cab to Wiesenstrasse. It was, I think, that cab's last journey, for on its next I am sure it will fall silently to pieces. However it had two horses and only cost one mark.

I clomb and I clomb and I clomb and at last arrived at a door with Bieder on it. I was admitted by a maid, but for a long time she and I failed completely to come to an understanding. At last it transpired that the Herr Doktor and the Frau had gone to the station to seek me. This shows you what kind of people they are. They almost immediately returned—just when I had had time to put on my more presentable coat and waistcoat—and greeted me with noise and laughter.

Dr B. is a tall fat hearty man with moustaches. If he was English he might be a bounder, but being a German he is perfectly delightful. The Frau showed me this morning a photograph of Bismarck and said of course I knew who it was. I said "Ja, gewiss, the Herr Doktor," and have been popular ever since for this striking instance of my *savoir-faire*. The Frau is nice-looking, smaller, and not stout: indeed she drinks no milk (I learnt this morning) for she trembles to become thick. She is very simple and delightful and knows English quite well. She is going to give me Stunden.

The Neuphilolog did not appear till Abendessen. He is thin, fair, and pale, with pince-nez and a nervous manner. He is like most booksellers' assistants to behold. Frau B. immediately told me in his presence that he was a "Bücherwurm" and he seemed to glory in the title. Apparently, like the too hasty widower of Bowes, "they tax him" about it. He knows no English to speak of and is very eager to be kind. There is also a mother upstairs, suspected by me of being feeble-minded, and at present "hid from me," though promised as a treat for Sunday.

My room has a window (which I pain the B.s by keeping open), a bed of decent length, and a washstand, a wardrobe, two tables and plenty of room besides. It is, like things in the advertisements, "all that can be desired" and errs on the side of excessive heat rather than cold. The flat has four rooms opening one from the other. My room alone is disconnected. The Neuphilolog lives upstairs.

After Abendessen, we all joined hands round the table and said Mahlzeit. The trio are very affectionate and slap each other's cheeks continually. Then came a pause and with an effort the question that had hitherto troubled each breast was delivered: My mother—was she dead? I overcame the lying impulse, and said No. Then in broken German I told the whole truth about the family.

Shortly afterwards a delightful thing happened. Dr B. asked me eight times if I liked music, with assistance from his wife and brother-in-law. I understood at last, and answered in the affirmative. Then the fat Herr Doktor opened a harmless looking piece of furniture, and behold, a harmonium. He sat down and played, his eyes closed with delicious enjoyment of the thick smug notes. I said "ich danke" a dozen times which seemed to please him. He is really an awfully nice man, and so are they all awfully nice people. Their one idea is that I should be "zufrieden[1]," and though they cannot reconcile this with my sleeping with an open window, they ensured it by offering me and allowing me a hot bath yesterday evening and by numerous other attentions.

This morning I got up (at eleven, I fear) and went shopping with the Frau. We eat thus: first breakfast 8.30; second ditto 12; Mittagsessen 4 o'clock, when the Doctor returns from the office; and Abendessen at 8. Schwerin is a handsome town, though all the streets are cobbled; and this morning we had the rapture of seeing the Grand Duchess drive into the Castle. At three o'clock I went (alone, to the horror of the Frau who was cooking the dinner) to get my box. It has been examined and has just arrived safely in my room.

[1] Contented.

The lakes are lovely. I intend to buy skates to-morrow, and go skating with the Neuphilolog, who always tumbles when he skates and prefers going softly, like me and Hezekiah. The Herr Doktor is on the Parliament of the town, and altogether a person of note.

I still find understanding difficult, except with Frau B. who translates words I do not know into English. I find it easier to catch the Herr Doktor's meaning when he speaks his native language. They are very comfortable, unselfconscious, simple people, and Frau B. is, I think, very clever, and should make a very good teacher. She taught my predecessor, and then exhibited him at ladies' parties. The rooms, if a little stuffy, are very comfortable, and the red-armed servant most obliging.

To A. E. Hutchinson[1]

A fragment from an earlier letter to the same correspondent explains passages in what was afterwards written from Germany.

Cambridge, 4 *January* 1914

I am writing this letter in the intervals of weeping over Beresford Webb's German Grammar. His gloom thickens every page. The only three complimentary adjectives he has yet introduced—to set against pages of tired, sick, idle, old, bad-tempered aunts who eat stale bread, use blunt knives and everlastingly are losing them—the only nice adjectives are very begrudging and left-handed—"pious," "industrious" and "amiable." And Lord! it is always the Count who is pious and the landlord who is amiable and Charles who is industrious.

[1] Of Marlborough College; second lieutenant, Northumberland Hussars, December 1914; Irish Guards, January 1918; M.C.

And can you, I ask you, imagine three more irreconcilable and impossible states of affairs?

I am just discovering Thomas Hardy. There are two methods of discovery. One is when Columbus discovers America. The other is when someone begins to read a famous author who has already run into seventy editions, and refuses to speak about anything else, and considers every one else who reads the author's works his own special converts. Mine is the second method. I am more or less Hardy-drunk. Read him, if you ever get hold of him, though he's dull in places. Of course at Marlborough he is non-existent.

Schwerin, 23 *January* 1914

I spent the week-end in annoying numerous Cambridge Old Marlburians by paying them visits. I put on my very oldest clothes to see Ridley in, which pained him horribly. On Tuesday evening I was sent off with more luggage than I have ever previously been responsible for, because my mother had a rooted idea that I would die of cold in Germany. As it is, the trains and the houses as well suffer from a thing called Central Heating (a euphemism for deliberate and organised stuffiness) so that my death will be due to excessive perspiration or to suffocation, not to cold. I took poison before embarking at Harwich; and then went to sleep. The stuff was reasonably effective, for it was not till three o'clock a.m. that I began to behave with any violence. But the boat arrived at 4.30 at Hook, so on the whole I was fortunate. I had then a twelve hours journey through to Hamburg, during which I lost a trunk and was lamentably weak-willed over the loss.

I arrived at this delightful place about six o'clock on Wednesday, and engaged in elaborate calculations as to what I would be doing in Marlborough if etc. I have either to subtract or add fifty-five minutes to get the English time, and this requires more effort than I am often capable of giving.

I live here in a pleasant (if stuffy) flat, with the two B.'s and Mrs B.'s younger brother whom they call with the utmost friendliness "the Bookworm." The three are, like the Count, amiable. They are very kind, very simple, very merry, but entirely deficient in Vice. A lovable over-anxiety that I should be in everything contented (which they have as yet failed to reconcile with my always opening my window), an overwhelming affection for their victuals (which I too possess), and a bad habit of playing the harmonium in the evening, are their only faults. After meals we all join hands round the table and say "Mahlzeit"—a greedy but harmless habit. They are all very fond of one another and slap each other's cheeks and tickle each other's necks with gusto. Soon, I fear, they will do the same to me, and I will have to return the compliment. I think they like me, as you've no idea how foolish and willing and humble—in a word how amiable—I can look and be. Besides yesterday Mrs showed me a beastly picture of Bismarck: "Of course I knew who it was?" "Yes, yes, of course, the Herr Doktor," I answered. Did you know before that I had such great tact?

They are very inquisitive. All the correspondence about my coming here was carried on by my father. This somehow got on their chests. So at dinner yesterday the awful question was at last put: My mother—

is she dead? If I had been really funny, I should have burst into tears and said, "Unfortunately yes" (which I have learnt from Beresford Webb); but I missed the opportunity and told the truth.

The time is now 5.15, and having subtracted fifty-five minutes, I am now contemplating with satisfaction the probability that you are enjoying at the moment the Best that Marlborough can Give in the way of Evening Hockey on the Common. "Third" is second hour on Fridays, isn't it? At least you probably get better exercise than me; mine consists in skating upon a lake which is really very beautiful. The Bookworm always accompanies; and, while obviously considering me feeble-minded, is very nice to me and I am inclined to like him very much. We find it difficult to come to a complete understanding (he knows no English), but each supplies his deficiency with wreathèd smiles.

To Professor and Mrs Sorley

30 *January* 1914

The Bieders continue "up." But I have somewhat changed my opinions of their relative merits and have made some important discoveries. First and foremost, Frau B.'s mother is not, as I had gathered, kept locked up in an attic-room upstairs on account of mental decay. Quite the contrary. She lives alone in another part of the town, and comes to Mittagsessen on Sundays, when she ate considerably more than I had thought was possible at her age. Secondly, though my opinion of Frau B.'s character is still in the stars, my opinion of her braininess has descended somewhat. I am having a lesson of an hour and a half every day at present (for two marks a day), and am learning, I think, a lot, but she is not what you might call "brainy" or quick. I have considerable difficulty in preventing her speaking English to me as she is always pressing me to be home-sick, and she considers the remedy for this is to talk English to me and overfeed me. However, I have managed to stop her, at last. But she is an extraordinarily nice woman and has a very pleasant face and figure, and quite a pathetic admiration for her husband.

The Herr Doktor is one of the men who, I imagine, make Germany what She Is. He gets up at 8.30, and goes to his office before 10. There he works till half-past three or often till half-past four, and then returns for Mittagsessen, in a state of overwhelming perspiration due, his wife tells me, to overwork. He works again from five till half-past seven, and after Abendessen, followed by a brief but memorable innings at the harmonium, goes into his room and works till 2 a.m. All this, as far as I can make out, is the dullest kind of work—chiefly copying and correspondence and dull little provincial law-suits about step-mothers, which get explained at Abendessen. He is very genial—I think "genial" is the right word—and behaves to his wife exactly like Torvald Helmer, calling her "sweet mouse" and "comic child." However she is fortunately no Norah—and is "thankful oh! so thankful" (she has told me) that her man is always happy and hearty, and not as other women's husbands are, who come back violent (as well as sweaty) from their day's work. They were engaged, like Jacob and Rachel, for seven years, and wrote to each other every day during the espousal. I was inclined to agree with her when she told me that

that was impossible in England. They have been married for eight years now, and hope next year to buy a house of their own.

But the "brainiest" of the lot is Junger Neuphilolog. He is a pleasant-looking fellow, with a growing moustache but no chin. He sometimes has me up to his room and reads Goethe's *Egmont* to me, "indicating," like Eliza's husband, "by changes in his voice which character is speaking." He is really very nice, and his only weakness is a love of bright ties. He often changes his tie as much as four times a day, and altogether has about sixteen different ones of surprising colour.

Tuesday was the Kaiser's birthday and treated like a Sunday. The Herr Doktor is a reserve officer of sorts and got himself up in a beautiful uniform. There was a parade in the morning, which I went to see. I had not expected such a funny sight. German soldiers have an unfortunate way of marching as if there were somebody in front whom they had to kick. The Battalion from Schwerin looked like an army of wooden dolls as they marched out of the Castle, jerking each leg quite stiff as far as it could go—marching in perfect time in this ridiculous fashion, with the explanation "sic itur ad astra" on a flag borne in front of them.

After the parade, the hero in his uniform rejoined us and took us to a restaurant and gave us all a glass of port, and for the first time in my life I drank the health of Kaiser Wilhelm. When questioned about the parade, I undid all my good work of the other day when I mistook the Herr Doktor and Bismarck, by saying I considered it "drollig." Such a storm arose that I had to put on my best stupid face and explain that I thought "drollig" meant beautiful, and stutter and blush and say how could they think I thought the parade comic.

I did not get getting to Church on Sunday, but we went for a long walk. The surroundings here are really quite fine, though the place is rotten with lakes. By the way, the supposition that I was going to die of cold in Schwerin has proved a mistake. After three days' skating on the Castle lake with the Neuphilolog, it has thawed and has turned quite warm, and my exercise now consists in walking: but when I am sufficiently remote and persuaded that there are no spectators—I run, madly run.

I can now make myself understood more or less, whatever I wish to say. But I still find difficulty in understanding. I can generally understand the Frau, for she talks slowly to me and about simple subjects: also the Neuphilolog. The Herr Doktor (of whom I do not see much) I find more difficulty with, on account of a stupid habit of his of interjecting English words when he knows them: to prevent me, I suppose, from being homesick. As he only knows the simplest English words, of which I also know the German, this only adds to the difficulty of understanding. But I can understand very little of what Frau B.'s yellow-faced friends say to her. They talk, I think, in a language of their own, as we might talk to the Nice One, and sooner or later get up and chase each other round the table. Indeed in one respect, the B.'s are very like us. It is the highest form of humour to say yes when you mean no, and to tell the Herr Doktor when he comes down in the morning that a letter has arrived, sacking him.

I am doing no Classics at present. I am doing chiefly

Grammar in my Stunde, and also we read a translation of the *Christmas Carol* together, which draws tears from the Gnädige Frau. By myself, I am reading Goethe's *Egmont*, lent to me and recommended by the Philolog —sterner stuff than the *Christmas Carol.* I also am reading some of Heine's shorter lyrics, whenever I have a loose quarter of an hour.

To Professor and Mrs Sorley

5 *February* 1914

We are at present suffering from a heat-wave, which is very delightful, because I can make a full acquaintance with the country round, to which, in spite of a patriotic determination to resist all temptations towards favourable criticism, I am becoming quite reconciled[1]. It is passing through the same stages of transmutation in my mind as A. M.'s friends in hers, and is now "really, I should say, quite beautiful": more than that, walking is not, as I had feared, confined to main roads, but there are innumerable cross-country tracks, and the word "verboten[2]" very seldom defiles the landscape. The country is inclined to be flat, but there are several little hills from which the view of Schwerin is not so ugly as on the post-cards I sent to the maids. So far, on each of my walks, I have found two new lakes, of which one is probably really new: and the country round is remarkably uninhabited, so altogether I'm not complaining.

[1] It is chiefly when I look out over this bare and arable landscape here that I damn myself for leaving: for after all it is the surrounding country that makes M. C., and the surroundings of Marlborough have a strangely attractive property.—Letter of 26 January.

[2] Forbidden.

The Frau Doktor and I are getting very thick. She is really an awfully nice woman, and very frank, and tells me whiles that I'm getting "eingebildet[1]" (you can look that up, if you don't know what it means) and asked me suddenly the other evening if my brother and sister always thought they were in the right as well. She is violently interested in the family, and perhaps has still a suspicion that we hate each other, for Jean lives in College when she might, if she wished, live at home; and Kenneth and I are deliberately going to Oxford, though at first she had an idea that a cruel father drove us there: and all this seems to her a little "funny." But she is as nice a woman as you could find (yes, and her cooking is excellent), and, by the way, she sends her greetings to you. The Herr Doktor, also, sends "his recommendations": the old fool has still a way of talking unintelligible English, which makes his good Frau very impatient. My respect for the wife does not embrace her worser half. He comes down to Frühstück late and looking enormously fat and vulgar, shouts out "Liebling" at the top of his voice as soon as he catches sight of her, sweats with the effort, sits down heavily, and grasping a knife with clenched fist proceeds to state that he feels as "fresh as dew!" (I have looked up the word and, with a different gender, it can also mean a rope: take which you please.) The devotion of the Frau is extraordinary: she sits up till one, copying for him, she spends hours rubbing out the ink-blots from his documents: and when he comes back late and hot to Abendessen, think of it, she strips his shrimps for him. A love of shrimps is our only common

[1] Conceited.

characteristic, but even here we differ, for I prefer that the hand that strips them should be my own.

I was introduced this afternoon by the earnest moon-faced Philolog to a man who is going to give me a game of hockey twice a week. There is an old stick here, belonging to my predecessor, so everything is very nice. But alas! I am not to get getting wearing shorts. In Deutschland, they do not exhibit their knees in a state of nature. And to play hockey in I must wear knickers *and* a hat!

I duly received a curt letter from my future tutor in which he drily remarked that I probably would not wish to forget all my Classics; he did not like men to read Mods books before coming up, but there were exceptions: and the list of exceptions was terrifyingly long and included none of the books I have brought. However the moon-faced Philolog has them, and he loves lending. But I think I shall not begin for another fortnight.

The Frau and I read together silly novels in the morning in our Stunde, which generally stretches to three hours instead of one and a half: because she has an English translation with her. In the evening, we read together lovely sentimental little things, easy to understand, from Heine and Geibel: and then I retire to my room at 9.30 (with the pleasant lie that I go to bed then) and hack my way through another scene from *Egmont*, which bears about as much resemblance to Geibel's lyrics as the downs to the forest at Marlborough: and then I generally (as now) write, when I ought to be in bed. My bedtime hour has been getting daily later, but I have not yet heard midnight strike.

To A. E. Hutchinson

7 February 1914

Thanks so much for your letter which arrived while I was in the thick of a new original and invigorating game with the Frau—which is already condemned by its name which is "Puffspiel." Immediately, I did my best to bring the new invigorating and original game to a close by playing deliberately abominably, but it was not for an hour that I was allowed to look inside your letter. Twopence halfpenny, by the way, *is* a very reasonable amount to put on the letter. I like writing to people in England very much, because it only costs me twopence; while, when they in common politeness have to answer, it costs them twopence halfpenny. So I somehow feel I make a halfpenny every time I write, but perhaps I don't really. However, I am sorry to hear you are not playing hockey, partly because it is embittering to think that my malicious satisfaction was inhabiting a fool's paradise, and partly because I am. I was introduced yesterday to a most interesting gentleman with two or possibly three fingers missing on his left hand—but he was needlessly ashamed of this and continually kept his left hand concealed, so that, in spite of the real British grit you impute to me, I could never get a satisfactory view. Anyhow, this self-conscious gentleman runs a club that plays hockey every Wednesday and Saturday, and for the future I am to take part. I have just returned from my first game. The rules of offside and any ideas about circles are still confined to your side of the North Sea. I distinguished myself vastly and scored eight goals; though I was thrown into the shade by a fat gentleman who scored eleven goals by the simple method of standing a few yards from his opponents' goal and getting the backs to hit to him and guiding the ball in. We played for a good deal more than two hours, and most of my eight goals were scored when the remainder of the players were enjoying an illegitimate interval, but none the less they were goals. An unfortunate incident occurred before I started. I was stealing out of the house looking very nice in clean white shorts (with a patch) and my cap-jersey[1]—looking quite Byronic. No sooner had I closed the door, than I was ruthlessly hauled back by the Frau's brother with averted eyes lest he might see my nakedness, and told that in Deutschland knees were not exhibited and ordered to change into breeches at once. However I enjoyed myself very much, and my cap-jersey was very much admired, as is only right.

It's a delightful place. The common people are worth gold. Only just now I "stepped" into a shop to "purchase" this note-paper and had a splendid time with the shop-keeper. I took half-an-hour to explain that what I wanted was note-paper—no, not brown paper but note-paper. I then took another half-hour to tell him that the reason why I spoke so badly was that I was a foreigner. However he failed to put two and two together, and got hold of an idea that the reason why I found it difficult to understand him was that I was deaf. So he started to shout. He shouted for half-an-hour. For a long time I could make nothing out, but by

[1] The cap-jersey is the jersey worn by possessors of a "forty-cap" or "sixty-cap" (equal to about second fifteen or third fifteen respectively).

standing as far away as I could, I at last discovered he was asking me, Was I a Swede? I thought the best way to still the tumult was to say, "O yes, I'm a Swede"; so I said so. Then the tumult commenced anew only far louder and more unintelligible, for he was now filled with the idea that I must be very deaf. A horrible fear came over me that his wife might be Swedish and he had started talking Swedish to me, and I would be publicly exposed as a liar. But such fortunately was not the case; he was merely saying—I at last discovered—that probably I had a great many very nice Swedish friends. But my nerves were by now strained to breaking, so I hurriedly left the shop with my note-paper, murmuring indiscriminate praise in broken German of my very many Swedish friends. I am much intrigued by my Swedish friends, and am thinking of writing a book about them.

Talking about books, my novel has not yet died, and I have written three brilliant chapters of it. I have reckoned it will take me thirty years to finish, and if it is then refused by brutal publishers, my heart will break and I will die. Is yours still living and growing?

I enclose a piece of verse which I composed through sheer boredom on the Kaiser's birthday, because they made me stand in the street for hours to watch a parade which was not much more impressive than an ordinary college effort, but slightly more amusing because at attention they march the goose-step. I hope it will not make the letter too heavy and force a phlegmatic but immovable Shipway to extract fivepence extra from you for overweight. If such is the case I shall have the satisfaction of knowing that I am the gainer, not this time merely by a halfpenny, but by five pence halfpenny by the transaction of writing to England.

Encourage your people to send you to Germany. They are a delightful people—the women and shopkeepers especially; and the country round Schwerin, I have at last been forced to admit, is grand. But perhaps you wouldn't like it, just as you won't like Camp, I should say. They eat so unashamedly. Anyhow I don't think you could do better than Frau B.

Still, in dreams they haunt me—he, Torwald Nijjikovsky with the curling Swedish lip and the true pale Swedish eyes, and he, swarth Nicholas Fjjordd with his pearly flashing teeth and swift swarth hair that seemed ever to proclaim "Six Norwegians, six Danes and seven Finns are not worth one Swede": and thousand others, large and small, weak and strong, handsome and hideous, but all of them one in their genuine sweet Swedishness and their ardent love for me, sitting in their delightful drawing-rooms—or do they have anything so civilized as drawing-rooms in Sweden?

The following is the "piece of verse" enclosed in the preceding letter.

Questions expecting the Answer Yes

Addressed to A. E. H.

I wonder, does that ancient bell still clang
  Welcome to new arrivals every day,
As up the hill and round, a small black gang
  With their inevitable coffin stray,
  Decked out in black, with flowers in white array,
And suitable stiff hats and heads that hang,
  And downcast eyes with ruts where tears have been,
  And all those other things which make Death mean?

And some strange sweaty creatures stop to see
On those bald heights—strange bare-kneed passers-by,
With scarves about their necks that they may be
(Do they still think it?) comely to the eye,
And say, In Marlborough they daily die,
And gape and pass on downwards to brew tea.
And having downward passed, do they still find
A mimic city filled with men who mind?

Still haunt blear bearded men, whose eyes are ill,
The basements? Does the man without a name
Still ride his washing waggon down the hill
Into the laundry? Is it still his game
To make in Court disturbance with the same?
And do the Widow and the Curate still
Get up at Vosse's, and go straight to cold[1],
And feed on Lyall's syrup coloured gold?

And on the Common is there still mock war,
Where many minds are sacrificed to one
Small Ball, and talk of it, not sorry for
Their meaningless behaviour? Is this done
Still? Do they still care whether they have won?
And is there still a Folly called the Corps
Allowed out twice a week and thinking then
It's learning how to kill its fellow-men?

On Sundays are there thirty chosen ones
Who wear white ties, because their lives are white,
Who spurn the Wrong, nor eat Duck's damp cream buns,
But eat fair Knapton's cakes, and choose the Right?
And do they still on Saturdays at night
Put out all best clothes ready, tons and tons,
For Sunday wear, because the Lord likes best
To see his faithful worshippers well-dressed?

And say, is Classroom changed into a den
Of bright-faced British youth that nobly tries
To follow in the steps of those great men
Who always fig-leaves wear, or made-up ties,
And sacrifice their lives to Exercise,

[1] The Widow and the Curate are names which he gave to two types of boy; Vosse's is the first bell in the morning; to go straight to cold is to take a cold bath without first washing in warm water.

And clench their fists and feed on Force, and when
Worn out by muscular and manly toil
Read chapters from clean, Christian, Conan Doyle?

And is there still a refuge, when each day
The same small life, the same poor problems brings?
Is there still change? O, is there still a way
Outward, across those many earth-risings,
A Comfort, and a place to find new things?
And are the downs, and are the downs still grey?
And is the Chapel still a house of sin
Where smiling men let false Religion in?

[N.B. Verse vi hopes for the Answer No.]

To Professor and Mrs Sorley

13 *February* 1914

I am so glad you enjoyed *Hippolytus*, which I have always liked for being the first Greek play I ever read. I agree that Artemis's appearance is all wrong and spoils the play. But I believe the very most Modern (with a big big M) people—the "ipso Verrallo Verralliores"—consider that Euripides deliberately ruined all his plays by the *deus ex machina*, just to show how wrong that sort of thing was. I am glad you liked Murray's translation: I suppose you could smell the violets. You may not have noticed the triolet in the *Cambridge Review* about two years ago that ran somewhat thus:

We do not read Euripides.
Only Professor Murray
Has time for that in days like these.
We do not *read* Euripides.
But when we snatch a little ease
We skim; and in our hurry
We do not read *Euripides*
Only Professor Murray.

The hockey—I have had two games so far—has been an entire success. We play on a beautiful stretch of ground high up above Schwerin, twice a week, beginning at 3 o'clock and madly playing till dark night forces us to stop. Fortunately all the players are very bad: worse than me. Indeed the two shining lights both come from North of the Tweed—the (a-hem) other being a fat round girl with spectacles who hails from Cupar-Fife. Most of the men play in their Sunday clothes with stiff collars that don't quite cover all their ears. They do not in the least mind making idiots of themselves, which is very delightful. We play at hockey here; in Marlborough we played hockey: and I think I prefer the former.

I don't think I told you last time about my nice Swedish friends: which reminds me that I really must get rid of that lying habit. I went into a shop to buy a post-card, and the shop-keeper, who wore whiskers and a jersey, was very difficult to understand. Unfortunately he was also a bit of a Sherlock Holmes, and at once jumped to the conclusion that I could not understand him because I was deaf. So he simply shouted at me, and I shouted back that unfortunately I was an Ausländer. Then a most horrible tumult arose, and by standing at the other side of the shop I at last realized he was asking me "Was I a Swede?" I saw there was only one way to make peace, so I roared back "Yes, yes, a Swede." But no. It did not stop, but began again ten times louder than before. A horrible white fear came over me that he had started addressing me in Swedish, and that was why I could not understand. But as I turned to flee, I suddenly made out what he was shouting. He was saying that he considered it perfectly likely that I had a great many very nice Swedish friends. And so I gave him a lovely smile, and hastily left the shop, blubbering out indiscriminate eulogies in broken German of those many nice friends I have left behind in Sweden.

On Sunday I got going to Church. It was really quite enjoyable and not half so Prot as I had feared. The music—at least to my Philistine ears—was magnificent, and it is a fine and spacious old church. I could make very little of the sermon, however.

My hostess and I are as great friends as ever. In spite of my having told her so many times that such a thing is quite impossible, she insists on my sending an invitation to either or both of you to come and stay with her now. I don't think she considers so long a separation of Parents and Child is either natural or right. Is Kenneth's fate yet settled? For I cannot imagine a nicer place for him to go to than this: though that would mean we could not be in the same town. But if we were in the same town, he might light on an unsatisfactory family.

Is Jena more or less settled as my fate? It is such a little quiet place, it seems. Fired by ecstatic accounts and post-card albums of the lemon-faced Philolog, my eyes turn longingly in the direction of Munich, which I have been led to understand is for some or another reason under a ban. And you don't have to walk thirteen miles to see a theatre. However, there is loads of time to see.

I am going for the first time to the theatre in a few minutes. The piece is Ibsen's last, *John Gabriel Borkman*, which the Frau and I have read together. I will finish this letter on return.

I have now (obviously) returned. It is a wonderfully fine play, far better than any others by Ibsen that I have read or seen, but I can imagine it would lose a good deal in an English translation. The acting of the two middle-aged sisters who are the protagonists was marvellous. The men were a good deal more difficult to hear, but also very striking. Next to the fineness of the play (which has far more poetry in it than any others of his I've read, though of course there's a bank in the background, as there always seems to be in Ibsen)—the apathy of the very crowded house struck me most. There was very little clapping at the end of the acts : at the end of the play none, which was just as well because one of them was dead and would have had to jump up again. So altogether I am very much struck by my first German theatre, though the fineness of the play may have much to do with it. It was just a little spoilt by the last act being in a pine forest on a hill with sugar that was meant to look like snow. This rather took away from the effect of the scene, which in the German is one of the finest things I have ever heard, possessing throughout a wonderful rhythm which may or may not exist in the original. What a beautiful language it can be!

The Grand Duke was there with his wife and several satellites. I am told he pays 500 marks every night the theatre is opened—i.e. five nights a week from October to May—but the money is his wife's.

To F. A. H. Atkey[1]

14 February 1914

I hope you do not object to my Scots habit of keeping tight hold of my tuppences and sending this letter via Kerr. After I parted from you at Charing Cross, I fed and then spent the rest of the evening in glory in the gallery at the Savoy. I had never read Galsworthy before, and I thought *The Silver Box* a most remarkable play for its restraint and the deliberate way the author ruins it by an impossible dull third act, in which what would happen and not what might happen happens. But *The Death of Tintagiles*, which came before it, was the most moving affair; it was the first time I ever heard real natural crying on the stage.

But all other dramatic performances have been shoved into the shade for me since yesterday when I went to *John Gabriel Borkman* at the theatre here—one of the best in Germany, being richly financed by an admirable Grand Duke. I took the precaution of reading the play first, so that I could follow very well. Do you know it? I think it is far finer than any other of Ibsen's. And it has far more poetry in it than the others I have read, even though there is the inevitable bank-smash in the background. The acting couldn't have been better—and the phlegmatic and un-emotional way those Teutons received the piece! I dared to clap, not Philistinely in the middle of a scene, but decently at the end of the play, and all the eyes of the theatre were turned upon me. However, I have no more accusations to make against the Germans, except, perhaps, that they will not

[1] Assistant-master (Classical Sixth) at Marlborough; afterwards Captain, Yorkshire Regiment; killed in action on the Somme, 5 July 1916.

let me play hockey in shorts. I am living with delightful people—at least the Frau and her brother are delightful. The Herr Doktor is negligible, being Torvald Helmer come alive. And this is a charming town, though, I am told, provincial. The surroundings are varied and very beautiful ; the shopkeepers charming—I cannot buy a penny pencil without having to tell my life history and hearing theirs in return. The unaffected way they laugh at me is, I think, doing me no harm. One shopman asked me to come again because he found it so funny hearing an Engländer trying to speak Dutch, and said this with the conviction of one who pays a compliment.

I am staying here three months, and then elsewhither. I want Munich, but there are forces at home that want Jena. However, wherever I end, I am at present delighted with Germany.

I am beginning to fear that you were right when you advised my staying at Marlborough. My present state of mind is Hang Classics. I am so intoxicated by the beauties of the German language and by *John Gabriel Borkman* that I have done nothing and thought nothing of Latin or Greek since I came here : only Goethe and Heine and innumerable books about *John Gabriel Borkman*, and the play itself, of course. But I hope to reform some time next week. But at present this new language is quite enough to keep me happy. Ibsen is a different thing altogether in German !

I am only reading English on Sundays when all Germany is asleep after Mittagsessen. I think it is then permissible. In the holidays, I shunted Masefield into a siding and "discovered" Hardy. Since then, like people in the advertisements, I have read no other :

though I prefer his earlier ones—but I like *Jude* very much on account of its being North Wessex, and Marygreen somewhere I suppose on the Lambourne downs. But I would give *Far from the Madding Crowd* the prize for the best novel ever written.

By the way I read *The Harrovians* in the holidays, having heard you talk of it. I thought it really bad. Smart perhaps and amusing, and the chapter on Confirmation I liked until he suddenly began to think he was casting down and not setting up, and so he began talking about the Dawn of Beauty in the Young Mind and the Soul behind the Mountains—obviously second-hand and ten times more insincere than what he had been laughing at. And what an unpleasant fellow Peter was!

I hope the Junior Lit. Soc. still flourishes, and that, in spite of early private tu., you are having a good term. I hope soon to return to Classics when I have ceased learning *John Gabriel Borkman* off by heart and acting it to myself in the privacy of my bedroom.

Delightful place Germany!

To Professor and Mrs Sorley

20 *February* 1914

Thanks very much for the letter. The Gnädige Frau sends the same, only in much stronger terms which it is too late at night to translate. I am very glad you think of sending Ken here, for he could not be among nicer people. About the Bieders' accepting there is no doubt at all. Up to the time of my predecessor, the Frau had such a lonely life that I wonder she did not go mad or commit some fearful crime. Du lieber Karl is absent practically all day and so she was left with the red-armed many-fountained Ida (the general) for company. The Philolog works practically all day, and takes his Mittagsessen with his mama. So altogether an English companion is by now more or less a necessity to her, for her friends in Schwerin are Alexander Bells[1], and she's not the kind of fat German Frau who's content with a life of husband-coddling and housework. So she was overjoyed to get the letter, though I had to explain that the sentence about my always being in the right was not really so revoltingly unmotherly as it seemed, but was "nur in Spass," a phrase that is getting a "Where-d'you-want-to-gow-to?" with me in the innumerable occasions when I try to be facetious; but my little jokes fall on the stony ground or among the thorns, and I have to explain them away. She is a remarkably nice woman. Ken cannot fail to get on with her. Perhaps it can be so arranged that our times may overlap by one or two days.

"He that maun to Jena will to Jena." I am amused that the place is so full of attractions, that you have chosen out the existence of a Zeiss microscopic factory to prove its desirability. However, since I have heard that they speak an utterly alien language at Munich, I am quite reconciled elsewhither. And, with the shades of all the Schillers about, Jena should be a most elevating place. And I do hope this plan of a flying visit in June

[1] "His name is Alexander Bell,
His home, Dundee;
I do not know him quite so well
As he knows me."
R. F. Murray, *The Scarlet Gown.*

will come to something. Only the family will be very critical to observe how much use Charlie has made of his time out here.

I am getting more unpatriotic daily. Yesterday evening, returning from a walk, the Frau and I were passed by several companies of soldiers on their return from a day's outing (I don't mean to the sea-side: I mean what we used to call a Field Day). I have never heard such singing in my life. The roar could be heard for miles: "Heimat, O Heimat, es giebt auf wiedersehen" or something equally senseless and satisfactory, simply flung across the country, echoing from Schwerin two miles away. Then I understood what a glorious country it is: and who would win, if war came. However, on that subject, the people here seem wonderfully pacific; they consider England is the aggressive party and affirm that Edward VII spent his life in attempting to bring about a German war. To which ideas I may add one or two other truths about England which I have picked up at random: such as, that when a German goes to England, the English refuse to speak to him: that they never say grace in England, but compensate for this by never reading on Sundays: that the English always marry for money: and that Queen Victoria was always tipsy.

Yet they stand no nonsense. I declared yesterday, in a moment of annoyance at being continually cross-examined about my likes and dislikes in food, "that all food was alike to me." The hands went up in horror and I was dared to repeat the blasphemy. I repeated it with magnificent calmness and conviction and left the room a victor. I remained a victor till Abendessen, when I found on my plate a gigantic loaf of bread and a mountain of butter. Nice things were offered round the table (particularly nice they were that evening) but Ida was told not to offer them to me, for all food was alike to Mr Sorley. But I quickly recanted and grovelled, sold my soul for German sausage and climbed down.

I have been reading many criticisms of *John Gabriel Borkman*, lent me by the Neuphilolog, and it strikes me more and more that it is the most remarkable play I have ever read. It is head and shoulders above the others of Ibsen's I know: a much broader affair. John Gabriel Borkman is a tremendous character. His great desire, which led him to overstep the law for one moment, and of course he was caught and got eight years, was "Menschenglück zu schaffen[1]." One moment Ibsen lets you see one side of his character (the side he himself saw) and you see the Perfect Altruist: the next moment the other side is turned, and you see the Complete Egoist. The play all takes place in the last three hours of J. G. B.'s life, and in these last three hours his real love, whom he had rejected for business reasons and married her twin-sister, shows him for the first time the Egoist that masqueraded all its life as Altruist. The technique is perfect and it bristles with minor problems. It is absolutely fair, for if J. G. B. had sacrificed his ideals and married the right twin, he would not have been deserted after his disgrace. And the way that during the three hours the whole past history of the man comes out is marvellous. The brief dialogue between the sisters which closes the piece is fine, and suddenly throws a new light on the problem of how

[1] To bring about human happiness.

the tragedy could have been evaded, when you thought all that could be said had been said.

Twelve o'clock! I must stop.

P.S.—I am glad to hear you like Flecker. I think he must be a Trinity or at any rate a Cambridge man, from his compliment to Verrall in the poem *Oak and Olive.*

To the Master of Marlborough

20 *February* 1914

I have been here a lunar month to-day: up to date I have done no Classics whatsoever: to-morrow I intend to begin: and I think there could be no more suitable time than the eve of my reformation, for reporting myself to you.

I am admirably pleased with myself, and consequently with everyone else. I can now meet all the members of the family with which I am staying on equal terms, and we discuss the deepest subjects, such as the English Public School system, and often understand what the other has to say. The Frau, who gives me lessons, I see most of. I began, in my way, by despising her utterly. Now all that is changed, and, to use the Irish expression, "Me to live a hundred years, I would never be tired of praising"—at least, I hope not. She has also a delightful little brother of 23, who is very nice to me. He is a student of sorts, and on account of his industry had earned the title of the Bookworm, till I came, I, whose industry was never appreciated at Marlborough, and (Gospel Truth) usurped that title.

But what has given me most pleasure is the existence

of a Hockey Club in Schwerin. I hope you will not think me ungrateful, but I enjoy hockey here ten times more than I did in your kingdom. You know I am not given to boasting, but, though I say it as shouldn't, I *know* I am far the best outside-right within ten miles round. Now in Marlborough they never thought that of me. Yes, hockey means a different thing than that cold-blooded performance on winter evenings beneath the eyes of an Officious and Offensive House-captain, that it used to mean. We now play twice a week, beginning at three o'clock and continuing till the sun goes down and Ἑσπέρα πάντα φέρων[1] drives us in darkness to bed. This Season (I think that is the proper word) I have already scored 37 goals (incidentally, the first 37 goals of my career), and when the modest blushing Invincible Outside Right is congratulated at the close of the game on his skill (yes, skill), he explains in broken German, that at the school in England he was considered a contemptible performer, and they open their eyes like Dick Whittington and think with reverence on the School, where Talent at Hockey is as cheap as Gold Nuggets in Eldorado. At least, I don't suppose they really do.

The only objection I have to make is about the absence of shorts : or perhaps I should say (the former

[1] The phrase is from a fragment of Sappho, thus translated by J. A. Symonds,

Evening, all things thou bringest
Which Dawn spreads apart from each other ;
The lamb and the kid thou bringest,
Thou bringest the boy to his mother.

Cp. Byron, *Don Juan*, Canto iii, 107, and Tennyson, *Locksley Hall : Sixty Years After* : "Hesper, whom the poet call'd The Bringer home of all good things."

might be misunderstood) the rule that nice gentlemanly knickerbockers that conceal the knees must be worn. The three German officers that belong to the club play in their Sunday clothes—boiled shirts, butterflies and spats. They have not yet hit the ball, but are still trying. Now isn't that delightful? Catch a beastly English officer making a public donkey of himself! I think it is the utter absence of self-consciousness that makes the Germans so much nicer than the English.

For just at present, my patriotism is on leave. I cannot imagine a nicer nation. I was coming back from a long walk with the Frau last night and we passed a couple of companies of military returning from a field day of sorts. It is truth that we could hear them a mile off. Were they singing? They were roaring—something glorious and senseless about the Fatherland (in England it would have been contemptible Jingo: it wasn't in Deutschland), and all the way home we heard the roar, and when they neared the town the echo was tremendous. Two hundred lungs all bellowing. And when I got home, I felt I was a German, and proud to be a German: when the tempest of the singing was at its loudest, I felt that perhaps I could die for Deutschland—and I have never had an inkling of that feeling about England, and never shall. And if the feeling died with the cessation of the singing—well I had it, and it's the first time I have had the vaguest idea what patriotism meant—and that in a strange land. Nice, isn't it?

And the language is so glorious. Thoughts that appear vapid or sentimental in English, are glorious when clothed in German. That's what I find. My attempts to translate have met with no success. I have been to the theatre here and seen Ibsen's *John Gabriel Borkman* magnificently acted. In English, the play would be wizened. These magnificent compound words! The prodigal will find his return to the defunct languages to-morrow a wet-blankety job.

I cannot regret for one moment having left. The temporary loss of many friends is entirely compensated for by the eternal discovery of a language. It is such a relief, too, to be clear of any artificial position of responsibility, which continually threatens to make one a prig, a poser, or a censor. All temptations to be always striving in the race of showing off, are gone. For try and show off here, and you get short shrift. One day, a little annoyed by the German honesty in not concealing the natural human love of food, I said, "it didn't matter to me what I ate. All food was alike to me." When we came in to Abendessen that evening, the rest of the family had the usual nice meal, but I was only given bread and butter—as much bread and butter as I liked—but as it was all the same to me, nothing more. It was not long before I withdrew my silly statement, and helped myself to sausage.

I have a kind of feeling that towards the end of January I left Egypt and arrived safely in Canaan. I know it's wrong, but if you had heard those soldiers singing

> Vaterland, mein Vaterland,
> Es giebt auf wiedersehen!

you would have felt the same.

To A. R. Pelly[1]

25 *February* 1914

This being Wednesday afternoon, and Wednesday afternoon being the time when we used to combine cleanliness with conversation, I have (obviously) sat down to write to you and thank you very much for your letter. Receiving such letters as yours is most refreshing—quite like the Dew of Hermon or that nasty ointment that got into Aaron's skirts, or anything else that the men of old considered pleasant.

I am sorry to bear of the moral and athletic disaster against Sandford s last Monday. But then I've always noticed that Heaven grudges us poor mortals "given" halves: there is always something occurs to put salt in the sugar. I think the Germans (I nearly said "we Germans") have it over you in the matter of athletics. That there should be such things as fury, hatred and (far worst of all) apologies about a game of hockey would seem this side of the North Sea a very good joke indeed. As you say, the penalty of belonging to a public school is that one plays before a looking-glass all the time and has to think about the impression one is making. And as public schools are run on the worn-out fallacy that there can't be progress without competition, games as well as everything degenerate into a means of giving free play to the lower instincts of man. That's why it is so dangerous to let people of a certain type stay on more or less indefinitely till their competitive instinct becomes so overdeveloped that they can't endure even the threat of a defeat. Perhaps in eight hundred years

[1] Of Marlborough College; afterwards Captain, Norfolk Regiment.

people will suddenly wake up to the fact that the superannuation rule is exactly the wrong way about. I mean, that common sense, reason and all except the most inferior religions can see that it is the successful that ought to be "supered." If I were the Master, I would "super" everyone who had been in the Sixth or XV or XI, or in a position of responsibility for more than a year: this might give a chance to the "Obadiah-stick-in-the-mires" to come to something. However, then there might be such a falling-off in numbers: that's always what prevents reformation—fear of the desertion it always causes at first. So perhaps it's better that I'm not the Master.

So much for the sermon! Now for the prayers. I hope all goes well with you, historically, athletically and socially: also, by the way, discursively. I am leading in every way a model Christian life. I play hockey twice a week with a very mixed bag of German officers in Sunday clothes, stiff shirts, and spats; bald German lawyers in pyjamas, who perspire most vehemently; pale German boys with vermilion caps and pince-nez; fat German girls who laugh incessantly: and a man with nasty animal instincts for destruction who puts me in fear of my life. However I have scored this "season"—yes, Pelly, it's perfectly true—37 goals in eight games. You can judge from that how high the standard of play is. I also get up ten minutes earlier than I need and do Forward-stretch and Back-bend and On-the-toes-rise and other such degrading actions before breakfast. I do two hours' Classics every afternoon, attend Church every other Sunday—and in every way behave like any admirer of the author of *The Christian Year*. However, I cannot do without a little touch of heathenism, and so (although I swore to read no English here) I do just occasionally give myself up to Thomas Hardy and am falling more and more under his influence.

To A. N. G. Peters[1]

The following letter was written to a boy who had to leave Marlborough two years before owing to a breakdown in health.

(?) *February* 1914

Perhaps you hardly remember me, for it is now two years since I saw you. I have no excuse for writing now, except that the period of reminiscence and reflection which follows the close of one's public school career (in your case immaturely cut short, in mine unduly prolonged) has made me want to hear from you—what you are doing now and where and why—and to tell you I personally was far more sorry at your leaving so soon [than] perhaps you imagine. However, I do not know that you missed so much. Personally I found that the best time at M.C. was the earliest—the days under Gould or later with Atkey in the Upper V: when one could dream of future greatness. But when that greatness came in half-fulfilment it was really the devil of a bore. I think now that you were really in some ways to be envied for leaving ripe and not staying stupidly on to deal "unequal laws unto a savage race."

I left M.C. in December much as it ever was. I really grew to like the Master very much. I left the school under martial law, Roseveare being senior prefect: and everything running as perfectly as a machine. I

[1] Afterwards second lieutenant, Manchester Regiment.

grew utterly satiated by the artificiality of the atmosphere of a public school. I think those artificial positions of responsibility (as if everyone in a public school were not *ipso facto* in a position of responsibility!) are a poison to the character of those who hold them; and you were lucky to leave before being forced into one.

I left Atkey in great form. He is a wonderfully nice man, isn't he? I think he is the sanest, humanest man in Common Room. And he has come on a bit as a disciplinarian since Upper Vth days. The amount of trouble he takes with the Sixth without thanks or reward is wonderful. I am so glad your old housemaster is going to Malvern. He certainly has long deserved a headmastership. You remember Crosse[1] doubtless? Perhaps you have heard that he has turned out a really wonderful preacher, since taking orders. His sincerity and directness is a splendid change after the dull conventional rhetoric of such as Blank—good soul! The younger beaks are certainly a vigorous lot.

I am at present in this delightful land, learning the language and getting to know a very delightful and simple and unselfconscious nation. I feel I breathe a freer air than the last few terms when in the prison-house of prefectship. Not but what I regret being away Λακεδαίμονος ἐξ ἐρατεινῆς[2] sometimes: as I daresay you did often. It is chiefly the downs I regret: also many of the people. It was wonderful how nice most people managed to be in spite of the horrible public school system that sets up rivalry between neighbours, not only in work and games but in daily intercourse, so that

[1] Afterwards S.C.F., D.S.O., author of *The God of Battles*.
[2] From lovely Lacedæmon.

everyone is tempted to score points at others' expense. The acquaintance of German boys has shown me how [much] better their simple day-school system is.... Yet there is something in Marlborough that I would not have missed for worlds.

Now what are you doing? I want very much to hear from you: rumours of you at Cape Horn were the last I heard. I hope you are fit and well again. I go up to Oxford—University College—in October. Any chance of seeing you there?

I hope you don't mind my writing. But I am really anxious to know you again. I always wanted to see more of you at M.C.—but there the beastly system got in the light: and then you had to leave—perhaps as well for you. I draw a bow at a venture in addressing this letter merely "York." But I do hope it will hit.

To A. E. Hutchinson

26 *February* 1914

Thanks for your two, especially the overweight one. I hope Henn conveyed my message about *The Harrovians* to you. I only meant that I didn't like to think of you spending on that silly book six shillings of your money, which might far better be given to the Little Sisters. However, it is not such a bad book to read if you can get it free. It is very amusingly written, but as a novel it is beyond redemption. The man has no idea what art is. The technique is pitiful. The only character that shows any attempt at character drawing is a most unpleasant youth. It is an amusing enough diary: but to masquerade as a novel is profanation.

Talking about books reminds me of your prize. I know those publishers' catalogues well and used to spend hours in their company when R. had banished me from my study by singing "The Girl in the Taxi." However, I assure you you could not have applied to a better person than me. I have chosen prizes for other people for years. To begin with, it is unnecessary to have them bound. I have always thought that the way they insisted on having all books bound was eminently typical of the public school attitude to life and humanity: "spend more than half always on exteriors; as long as the outside is nice and showy, Lord! what do the contents and kernel matter?"...

My "poem" is, I am afraid, copyright. It is not meant for all eyes. The six escaped criminals, who sit behind big black desks in the [*Marlborough*] *Times* office and look like clerks, had a wonderful habit of emending my verse whenever they considered that "same" (as shops say) was likely to corrode the morals or religion of the school. Therefore I shudder to think what their united efforts would work on it.

I cannot satisfactorily discover to what extent La Chasse exists in Germany. In one of my grammars there is a Hunter who constantly comes in, is cruel and shoots bears. But then there is also a Heathen who is always dragging Hides across a Heath to-day—always "to-day"—and I can imagine him meeting a Christian (the Christian of course dragging nothing) and the Christian saying to him mockingly "Jam yesterday, jam to-morrow, but never jam to-day," and passing on rejoicing, and the Heathen looking ruefully at his nasty bloody hides which he *must* drag and thinking to himself

"Yes that is at once the advantage and damnation of Christianity. For them it is always jam to-day."—But Lord! what am I talking about? I mean I don't think there is any such thing in Germany. For the Cruel Hunter in my grammar (whom the author occasionally and with great unwillingness allows is also "bold") always "shoots," and my enquiries from the B.s have corroborated this statement. However, I have read a ripping poem about dogs who were not allowed to go out hunting. "So bleiben die Hünde zu Hause zurück—zu Hause bleiben die Hünde," and that may bring hope.

Yesterday I ruptured the Sabbath badly and was well punished. I went to an Opera called *Carmen* with the rest of the family and was miserably bored. The Frau was bored too, so that healed things a little. However, I know not to go to an Opera again; though the first time I went to the theatre here, I saw the finest modern play—*John Gabriel Borkman*, Ibsen of course—very well acted.

I apologise for the scrappiness of this letter, but I have been so engrossed in *Jude the Obscure* that I cannot properly think of anything else. Such is Thomas Hardy! However, I hope to be in a better mood and have a better nib next time I write—perhaps I will then even contrive an overweight letter, who knows? But T.H. has temporarily taken possession of myself: horrid old pessimist and scoffer though he is, there is no one like him—except yours ever.

To Professor and Mrs Sorley

27 February 1914

We have had a little snow here, by way of a change, and the place looks quite nice, although hockey is temporarily prevented. The snow, however, has re-opened the old sore about open windows: and I nearly managed to work up "Du lieber Karl" to write to you and ask if you really allowed your son to behave so recklessly at home.

Last week-end was enlivened by a visit from Karl's little brother Hermann, who weighs 16 stone. He is a farmer in the neighbourhood and had come for a visit to Schwerin for the Time of his life. He was accompanied on arrival by a huge cake, not quite as big as himself, which he presented to the Frau, amid shrieks of delight from Karl, as a kind of entrance-fee. It was a goo-ood cake, though I regret to say there were "quarrels" over when it should be eaten—as a kind of pick-me-up between meals? or during Mittagsessen? and, if the latter, after the soup or with the coffee at the end? The latter was decided upon, till suddenly, half-way through Mittagsessen, Du lieber Karl struck and insisted on having his piece before the oranges. Having had it, he repented and had another piece with us with the coffee. Clever man. The great question for discussion while Hermann was there was, Which do you think is fatter, Karl or Hermann? They were eventually measured, and Hermann won. They are dears—but I prefer the Frau's side of the family.

I am sorry to say I broke the Sabbath and was taken to the theatre. However I was punished, for I found it decidedly boring. I thought I must go to an opera sooner or later, so as the others were going, I accompanied them. The piece (I suppose you know it) was entitled *Carmen*, by a man whom I probably ought to have heard of before, called Bizet. There was one tune in it—I know "tune" isn't the proper word, but still—that I had heard before and always liked, that Bullfighter's song, I suppose you know it. But the unreality of the whole thing was so absurd, that except when the Bullfighter air recurred, I felt rather out of it. However I shall know not to go again.

I have this week begun Classics again and am trying to get in two hours or at least an hour and a half a day. They are much more pleasant when not read for the sake of reproduction in a few hours' time: but my tutor's prescription is uncomfortably large.

Thanks for *Punch*. Granville Barker seems in danger of becoming a crank, so perhaps *Midsummer Night's Dream* is hardly worth seeing after all.

To Professor and Mrs Sorley

6 *March* 1914

Thanks so much for the letter. The enclosed picture[1] I passed on to my hostess, who considered it "furchtbar nett von meiner Mutter" to have sent it to her.

Although, when I came here, I rather foolishly swore to read no English except for the hour following Mittagsessen on Sundays while the rest of Germany sleeps—*Jude* of course made me break the oath, and

[1] The second portrait in the earlier editions of *Marlborough and Other Poems*.

I finished it at a rush the other day. I have since re-read it in great part, though I didn't ought to have in a foreign land ; and the second reading has strengthened and increased my first opinion that it is quite the finest novel I know. It is simply not to be compared with *Tess.* Though apparently Hardy had two purposes in writing it : (1) to produce an anti-marriage tract, and (2) a tract to show that life is not worth it, and the sooner the human race die off the better : the novelist in him has completely ousted the tractarian, and Jude is the finest character I have ever met. What he has proved is that continual thwarting is far better than attainment, and for the way in which the reader sees Jude visibly becoming nobler before his eyes, it is on a level with *Oedipus* and *Lear.* Any outsider measuring the character of Jude would say : "Here was a man of high ideals but insufficient determination who ended by going to the bad." But Hardy never lets the reader count any of Jude's visible sins against him. I think you will agree, when you have read the book, that Jude is one of the finest, because most unpityingly conscientious men you have ever met in a book. As with Oedipus and Othello, it was his conscientiousness that did for him.

The heroine I also find convincing though I did not at first : but on that subject I have not the experience to judge. She also comes to grief through over-conscientiousness. But part of the tragedy of the book is that the great sorrow of their lives—their children's death—narrows and warps her outlook on life, while it only enlarges and perfects that of Jude. The glory of the book is its failure : I mean that Hardy, setting out to show that it were better for Jude if he had never been born, shows exactly the reverse. Though Jude dies quoting Job to that effect, you see that he is wrong. Among other things Jude has stimulated me to reading Job. Hardy's outlook on life seems to me very like that of Job : only Job was in the end convinced when God spoke to him out of the whirlwind, Hardy not.

Another reason why I like the book so much is that it is North Wessex. The first part takes place at "Marygreen" one of those ricketty villages that I know so well by the Icknield Way overhanging "Alfredston" (Wantage)—about fifteen miles from Marlborough. There is another part at "Melchester" (Salisbury), and quite a lot at "Aldbrickham," which is Reading, and "Kennetbridge," which is Newbury. And a third of the whole is at "Christminster" (Oxford) which the honorary fellow of Magdalene College, Cambridge, regards with suitable contempt. And one or two of the best scenes in the book take place on the north-east Berkshire downs, which are cousins to the Marlborough downs.

Like in *Far from the Madding Crowd*, there are four protagonists, all clearly and convincingly drawn, and a chorus. The chorus in *Jude* is Jude's great-aunt, and after her death the widow Edlin—two of the most delightful characters in literature. The only fault of the book is that they don't come in enough.

I shall send the book home with my winter clothes, for I'm sure you will like it. If you want it earlier, do say so. I'm sure you'll agree it is one of the great books of the world.

I heard from Atkey yesterday—such a nice letter. He had been to *Midsummer Night's Dream* and said that he was very struck. He said that Owen Seaman in his review missed the whole point—that lack of scenery was not a pose but a means of preventing long distracting pauses and consequent cuts. He also approved of the gilt faces.

By the way, did *you* know that Thomas Hardy married his secretary three weeks ago? I hope you didn't for I, who do not even know whether Ulster or England have yet won, feel great pride in conveying such news from Germany.

As I kept on forgetting to send for old *Marlburians*, I am sending herewith some of my efforts composed while devouring "curry in cloud-cuckoo land," as I gathered you wanted to see them[1].

To A. E. Hutchinson

March 1914

That is the worst of public schools. The artificiality of the atmosphere entirely unfocusses the eye. The real reason (though I don't believe I ever mentioned it to you) why I kept on beseeching my father to disregard Gidney's sermons and take me away, was that—though the surroundings of Marlborough and one or two of the inhabitants of the College were almost un-do-without-able—I simply couldn't endure the position of Head of House any longer. I had a dreadful warning at the beginning of the term when I talked public-school-story rot instead of refusing to make a mountain from a mole-hill, and preached a sermon

[1] Nos. ii, iii, v, vi, ix, xiv, xix in *Marlborough and Other Poems*, 4th ed. The phrase in inverted commas in the previous line was made by combining two criticisms in school reports.

instead of bursting out laughing. I couldn't risk degrading myself again, in case —— tried a similar joke a second time: but in such a position it is almost impossible not to. "My heart! how young we were"—and are still for that. I don't mean that positions of responsibility are immediately poisonous; like many things they are an excellent medicine at first, but develope into a poison. One or two terms are very good, I should say, and that's why I hope you'll stay on till the Christmas term. But Heaven pity poor prefects! You have to act from day to day and say what you don't think in dormitory and think that you are good and become a prig. It has ruined many people.

Sidney Webb besides being a Fabian is beyond all other things a Husband. Every week in *The New Statesman* many articles on Socialism appear by Sidney and Beatrice Webb. Whether Sidney dictates and Beatrice writes, or Beatrice writes and Sidney applies the blotting-paper, or Sidney's soul and Beatrice's soul work in such close partnership (as is so fashionable now-a-days) that they both think of the same thing at the same time (like the seventy clerks who translated the Septuagint, all working in different cells and having no communication with each other, and they all finished at the same moment and the seventy results were word for word the same: which proves that Abel really lived and God wrote the Bible)—I don't know. And at the Fabian Summer School the same sweet conjugality hovers around. On Monday afternoon, Beatrice Webb will give an address to Mothers on the Necessity of State-motherhood, and Sidney Webb will take the chair. On Monday evening, Sidney Webb will give an address to Men of Full Age on Statecraft and the State-soul: the chair will be taken by Mrs Sidney Webb. They live in a perpetual halo of mutual admiration, put their trust in figures, write articles to show how easily the whole world could be put right, but have not up to date succeeded in making it any better.

Things continue well here, though a little slow. I have been able to obtain no clear information about harriers. I hope you are flourishing, and Christian relations between you and your form-master continue.

What more shall I say?—as Paul said when he wanted to fill up space. Do I write nicer letters than Paul? I hope so. But I feel this evening I have rather given way—like Paul—to my old vice of preaching.

Atkey wails over Dyson's leaving in his letter. He is quite right. A man like Dyson without a public school education and a mind that never curled itself up, but was always ready to receive new things, was invaluable at Marlborough. Dyson and Bicker left! If the last of the trio—Atkey—also leaves, there's an end of Marlborough.

But I ought to be doing Classics.

To Professor and Mrs Sorley

13 *March* 1914

A "lovely little" letter, two *Punches*, a postcard, a *Cambridge Review* and a *Times Lit. Sup.* on Dryden, all just arrived. Thank you so much for them all. The Frau sends a message of sorts. I suppose this exchange of compliments will continue every week in Ewigkeit. I am glad the letter was so nice for so is the writer.

I am so glad the presentation of the portrait[1] was such a success. Was Balfour there? I can imagine what a Germany Dr Ward was in. Even now the magic word "Achtzehnhundertsiebzig" produces a transformation, and even the Herr Doktor stops eating (to which he is more sympathetic than anything else) and bursts into poetry (though ganz und gar unpoetical)—and the frog of the fairy story is turned for a moment into a prince.

Yesterday I had a great evening. An agnogger from the South of the name of Professor Drews burst into Christian Mecklenburg and was invited to speak at a "Vortrag" in Schwerin. We all went, the Philolog armed with a note-book and pencil, the Herr Doktor in a state of bottled wrath and sulks at having to go and hear a lunatic (all who disagree with Herr Dr B. are lunatics), and the Frau very anxious to go and with some humour declaring that her character in Schwerin would be lost for ever. The hall was full of people, half very respectable, and half with red carnations in their buttonholes—Social Democrats—ugh! We sat among the Pharisees, of course. The agnogger was a little man, like Uncle George to look at. He agnogged in spite of interruptions for two hours, and I could follow him fairly well. As long as he was insulting their religion he only produced smiles of contempt from the righteous and polite noddings of the head from the red carnations. But when he began insulting their State there was an uproar in the house. The red carnations rocked with pleasure, the righteous looked as if they were trying to be sick. At last, when he

[1] Of Professor Ward to Cambridge University, 28 Feb. 1914.

yelled at the top of his cracky voice that the Christian Germans who omitted to wear red carnations were slaves, there was nearly war. Many left the house to prove that they were not. Others proved they were not by standing up for the rest of his speech. Some spat and others fought the empty air with fists. The red carnations were awfully pleased. The tumult was at last stilled, and the agnogger fought like a terrier for another hour.

I was very grateful to him, for his delivery was remarkably precise and clear, and I understood better than I had ever hoped. He was very clever and, I should say, earnest, but hopelessly lacking in controversial dignity: as indeed were many of the speakers. The debate continued for about two hours more. He was reproved by a very nice man called Hermann Turck who lives in Schwerin and has written a book (think!); by a ranting lawyer, one of the chief in Schwerin, with a mind as narrow as his second chest was broad; by a gentle thin-faced Baptist minister with a thin black beard, rather like Jude to look at, and far more reasonable than I imagine his Lutheran brothers to be. He was supported by cranks from among the red carnations—awful men with hair falling about their shoulders, with no collars and obviously dirty beards—strange creepy creatures that I thought only existed in England. I could understand them very little, but it did strike me that the tone of controversy was very low. But the whole thing gave me a different idea of Schwerin. It is not such a provincial place as I thought by any means. It seems that it is only the lawyers and officers—the highest grade socially—that are the lowest intellectually.

Those people in the Vortrag (not only the red carnations) with whom we don't 'sociate—actors, journalists, Jews—seem to lead a much freer life than their social superiors. I got a little scolded by the Herr Doktor for clapping Otto Drews; he was much disgusted by the whole thing, and *schimpfed* dreadfully. But it was nice of him to come, for he didn't want to. The thing went on till past midnight.

I am so glad this blessed baron can't be bothered. It is very kind of Mr F., but I am very afraid of these grey-coated officers who look as if they wear stays.

I was pleased to see the Dyson cutting [from *Punch*]. I have not yet outgrown the stage of being very pleased at seeing the word Marlborough (otherwise than Duke, Suburban Theatre, Palace or Police-Court) in print. It is very sad, Dyson's leaving. Music apart, he was invaluable at Marlborough, being the only member of Common Room without a public school education.

The Frau and I have read together several plays of Ibsen's, several technically beautiful but slightly sentimental stories from Theodor Storm, and are doing now the last book of *Wilhelm Meisters Lehrjahre—die Bekenntnisse einer schönen Seele*. By myself I have finished *Egmont* and am about to start *Faust*. But lately I have been trying to give two hours a day to my old enemies, the Classics, so I have not had so much time.

To Professor and Mrs Sorley

20 *March* 1914

Thanks so much for the letter and enclosures, and the three papers that arrived the following day. I am so glad the *Times Lit. Sup.* is now on its own, for it is really the only kind of newspaper that I had previously missed out here.

Yes, the name is Arthur not Otto. It is the abominable way they have of pronouncing Arthur. Drews is pronounced to rhyme with "slaves." He is a professor in some technical High School in the South. I have looked up the report of his speech in the paper. He did not insist on his Christ-myth idea, but he did put everything about that time in a very hypothetical way. Nor did he state precisely he was a Sozialdemokrat. Only it was the Social D.s that had got him down to talk, so of course he patted their backs for them. His speech put forth no special theory, as he was addressing amateurs. Its title was Der Verfall des Christentums, so he did not trouble about building up a substitute. And the Christianity he attacked was merely the North German Christianity, which needs attacking. Altogether his matter was very reasonable and temperate.

I have been writing German for some time. After about three weeks I began translating gobbets from *Jude the Obscure* (which distressed them at first, because they thought Jude meant "Jew" and a book—other than the Gospels, of course—whose hero was Jewish couldn't be a nice aristocratic book). Since then I have written a certain amount of essays, subsequent on which we argue furiously for hours. Now, however, I have rather given up the habit, preferring to read more. But I shall start it again, for I am a terribly inaccurate speaker, and have never the patience to wait till the end of the subordinate clauses for their verb. I have occasionally pamphlets and documents in English to translate for Karl, which is good fun.

I have this minute returned from the theatre and got the second letter, for which many thanks. I have given the enclosure to the Frau, who, being the kind of person who feels other people's disappointments far more keenly than her own, is overcome with distress and sympathy for Ken. We had such a clear view of the future for us two Zwillingsbrüder[1] a month ago, that it is no surprise that it should prove an illusion. But I am so glad it is nothing radical and will only prove an episode. And I hope it does not mean altogether the giving up of the idea of Oxford in October. But if it is to purchase good health, I should think anything is worth it.

It may be "sex hatred," but I cannot stand Mrs Meynell, since I read *The Lady Poverty*, which simply asks for the answer "I adore that dirt!" When she says in another poem that "her thoughts are sheep" she always seems to me to tell the truth. She is far too precious as far as I have read her, but perhaps M. has introduced you to something written with a thicker pencil.

Three days ago I was at *Richard the Third*. It was excellently staged, without being overdone, but at the cost of many maddening pauses which Barker's Liberty curtains and twopenny tubs would have avoided. The scene in Richard's tent in the last act, with the flap half lifted and a cold darkness without and a wild appealing bugle sounding at uncertain intervals, was a masterpiece of mimicry and reminded me exactly of—the O.T.C. camp! You could smell the night outside. But the cost of this good staging—besides maddening pauses, giving opportunity among my neighbours for the discussion

[1] Twin-brothers.

of the price of eggs with an eagerness that I thought was only known in arithmetic books—was one or two serious cuts. Much of the female parts was cut—and the women are wonderfully good in *Richard III*; while the uninteresting parts about Hastings, Rivers, Vaughan and Grey and such impersonalities that seem to be killed and come alive again in all Shakespeare's historical plays—all that was left untouched. The best scene was the "Clarence is come, false, fleeting, perjured Clarence" one in the Tower, though that particular line dies in German. The part of Richard (which is the whole play) was taken by the same man as did John Gabriel Borkman, and who acts the part of megalomaniacs very well. But he could have been much better, was not half ugly enough and indeed looked most attractive, leaping about in bright gold armour and offering his kingdom for a horse. His fine opening speech he declaimed Macready-wise to the house, not as a soliloquy, but as a kind of prologue. But towards the end he acted very finely, and the production, though in very many ways imperfect, showed that Richard, bar Margaret of Anjou (who was a Richard in her day), is the only noble person in the play. And after all, the best a production of Shakespeare can do is to suggest to each of the audience what he would consider the perfect production : which it has to me : therefore I am very critical thereof.

This evening I have seen the most famous actor in Germany and reputed one of the best in the world. His name is Paul Wegener, and if I had not heard of him before, I have seen him now. The piece is *Gyges und sein Ring* by Friedrich Hebbel : a very good play, without being earth-shaking. I cannot criticize because I do not quite understand it: the characters are so inconsistent, even for Orientals. As I read the play beforehand, the smooth beauty of its blank verse and its seeking after greatness and finding none, also the fact of a fairly modern writer writing under ancient stage conventions, kept on reminding me of Stephen Phillips: though I should now put it on a much higher level than that. As a whole the piece is unsatisfying: but there are fine bursts of poetry and one or two real remarks. And the part of Candaules was wonderfully played by Paul Wegener. He was incredibly passionate and startling, without ever descending to the melodramatic. Now that I come to think of it, it is certainly a remarkable play: it bears towards the end some slight resemblance to *Antony and Cleopatra*.

TO A. E. HUTCHINSON

20 *March* 1914

I fear we are not so like Sidney and Beatrice after all. For never once did I think of whiling away the slow hours spent in Chapel in the interests of religion, by pretending it was Parliament. I certainly sympathized with you two Sundays ago, but I had no idea you would be sitting on red forms and debarred from praying in the conventional way.

Here we are also in the grips of an approaching confirmation. The shops are making a great profit from it. There are many special windows labelled "suitable presents for confirmation candidates." I hoped that the presents were prayer-books, watch-chain crosses, texts for bedroom use, etc. But no; the presents were all tooth-brushes, hair-brushes, nail-brushes, soap, scent, sponge-bags and complexion-creams for confirmation. But don't think the Germans are without a sense of humour. A beastly little rag-and-bone shop quite near displayed in the window a pair of decayed kettle-holders with "suitable present for confirmation candidates" engraved thereon, in satire of its finer brothers down the street. The owner of the shop who first thought of presenting all intending Christians with a kettle-holder on their entry into the Church, was a man of real genius. I bow.

Good luck to Robert Browning as interpreted by the Master. I have on the whole less respect for Browning than I have for Paul, who was also called Saul. But that is of course entirely my loss, and, as the Master once laboriously explained to me, I must not therefore think that St Paul or Browning mind very much. Do suggest something absurdly atheistical to the Master (as I suppose he approaches Browning from the theological and never from the literary standpoint). Browning has (I don't know whether you have noticed it) a hearty bounding incorrigible optimism which must be very comforting to Christians. He was always content with second best.

Your attempt to explain the "sacred miracle of the Septuagint" is "perverse ingenuity." I learnt all about it from your spiritual pastor and master Moule: as also these two phrases above.

Thanks for the news about Mrs Stevenson. I tried to be sorry but failed. I once met a friend of the lady's who said in gasps "that she always came down to breakfast at 11 o'clock in a (sigh)—teagown! and besides she was divorced from her first husband." I never knew what a tea-gown was, but imagined it to be a nice soft dressing-gown with frills: and with the help of the bird's-nest hair can make up a very pretty picture of her eating shrivelled toast and greasy eggs and bacon and schimpfing at Louis' endearments at 11.30 a.m. We might make up a poem about it:

Women who seek, obtain, employ Divorce
Are only fit for men of Greed and Force.
Women who take their Breakfast three hours late
Are only fit for men of Spite and Hate.
Women who wear a Tea-gown all the time
Are only fit for men of Vice and Crime.
But women such as get Divorced, and then
Come down to Break their Fast at e-lev-en,
Garbed in a Tea-gown (ye Commandments Ten!)
—Are only fit for Literary Men!

That would be a nice epitaph for her coffin, and you supply the wreath.

I have been lately very "gay." The German supper is a terror. The people come at seven and talk about the rise in the price of butter till 8. From 8 till 9.30 they eat and drink and talk about the niceness of the victuals, and ask the hostess their cost. From 9.30 to 10.30 they talk about the scarcity of eggs. From 10.30 to 11 they drink beer and cross-examine ME about the Anglo-German crisis. From 11 to 12 they make personal remarks and play practical jokes on one another. From 12 to 12.30 they eat oranges and chocolates and declare they must be going now. From 12.30 to 1 they get heavy again and sigh over the increased cost of living in Schwerin. At 1 they begin to scatter. By 2 I am in bed. However don't let this put you off Germany.

The only interesting person I have met in all these gay Lent supper-parties is a twisted man, with only one lung and an ear-trumpet, who had the ghastly assurance to tell me to my face that he knew the whole of *Richard the Third* off by heart. I whistled and bellowed down the ear-trumpet that this was impossible. But he stuck to his guns and, in order to cast his previous exaggeration in the shade, he perpetrated a far grosser one. Standing on his tiptoes he bellowed at me, like Humpty Dumpty to the Keeper of the Little Fishes, "And it isn't the only play that I know right off by heart. I know very many of his pieces off by heart. And (hiccup) I think him (hiccup, bellow) a good poet!" It was not till afterwards that I realised all this gross perjury was merely committed to please me and fill my patriotic heart with pride. But if it were true! Think of the pathos of the thing! A hideously deformed little dwarf, with a six-foot wife; lame (because a big dog once knocked him down and rolled him about the street, thinking he was a doll); deaf and overworked; and knowing *Richard the Third* (why *Richard the Third*?) off by heart, and having no opportunity to make use of his hard-won knowledge. Perhaps he repeats bits in the bedroom, when She isn't there, all to himself, and imagines sometimes that he is a Richard and "descants on his own deformity" and is "determined to prove a villain." But it's rather silly to make all these "baseless conjectures" (Moule), considering I have only seen the couple once in my life.

It is 12.30, and I can't go on for ever like Tennyson's beastly brook.

I envy you this part of the Lent Term. I always liked

it, so far as it was not interfered with by Sports. Decent weather, no hockey, no exams, heaps of time: and there is certainly something exciting in the annual arrival of spring. Savernake canal and the Bedwyn side of the forest are at their best then.

To Professor and Mrs Sorley

27 *March* 1914

I hope the day in London—though spent for a rather different purpose than the accustomed day in London—brought satisfactory results and "a lovely little home" for Kenneth.

Do *force* him to take some Hardy to the Nursing Home. In my busybodyish way, I am very anxious to thrust it down his throat, and I'm sure that with *Far from the Madding Crowd* and *The Trumpet Major* (which I can later send) Nursing Home were paradise enow.

Karl sends his "recommendations" which he does monthly. He "finds so kind" of you to ask him and his wife to pay a visit, but it is quite impossible. Heavens! he is fat.

We are having some very inspiring weather and Schwerin is looking highly picturesque. Hockey is going strong, though one or two officers have very sensibly taken to playing in spurs, so that when they get the ball their way to the goal remains undisputed. The ladies have also taken to playing in cameras, so that one cannot oppose them without being snapshotted or breaking the camera. O, we such are dogs getting! My, such goings on!

I have been to *J. G. Borkman* a second time with great pleasure: otherwise the week has been quiet. I have taken to reading the papers with diligence, now that things are coming to a head. They purr a little, naturally, but are never really schadenfroh[1], and rejoice more at the failure of a Liberal and would-be democratic government to keep its subjects in order (for they are sound conservative papers) than at the possible self-inflicted wounds of the rival nation.

Faust is to be given here on Easter Monday, so the Frau and I are reading it. So far it seems to me more a wonderful collection of "very good remarks" than a dramatic masterpiece, but as I have only read half so far, I oughtn't to be talking; and it is as much as my life is worth to express that opinion with the Philolog near. He examines me and the Frau every evening on what we have read and our understanding thereof, and turns a deaf ear to his sister's chaff. I never knew how nice and natural and interesting a pedant could be till I met the Philolog.

I am still being naughty with my Classics. I am bobbing through the *Odyssey* at the rate of two books a week, and I have read one play of Euripides, and begun one of Aeschylus: but I am reading only what I enjoy. In obedience to the tutor man I have spent about fivepence on a certain amount of molehills made into mountains by that short-sighted swelled-headed narrow-minded windbag Demosthenes, but the leaves of the ugly yellow books as yet remain uncut. The *Odyssey* is a great joy when once you can read it in big chunks

[1] Malicious. (But the word has no exact equivalent in English or French.)

and not a hundred lines at a time, being able to note all the silly grammatical strangenesses or else a pained Master. I could not read it in better surroundings, for the whole tone of the book is so thoroughly German and domestic. A friend of sorts of the Bieders died lately; and, when the Frau attempted to break the news to Karl at table, he immediately said "Don't tell me anything sad while I'm eating." That very afternoon I came across someone in the *Odyssey* who made, under the same circumstances, precisely the same remark[1]. In the *Odyssey* and in Schwerin alike they are perfectly unaffected about their devotion to good food. In both too I find the double patriotism which suffers not a bit from its duplicity—in the *Odyssey* to their little Ithaca as well as to Achaea as a whole; here equally to the Kaiser and the pug-nosed Grand Duke. In both is the habit of longwinded anecdotage in the same rambling irrelevant way, and the quite unquenchable hospitality. And the Helen of the *Odyssey*, bustling about a footstool for Telemachus or showing off her new presents (she had just returned from a jaunt to Egypt)—a washing-tub, a spindle, and a work-basket that ran on wheels (think!)—is the perfect German Hausfrau.

Which reminds me: I have read Schiller's *Lied von der Glocke* as advised. It struck me there was something rather too domestic and conventional about it. I found the whole tone a little contented, and I did not like the compromise between fact and ideal that seemed to me to be one of its chief motives.

Thanks so much for *Punch* and *Times Lit. Sup.* which came this evening. I shall attack that article of Henry

[1] *Odyssey*, iv, 193, 194. See below, p. 148.

James to-morrow. At present, I have not the clarity of mind and concentration which his style seems to demand.

To F. A. H. Atkey

Early in April 1914

Thanks very much indeed for your letter. I hope your walking tour will be a great success. However, I shall not have the pleasure of seeing you. The reason is still a little dark, but I am not being allowed so far south as Munich. There is still a hope of Berlin. But I think it will be Jena, which seems to be most like Oxford or Cambridge of the German Universities. And I daresay it will be very stimulating with all the ghosts of all the Goethes and all the shades of all the Schillers in the neighbourhood. This provincial part of Germany does not seem to me to have yet recovered from the influence of Goethe and Schiller. Their family guide to conduct is the *Lied von der Glocke*, which has such a horribly domestic conventional and compromising tone, that I cannot stand it. Their outlook on life here seems to me 140 years old. However, that is because I am naturally only allowed to 'sociate with the very best people in Schwerin, the officers with minds like kittens and the lawyers with minds like tom-cats. But down in the "slums" of Schwerin they seem to be a very breezy lot. They have religious debates every week, which I am now allowed to attend, and distinguished agnoggers from the South come and speak to them. They are really tremendously enjoyable debates, and most pugnacious. But the leading spirits are not "our class," besides often also hailing from Morgenland (as they say here: a great joke), so I never see them personally.

Still, I still like my people immensely. They are liebenswürdig to the ground of their hearts. It seems to me a typical difference between the two nations that, in English, a charge of "amiability" is an insult while here "liebenswürdig" is the highest praise. But such contemporaries as I have met at hockey here (the spirit in which hockey is played might be imitated with advantage by Marlborough) are very nice indeed and extraordinarily earnest. They wear white caps that the world may know they are in the top form of the gymnasium, and ask me to repeat the first line of the *Odyssey* that they may mark the difference between the German and English pronunciation of Greek. The fact that I did not know what the first line of the *Odyssey* was must have nipped many potential friendships in the bud, for that made them pity and ultimately, when they tried me with the first line of the *Carmen Saeculare*, despise me, even though I am much better than them at hockey (though I say it as shouldn't). At Marlborough we were always encouraged to despise and reject such as knew the first line of the *Odyssey* and the *C. S.*, and to love, honour, and obey such as were better than us at hockey. Here the reverse. Hard on me, because at Marlborough I was if anything on the side of the angels who knew the first line of the *Odyssey*, and now I am among those whose hockey is their fortune. However, I bear up wonderfully in spite of it and am still enjoying the place enormously. Also my failure in the first line of the *Odyssey* moved me to spend threepence on that work, and I have already got as far as where the poet explains that the immortal gods always recognize one another, even the ones that have houses far away: which I need not remind you comes at the beginning of Book V. I feel I could not read it in better surroundings. The domesticity, the hospitality, the love of eating, telling long stories and giving gifts in the *Odyssey* is so very Mecklenburgish. I have also read the *Ion*: thought Creusa first-rate, but was immensely sorry for the poor Xouthos.

I saw of Mr Dyson's leaving first in *Punch* with a joke appended, then from many correspondents (besides you) with a wail following. It is now an "I only am left" case for you, of the triad that invaded Russia. It is a great pity for Marlborough—I mean that the others are gone, not of course that you are left.

I am sticking at present to Schiller and Goethe, but I hope soon to get on to "those modern fellows," as Mr Gidney calls them, Sudermann, etc. I have however found time for *Peer Gynt* and *Brand*, and entirely agree with you about them. With an excellent theatre here I am having a pretty full time. The immense relief of entire freedom from those warping artificial "positions of responsibility" (that delightful phrase which the supporters of public schools use under the impression, I suppose, that only such people as they delight to honour have responsibility in a community)! What now seems to me such a pity was the way the public school atmosphere deliberately overdevelopes the nasty tyrannical instincts. One is positively encouraged to confuse strength of character with petty self-assertion, and conscientiousness with Phariseeism. And, as you say, as far as one comes into relation with masters, things are made difficult, and as a pupil I was always a child. Give me your German day-school that makes them so earnest and lemonfaced and pincenezed and unashamed of the pursuit of learning: and not the public school that makes one self-conscious, ashamed of knowledge, always seeking to impress, and regarding all contemporaries as possible rivals. However, if I had been at a German day-school, I should have said exactly the opposite. Theoretically it seems there is not a thing to be said for our public school system. But yet it has given me and heaps of others five years that could hardly have been more enjoyable. I wonder why. Perhaps because human nature flourishes better in a poisonous atmosphere.

But look here, I must stop this. I should not be burdening you with all this egoism. I have been, by the way, to *Richard III* here, magnificently, almost Beerbombastically, produced. It brought out splendidly what you said about Barker's production of *Midsummer N. D.* My neighbours could not agree about the price of eggs. I would almost have preferred an orchestra.

In three weeks my time in a provincial German town will be over. It has been fine. I have also now got a reasonable hold of their fine shaggy language. We live opposite the barracks, and Stevenson, who used to give pennies to children for looking happy, would not have had any left if he looked long across the street from my window into those red pancakes. And when 400 of them sing at once!

To Professor and Mrs Sorley

3 *April* 1914

Thanks so much for the letter and the post-card. The former I was very glad to receive after returning from my sixth visit to the theatre. The piece was Schiller's *Wilhelm Tell.* I had read it before, and thus lessened my disappointment. It seems to me the most commonplace play. The only point which I could find in the reading of it—that Tell's real victory was not in freeing all those beastly Swisses, but in the last scene but one, when he concealed the contemptible Johannes Parricida from punishment—disappeared entirely on the stage owing to the important scene being three-quarters cut. If Schiller did mean this to be the point of the play, he might have brought it out more clearly and prevented the producers from cutting it. Otherwise it is only the history of the freedom of a country, and one can't be interested in the freedom of a country on the stage. There is a perfect web of underplot and no clash of character at all. Schiller makes the tyrant as black as he can, and, as I am always on the side of tyrants, this annoyed me. A fat pupil of Max Reinhardt's, who was born hereabouts and was paying a flying visit, took the part of Tell. His technique was marvellous, so marvellous that he might just as well have been a machine. But the local actors were all as good as usual—the megalomaniac, who is one of the finest actors I have ever seen, doing his best with the part of the tyrant, with whom Schiller has no sympathy. What I have read of the man leaves me quite cold. When I suggest this with many "abers," I am told that he had such a beautiful character, such bad consumption—and was so good for Goethe. However I must read *The Bride of Messina*, which I have heard has something wonderful in it.

No, Sudermann and Hauptmann have not yet come so far north as Mecklenburg. Even Ibsen is suspected. It is certainly far off the lines. I do not wish to be disrespectful to my host, but unless it is the [case] that lieber Karl thinks it necessary to cloak all pretence of having any sense whatever as soon as he enters his own house (like a lot of schoolboys, when they enter the classroom)—he is really a most extraordinarily vacant creature. He simply refuses to speak about any reasonable subject whatever. The only two times he has spoken reasonably were (1) to stand up for a pastor whom we had just heard preach a sermon against the growing tendency to cremation, on the ground (seriously) that Christ was not cremated: and (2) this evening, when he disputed the right of criticizing an actor on the ground that that actor could act better than his critic. It seems to me that among the Upper Classes of Schwerin the only person of any ideas is—Frau B. As you mention the subject, it is really extraordinary in what a primitive backward state is this city (not two hours from Berlin). This, of course, makes it all the more delightful for a three months' visit. But to live here must be appalling. Their view of women, too, is pretty low: they are strictly limited to being Hausfraus, and any practising on the violoncello must be carried on in the strictest secrecy[1].

Well, I am sorry St Giles' has bodily declared for Ulster. When I heard of the Archdeacon's successful

[1] See *Pendennis*, vol. II, chap. 6.

lures in the 'bus, Mrs B.'s remark "One always gives one's self away in the 'bus" occurred to me. The local newspapers (we only take in local ones) give a certain amount about it, chiefly chippings from the *Times*. I suppose one of the cartoons in this week's *Punch* was Asquith as Lady Macbeth and Seely as Macbeth—"Infirm of purpose! Give me the dagger." I can't help having a great admiration for our Prime Minister.

The family's ideas on the subject are not very helpful. Du Karl, except for a fixed idea that England is just waiting for a suitable opportunity to attack poor Deutschland, has no interest outside Mecklenburg. The Frau of course is indifferent to politics. The Philolog, and one or two others who have spoken of the situation, seem to think it inconceivable that the army should refuse to obey its government. The assertion that such things could never happen in Germany seems to sum up for them the situation.

We have been indulging in supper parties lately. The Germans feel the difficulty of rising very much. They come at 7 and do not leave till one. At first I was a little taken aback when old ladies waddled up to me and told me with serenity of their buried love-affairs, but now I am quite accustomed to it. One delightful old thing, that side seventy, on being introduced to me and thinking probably that conversation would prove rather difficult, began boldly "You wouldn't think that I've been engaged three times and not married yet, ha, ha!" All three broken hearts had some kind of connection with some of the other guests, who were occasionally called in to vouch for the truth of her statements. I have also met a man who is both deaf and lame, five feet high and toothless, who knows *Richard III* off by heart. His character is as beautiful as the White Knight's. For, he explained to me, a dog once knocked him down and made him deaf. But not to be beaten by no dogs, he learnt *Richard III* off by heart. So now he can go to see *Richard III* as often as he likes, and enjoy it just as much as if the dog had never knocked him down. So the time passes pretty quick.

The news of Cambridge's victory[1] crossed the North Sea all right and got into the local paper. I missed it myself, but Karl very kindly drew my attention to it.

We have been having beautiful weather, and the beauty of the country grows on one. I see now, it was ploughed fields without hedges that put me out so much at first.

To A. E. Hutchinson

April 1914

"When I survey that wondrous Cross
On which the Prince of glory died
My richest gain I count but loss
And pour contempt on all my pride"
John Newton 1771—1830.

But as the nature of hymns demands that the word Cross should recur pretty frequently and all their ideas are drawn from a common stock, perhaps Cardinal (John Henry) Newman and Catherine Winkworth have used it too, for of course "loss" is the only decent rhyme for "cross," though "purge my earthly dross" can come occasionally. However, if you are ever again in any difficulty about hymns, my boy, apply strait to

[1] In the boat-race.

me. (I quite recognize that I've spelt "strait" wrong, so you needn't laugh at me. *You* spelt Harvey with an *e* and cried "cryed.") For (to continue) I know all College hymn-book off by heart[1], from Bishop Ken (1590—1660) who did dread the grave as little as his bed, as if he *was* just a little afraid of his bed, to Frances Ridley Havergal (1840—1895) whose name gives no clear clue to its sex, but who asked the Lord in one swift and passionate sacred poem to take its heart, soul, mind, voice, intellect and feet and do whatever he liked with them.

I had forgotten the bishop's edifying story, but it is truly typical. Nothing riles me more than the ceaseless flirtation between the Church and Army. But after all, why shouldn't they? They are so very similar. They are both out of date institutions, financed by the State, and have outgrown their use. They are both run on the fallacy that it is enough to tell a reasonable being to do this or that, without explaining why. The officials of both wear ridiculous clothes to mark them out as State pensioners. They are both supposed to fight, but have no one to fight with, other nations having become too civilized to try the strength of the one, and the very existence of the Arch Enemy of the other having fallen into discredit. So bishops seek to curry favour by telling boys how they have preached to soldiers. But since they enjoy themselves immensely in their fools' paradise and give you and me something to laugh at, I'm not complaining.

I was interested to hear your criticisms of the "play" acted by that society which for the last year has profaned

[1] But not very accurately, as the dates and quotation show.

and purloined the name of Shakespeare by much the same unwarrantable licence by which the present popular form of Paulinism has purloined and profaned the name of Christ. It must be almost impossible to write a parody of melodrama without being often cheap. But I wish I could have seen it, all the same: not taken part in it, as you suggest, for I am one of those appalling "drags on the progress of humanity" that hate doing and love criticizing. Besides, as a dramatic critic, I have a tremendously high opinion of myself.

Curious that you like P. so. When I see a good-looking and well-dressed person, I immediately instinctively dislike him. My nasty, catty, jealous nature, I suppose.

I am in terrible trouble—you must help me. A cousin of mine, as yet unseen by me, has got engaged. My mother says that I must write to her a nice letter of congratulation. My aunt has written to me and told me to do the same, for "the little thing is so happy." Now tell me what shall I say? I now know she is little, know she is happy and suspect she is feeble-minded. But what shall the tone of the letter be?

Come, nephewish and burly?
Or sonlike, sour and sparse, eh?
Or cousinly and surly?
Or brotherly and blasé?
Or uncleish and "old-girl"y?
Or fatherly and formal?
Or man o' the world and curly?
Or neighbourly and normal?

Excuse me. But in times of excessive emotion my words always rhyme.

The reason for all this nonsense is that Du lieber Karl

has got an Order. An "order," of course, to your P. M.[1] mind suggests a piece of paper on which the signature of a more or less strange man enables the bearer to obtain clothes. It is not this kind of an order Du Karl has got. It is an orange-coloured Maltese Cross which might at a distance be mistaken for gold. The Grand Duke gave it to him this morning, and the reason was his Faithfulness. I suspect it was given to him on the same system that the two quite ungiveable-prize-to boys that are found in every orphanage home are given at the annual jollification a Prize for Collects and a Prize for Improvement, to prevent their being aware of the boundless incapacity of their minds before they are old enough to bear the discovery. Lieber Karl (whose mind has failed to expand since the age of six) made us drink wine all this afternoon in honour of his Faithfulness. It was perfectly beastly and it nearly did for me. The amount of alcohol the German stomach can stand is a marvel. And not to drink fast was to insult Karl's Faithfulness. However, he won't get another for five years, so don't be afraid, but come and see the man who gets an order for Faithfulness and yet is not ashamed.

Heavens! More wine! Called away at 10.30 p.m. to drink a huge tub of wine and consume a mountain of poisoned oysters in honour of Karl's Faithfulness. Frau B. hates it, I think, almost as much as I do, now. I have been so many times asked whether his order "makes me joy" (why the devil should it?) that my face has assumed a permanent grin to render further such questions unnecessary. I have now discovered that Karl is the

[1] Present Marlburian.

first man in the world to have received this particular order before the age of sixty, and that is the reason why he is playing so many hymns at present. You must come to Germany and see Karl. You will also see his wife—who is hewn from another rock altogether: and *there* is someone to admire.

I do hope you are having respectable holidays. During your peaceful sober English Easter think of me being made to hunt for Easter eggs (stale chocolate or rotten marzipan) and, having found them, having to eat them, and smirk at Karl's order and drink toasts to Martin Luther and listen to Karl reading out the Wit of the Week from *Happy Hours or Christ and Laughter*, and being asked sharply at every pause, Has Mr Sorley understood? Did Mr Sorley laugh? O, Mr Sorley can't see jokes! O yes, he can. He makes very good jokes sometimes! Mr Sorley (is he listening?) we like jokes in Germany! Poor me, with my Easter eggs of weary marzipan, my much enduring stomach, my willing ways, my permanent grin. No! the secret will out: though spread it not abroad: I am really growing almost—God save us—patriotic!

To Professor and Mrs Sorley

10 *April* 1914

Du lieber has received an ornament: an orange-coloured cross, striped with red. He is the first known man in the world's history to have received this particular ornament before reaching the age of sixty. Hence he has produced no end of wine—slimy white wines, sour red wines, and crimson frothy sparkling Rhine wine.

I have been put through them all and come out of the ordeal with credit. But that is not the only thing. There is a secret dabei. I must not let it out for four years, but then I will tell you. It is something to do with Karl's title being in the course of time converted and ennobled from Herr Doktor Ministerialsekretär B. to Herr Doktor Re—but hush! Not a word on this subject. But in four years' time the odious word Ministerialsekretär ("the people might think me a common servant. I don't like it," says he with delightful frankness) will disappear, the morning will awaken, the shadows will decay, and this true-hearted servant will be crowned with the title of Regierungsrat, but there! I have let the cat out. Only you mustn't tell all your friends in Cambridge this. I must say that I feel a little sorry for Frau B. in Karl's great joys and sorrows over his ornaments and titles; for one can see it is an effort for her to share them completely.

We have had a rather muddled week owing to the failure of Ida's uncle to believe in the Hell. Frau B. was really awfully humorous about it. Ida appeared to her in tears and told her that her uncle didn't believe in the Hell and could she go home at once? So for two days we had to manage for ourselves, or rather Frau B. had to do all the work. Then returned Ida. "Well, Ida, have you seen your uncle?" "Yes." "And—how is he?" "Well, he says he will go to Church every Sunday, if we like, but he doesn't believe in the Hell yet, so he can't be said to be quite in the right way." "And what did you do all the time, Ida?" "O, we talked about my uncle." "Wasn't he there?" "O no, we wouldn't have anything to do with such a one." "And did you talk much about it, Ida?" "O no, I slept." Apparently the root difficulty was the united refusal of the Mecklenburg clergy to confirm the children of this budding agnogger. I have no doubt Ida's presence was a moral support and very stimulating to the family in their distress, but we were a little sore Ida should have left us in the lurch merely to sleep in her father's house. If she had managed to shove this poor unwilling harassed uncle quite into the right way, that would have been another matter. I shall never be able to see a flock of sheep again with the inevitable One, who flops off into the ditch or up a wrong turning, and shepherd, shepherd's boy and dog pursue it with violence and cries, and the poor muddled thing flounders about and bangs itself on gates but can't get quite into the right way yet though it is willing to do anything it's asked, even go to Church every Sunday, but won't give up its conviction that I'm right and all the others are wrong—I have occasionally noticed such a sheep trying not to be a sheep and all the world against it—but I shall never see it again without thinking of Ida's uncle. If you knew Ida—her red arms and her vacant vacant face, her dumb eyes and her listless repetition of the formula, whenever she is dealt with, "O Frau Doktor, I would go through the fire for Frau Doktor"—and so she would, too, not joyfully shouting like Shadrach Meshach and Abednego, but listlessly and mechanically picking her way through the coals, the true daughter of this province of slaves where the first light of freedom is even now breaking in one of those stumpy brick-built hamlets in that waste of unhedged arable upland to the north, where Ida's uncle is not going to believe in the Hell, not for no amounts of parsons and relations and neglect. I should like to capture him and bring him over to England, where he could run our messages after Cockburn's death, and write us intellectual letters in the holidays and generally get his sphere enlarged: we being, of course, the only people in the world capable of performing that office.

I see that Monday is the 27th of April, when I believe you go North. It would be very nice if Ken could also travel that day, arriving in Schwerin on the 28th. I need not depart till the 30th. It would be very nice and touching, and might give the B.s a higher opinion of family relations in England.

I am glad you like *The Melting Pot*, though my recollection is that Sir Owen Seaman didn't. However, he is generally unpleasant to plays. I feel that this visit to Schwerin will spoil me for the theatre for the rest of my life. I have never ceased to see *John Gabriel Borkman* mentally since my second visit to it (when the acting was even finer than before and struck me as a perfect presentation of a perfect play). My only regret was that the whole family wasn't there as well. I should so like to talk it over with you: and the way that at the very end of his last play Ibsen sums up the object against which all his battle was directed: "Es war viel mehr die Kälte, die ihn tötete." "Die Kälte, sagst du, die Kälte! die hat ihn schon längst getötet."..."Ja, die Herzenskälte[1]."

The next four days are Easter, which they take very seriously out here! By the way, on a long walk yesterday I saw four curiously shaped birds straining slowly north-

[1] "It was rather the cold that killed him." "The cold, say you, the cold! Why, that killed him long ago"..."Yes, coldness of heart."

wards. On my return to the town I heard a great rattling and saw them already making themselves at home on the housetops in the middle of the town. And the street children were accosting them with the song :

> Liebe Störche, schönste, beste,
> Bringt mir eine kleine Schwester.
> Liebe Störche, seid nicht spröde,
> Bringt mir einen kleinen Bruder.

So I suppose summer has come.

On Tuesday *Faust*: a famous actor from Berlin coming down to take the name part. I am busy going through it the second time.

TO PROFESSOR AND MRS SORLEY

17 *April* 1914

About my arrangements [at Jena]—the B.s, you must know, love me very much but think less of my ability than my amiability. The idea that I should go to Jena —poor lonely lamb!—and hunt for rooms by myself, is repulsive to them, though very attractive to me. Anyhow, in this State, where the "youth" is warned off independence and even the Philolog "lets his sister do his dirty work" (i.e., buy his underclothing), I am not at present allowed to take my fate in my hands until another method has been tried—and you know what a crumpled poppy I am when my family aren't there to support me. The other method is this. The Philolog has a Jonathan in Jena. He has written to Jonathan and told him to get a bed-sit. for me at from 80 to 90 marks for the three months, which seems the usual and a reasonable price. If he cannot be bothered, I shall be forced to pack up in a week's time and dance away to

Jena, for one must be there pretty soon in order to get a room that doesn't look out on a slaughter-house. If he plays up, on the other hand, I can stay here over the next Sunday—and this is the real reason of all this intrigue—in order that I may see again the admirable Klemm.

Who, then, is the admirable Klemm? He was our Easter hare. He arrived late on Thursday evening with a cake designed like a pyramid, a palm-tree for the drawing-room, and no end of Easter eggs. But he brought much more than that. He woke the whole place up. He is an old student-friend of Karl's, and this fact does Karl enormous credit. He is something very high up in the Admiralty and has travelled all over the world in that capacity. The way this extraordinarily alert and bustling man from Berlin laughed down all Karl's Mecklenburgish ideas was charming to see. Karl is only gradually recovering. He was a really perfect guest and the most interesting man. Karl, in his vulgar way, introduced me to him as "Herr Klemm—who in six months is going to be an Excellenz." He is entirely different from any other German I have ever seen. He has a really beautiful and rolling accent, an excellent figure, and a very handsome face, had he not been so fond of duelling in his youth. It is impossible to believe that he belongs to the same nation as any of the jurists here. So we had a very lively Easter with him, and the weather, as in Cambridge, was glorious. Unlike Cambridge, however, the service was a disgrace. Schadenfreude is the only word for it. Wasn't it nice to think that we were all of us rejoicing on Easter Day and those nasty Buddhists out in the east and those wicked Social Democrats at home had nothing special to rejoice over? Karl thought it magnificent. It expressed his views exactly. Karl, like all the very best people here, is so safe in the right way that he need only go to Church on Easter and Christmas and stays in bed most of the other Sundays.

Anyhow Klemm pays another visit. And if I hear from Jonathan that he has got the refusal of a decent room in Jena for me, I can stay on here till the end of the month. I have received a "prospect" of Jena (prospects, albums, and enlarged photographs are the first necessities of life here). From it I see that the price of a room varies from 70 to 110 marks the Semester; that Mittagsessen at various inns comes to from 5 to 6 marks a week. Of university expenses the Philolog is rather hazy with his information. But he says that at Munich and Berlin he managed easily with 150 marks a month, and these two, I imagine, are expensive: while the prospect and the Philolog both agree that Jena is one of the cheapest universities.

I went to see *Faust*, First Part, well prepared. I had read it twice, and the Philolog had kindly read me a résumé of the second part. The performance was so magnificent, that its unsatisfactoriness was all the more glaring. The unsatisfactoriness lay in the attempt on the part of the producers to make a dramatic whole out of the first part. They did this by giving undue prominence to the Margarete episode—which is only an episode in Faust's career—and, instead of cutting two scenes towards the end in which Margarete sentimentalizes very prettily, they cut the two scenes in which Faust begins to kick against Mephisto, and also parts towards the beginning. It was necessary of course to cut a lot—as it was, the performance lasted nearly five hours—but they should have given us as much Faust as possible, as he is the subject and Margarete merely a temporary object, and left the First Part, as it is, merely a fragment. This was all the more necessary as Margarete was played by a local actress, very charming and of excellent technique, but nothing extraordinary: while Friedrich Kayssler, from Berlin, is the kind of man whose mere presence on the stage fills the theatre. In the scene in Auerbach's cellar when he sits at one table and watches, just watches, Mephisto and the others carousing, without moving or speaking, the expression of weary and tempered scorn on his face was wonderful. He is far the finest-looking man I have ever seen. He is one of the foremost modern German poets, but no real actor: that is to say, he can only play parts to which he feels perfectly sympathetic. His Oedipus is said to be magnificent. Thus to a certain limit his Faust was marvellous: and all through, he was living and not acting; but, after Gretchen's appearance, his Faust, according to the Philolog and the critics in the papers, was all wrong. He was never the passionate sensual lover, but an earnest elder brother, who seemed not to know why he was saying all those loving things. The love-scenes were the most mournful in the evening, and Kayssler appeared to be far too fine a nature to act the sensualist in action—though afterwards, in that great soliloquy, "Erhabner Geist, du gabst mir, gabst mir alles," where he is the sensualist repentant, he was wonderful again: and also in the one scene with Gretchen when Faust preaches a little and confesses his faith. In the last scene, Gretchen was so bad that he had no chance, and the expression on his face when he obeyed the command "Her, zu mir," from Mephisto was one of intense relief. Thus throughout he was Friedrich Kayssler and not Goethe's Faust (as interpreted by learned philologs): but I'm not objecting.

His idea of Faust, as far as I could make out from his manifest uncomfortableness in the love-scenes, was that Faust indulged in this love-affair with Margarete merely in obedience to his previous passion to know all mystery and all knowledge, merely for the sake of an experience and much against the will of his finer feelings. Having had this portion of his passion satisfied, he finds that satisfaction is worse than unrewarded effort ("O dass dem Menschen nichts Vollkommnes wird, Empfind' ich nun")—and visits Gretchen in prison in the last scene and tries to get her away not out of love, but merely pity and a feeling that he must pay the price of satisfaction. Hence the relief on his face when Mephisto snatched him off and prevented him being saddled with her. This idea is inconsistent, I think, with much of the text: and the critics were unanimous in condemning his performance as inexcusably unconventional. But his personality was a sufficient excuse, and, though his Faust may not have been Goethe's Faust, it was a tremendously living and convincing Faust that I shall never forget. And to speak out long soliloquies in metre and rhyme without the audience ever remarking that it rhymes and scans, is a feat which shows his genuineness.

The devil was perfectly delightful and so humorous. The part was taken by John Gabriel Borkman, Richard III and the Landvogt (in *Wilhelm Tell*), and he is really a fine actor. He is the head of the local staff. Auerbach's cellar was one of the best pieces of comic acting I have ever seen—until one caught sight of Faust sitting impassively regarding in the corner. I never knew Faust was so young, before. He wore a dressing-gown throughout the play, which was typical: as, according to the Philolog, Max Reinhardt's Fausts put on tights and frills when they fall in love with Margarete. But this was a Faust who had thought it all out for himself and played the part therefore with doubled love.

I have sent off a box full of green shirts and *Judes the Obscure*. According to the station officials it will arrive in four days. Multiplying that by three (I sent it off on the 15th), it should arrive on the 27th, which will be just too late. Being the first box in the history of the world that has ever travelled by itself from Schwerin to Cambridge, there was dreadful difficulty. I had to plunge into the slums of Schwerin to find the only inhabitant capable of dealing with such a vagrant. He meanwhile had gone to the station to find me (my fame having gone abroad) and, after criss-crossing like this about six times, we met at last but did not get on very well, as he had an uncomfortable habit of substituting the English word in his speech whenever he knew it, so that all the simple words were English and the hard ones were German. We had searchings of heart, dreadful, when he said "Wo ist Ihre Ahbitahtzione?" I thought an Ahbitahtzione was some extraordinary form or voucher, which made it possible to send a box from Schwerin to Cambridge. I answered brightly that I had none, but would be much obliged if he could supply the want. His treatment of me thereafter as a homeless orphan lunatic at last opened my eyes to the fact that he meant Habitation—the kind of word that is only used by railway companies—and he had put it in to make me feel at home. In their kind German way they would not let me pay anything. I only hope it will be seen again.

To the Master of Marlborough

23 *April* 1914

Thanks so much for your letter. Not wishing to spoil your breakfast by another shock about an angry parent in foreign lands, I have not dared to answer it till the "holidays." Things are still very bright here, though my previous enthusiasm has been sobered to a decent critical appreciation of German provincial life, which is still delightful from a spectator's point of view—but preserve me from having to live it for ever! Also I confess to weaker moments in which I consider that my absence Λακεδαίμονος ἐξ ἐρατεινῆς[1] has been almost long enough. However, I bear up wonderfully, and am really behaving myself. I have read, with the greatest care, as if in preparation for a quarter-sheet of paper to be filled up somehow by five answers, the first *nine* books of the *Odyssey*. If I had the smallest amount of patience, steadiness or concentrative faculty, I could write a brilliant book comparing life in Ithaca, Sparta and holy Pylos in the time of Odysseus with life in Mecklenburg-Schwerin in the time of Herr Dr Bieder. In both you get the same unquenchable hospitality and perfectly unquenchable anecdotage faculty. In both, whenever you make a visit or go into a house, they are "busying

[1] From lovely Lacedaemon.

themselves with a meal." Du lieber Karl—I mean Herr Dr Bieder—has three times, when his wife has tried to talk of death, disease or crime by table, unconsciously given a literal translation of Peisistratus's sound remark *οὐ γὰρ ἐγώ γε τέρπομ᾽ ὀδυρόμενος μεταδόρπιος*[1]—and that is their attitude to meals throughout. Need I add the *ἀγλαὰ δῶρα* they insist on giving their guests, with the opinion that it is the host that is the indebted party and the possession of a guest confers honour and responsibility: and their innate patriotism, the *οὔ τοι ἐγώ γε ἧς γαίης δύναμαι γλυκερώτερον ἄλλο ἰδέσθαι*[2] spirit (however dull it is)—to complete the parallel? So I am really reading it in sympathetic surroundings, and when I have just got past the part where Helen shows off to Menelaus her new work-basket that runs on wheels, and the Frau rushes in to show me her new water-can with a spout designed to resemble a pig—I see the two are made from the same stuff (I mean, of course, Helen and Frau B., not Frau B. and the pig). Also, I enjoy being able to share in a quiet amateur way with Odysseus his feelings about "were it but the smoke leaping up from his own land."

I'm off in a week to Jena, for the Summer Semester there. To show there's no ill will, I first am going to see a twin-brother installed here and then creep off to Jena and wonder if they'll notice the change. There are very few lectures on pure Classics at Jena, so I don't know whether I shall profit much in that respect. But

[1] I do not like having to lament during supper.—*Odyssey*, iv, 193, 194

[2] I for my part can see nothing sweeter than one's own country.—*Ibid.*, ix, 27, 28.

it is said to have the closest and most vigorous University life in Germany, and is only 15 miles from Goethe's grave, whose inhabitant has taken the place of Thomas Hardy (successor to Masefield) as my favourite prophet. I hope (if nothing else) before I leave Germany to get a thorough hang of *Faust*. I have already got well hold of the first part: and have seen it wonderfully acted here (the best Faust in Germany, himself a poet of distinction, having come down from Berlin). The worst of a piece like *Faust* is that it completely dries up any creative instincts or attempts in oneself. There is nothing that I have ever thought or ever read that is not somewhere contained in it, and (what is worse) explained in it. So I must busy myself therewith, with the *Odyssey* for a recreation: and then come over to England and climb down to Demosthenes (I do abominate Demosthenes) and Cicero for Honour Mods.

You seem to have had a very reformatory Lent term at Marlborough, and there's nothing now left to write to *The Marlburian* about. I hope, by the way, that you have found a successor to Mr Preston, who will *not* on his arrival *join the corps*. It has been a source of great grief to me that all the new members of common-room for the last two and a half years have arrived positively bespangled with medals, trailing records of past years of wonderful efficiency behind them. I do like a nice quiet civilian.

Do try and persuade other second class scholars who have no chance of the leaving-scholarship-bait to desert at Christmas and come over here. I'm sure it's better than to stay on "an idle king" and "mete and dole unequal laws unto a savage race": especially as the other is really much pleasanter. And if they want an address, they simply couldn't do better than Wiesen-strasse, Schwerin, where they'll find the *αἰδοιοτάτῃ*[1] of hostesses, and excellent food thereto.

To Mrs Sorley

24 *April* 1914

Many happy returns of the 28th. I hope this will reach you before you set out. Why is it that you always travel either on your birth- or marriage-day? Is it to prevent the feeling of mistaken festivity that is apt to accompany a birth-day spent at home? I don't mean this as an insult, but you know how days set apart for jollification are apt not to play up if given every chance. However, if you are not after all travelling and have got K. back, you don't deserve my pity.

Frau B., dragging out of me the date of your birth-day, is sending photographs (taken by the Admirable Klemm or by the Philolog with the A. K.'s camera) of various parts of me: one of my back, one of my front, and one of my new grey suit with the trousers so nicely creased, which made its début on Easter Sunday. This is a kind of appeasement to excuse my not yet being certain of your real present. K., to whom I confided its nature—Bickersteth's *Carducci* was your last choice, wasn't it?—said he didn't yet feel quite well enough to face a bookseller with it. So either—have you but the time and has he but the brains—tell him what it is again and try to be surprised when you get it: or wait and I will get it for you, when I return. I should think it will be a very interesting book.

[1] Most deserving of respect.

I'm afraid the kettle-holders are all gone. The man told me there was a great rush on them by people who wanted *really suitable* presents for confirmation candidates. Perhaps they exist in Jena also. I will try.

The A. K. is here at present, though he arrived without an entrance fee this time. But he is still taking photos. Frau B. has just come in with her letter and photos. There are many more than I thought. You can easily pick out the members of the party. Fat and liebenswürdig = Karl. Thinner, smaller, also moustached = A. K. Thin, unmoustached, and tall = the Philolog. She asks me to excuse her English, because she was cooking crabs the while.

I send—in case they may interest you—three other poems[1] (never properly rounded off, since they were all three done entirely in the open air), which I did not think worth sending with the others. 'Autumn Dawn' has too much copy from Meredith in it, but I value it as being (with 'Return') a memento of my walk to Marlborough last September.

The following sentences are from the letter enclosed from Frau B., and from one written ten days earlier. They were written in English and are given here without change: "I will miss your son very much, he is with me like a real friend, I always forget his age, he is in his spirit so much older and so we speak as if there were no difference in the age, you can be proud for him, his intellect, his heart and his behaviour." "Wednesday your son will lieve us. I wish he could stop much longer, but there is no possibility, so I try to think how nice these three months were and think we will meet Charlie perhaps next year in England....And now I say you good-bye. Again and again I thank you with whole my heart that you have send me your son, the time with him was like a holiday and a feastday."

[1] Nos. i, iv, and viii of *Marlborough and Other Poems*, 4th ed.

To Professor and Mrs Sorley

End of April 1914

Thanks very much for the letter. Jonathan has found me a room, 25 marks a month, coffee included. I call that cheap. It remains to be seen whether it is nasty also. Jonathan says the view is beautiful, it is three floors up, and the sole objection is that the only entrance into the room is through the landlord's dining-room—but this is made a positive pleasure by the wonderful charm of the landlord. His letter to the Philolog was charming, all about a blond son of Albion and a fair-haired cousin from across the Channel, whom I take to be me. I shall probably go on Wednesday.

Good luck to Helen of Troy. As you say, she loved her own sex as well. Her last appearance in Homer is when Telemachus was just leaving her and Menelaus after paying them a visit in Sparta, "and she stood on the doorstep with a robe in her hand and spoke a word and called him 'I also am giving thee a gift, dear child,—this, a memorial of Helen's handiwork, against the day of thy marriage to which we all look forward, that thou mayest give it to thy wife : till then, let it be stored in thy palace under thy mother's care.'" But she never gives to me the impression in Homer of being quite happy. I'm sure she was always dull down in Sparta with fatherly old Menelaus—though she never showed it, of course. But there is always something a little wistful in her way of speaking. She only made other people happy and consequently another set of other people miserable. One of the best things in the *Iliad* is the way you are made to feel (without any statement) that Helen fell really in love with Hector—and this shows her good taste, for of all the Homeric heroes Hector is the only unselfish man. She seems to me only to have loved to please Menelaus and Paris but to have really loved Hector—and naturally, for Hector and Achilles, the altruist and the egoist, were miles nobler than any one else on either side—but Hector never gave any sign that he regarded her as anything more than his distressed sister-in-law. But after Hector's death she must have left part of her behind her, and made a real nice wife to poor pompous Menelaus in his old age. She seems to have had a marvellous power of adaptability.

Thank you for the new point of view about the Gretchen "episode[1]." I quite agree that *Faust* is far bigger than anything of Shakespeare's ; but it was the work of sixty years, and *Hamlet* I don't suppose more than six months. I shall expect disappointment on further acquaintance with Goethe. The only other things of his I have read are *Egmont* (on the same level as *Henry V* exactly) and *Bekenntnisse einer schönen Seele*—a most egoistic young woman : at times it might almost have been written by A. C. B.

I have drawn out a plan of lectures from the list, which I shall probe. There are only two lectures on pure Classical subjects unfortunately, but still. Eucken

[1] This is in reply to a comment by his mother on his description of Gretchen as "only an episode in Faust's career" (p. 143). She had written somewhat as follows : " I am interested in your calling Gretchen's part of the story an 'episode.' I wonder, was it that to her ? Women suffer for you, struggle for you, sin for you—spend themselves utterly—and, in the latter end, are apt to be labelled merely 'episodes.' I suppose it is 'the man's point of view,' and perhaps a law of nature. I'm not complaining, only interested."

gives once a week lectures on Einleitung in die Philosophie, which sounds as if it were for beginners, so I shall attend that. It is at the peculiarly un-philosophical hour of 7 a.m. on Saturdays.

When I have an odd ten minutes at present, I just read a chapter of *The Trumpet Major*. It is a most restful book. All the fury with the world which comes down in a storm in *Jude* is only just traceable in the thinnest and finest irony that runs throughout *The Trumpet Major*. Hardy always seems perfectly at home with really good steady characters like Gabriel Oak and the Trumpet Major. There is a lovely chapter all about food. And all the characters are simple and it makes no demands on the intelligence whatever.

A good journey northward. I hope *Jude* will not prevent your looking out of the window when the drystone dykes begin.

CHAPTER IV

THE UNIVERSITY OF JENA

To Professor and Mrs Sorley

Jena, 1 *May* 1914

Here they are trying to refuse to matriculate me or even allow me to attend lectures until I have got a passport. The man in the office had got the word "passport" well into his head, and not even the brilliance of my logic and my Higher Certificate could move it out. So I had to look up my list of lectures and find the address of the English lector—the nearest approach to a Cook's homme I could think of. He was very noble and got me leave to attend lectures and says he thinks it will be all right about matriculation too, and that no passport will be necessary if you only give them time. And to show my independence I went straight off this evening and heard a most engaging gentleman called Nohl give the first of a course of lectures on Ethics.

I left Schwerin on Wednesday [at] 9.30 and travelled, with one change, among an amount of petrifying Prussian hussars through incredibly flat and tedious country to Halle. There I was left in a waiting room for an hour and a half. They would not let me go out and see the beauties (if any) of Halle, without giving up my ticket. It was the hugest waiting room I have ever been in, and, except for a few old broken men, who produced brown paper parcels containing the end of a black sausage and a roll and ate them with the assistance of pen-knives, and one or two broken-hearted babies who endlessly squalled, I was left alone with it. When at last I "boarded" an express from Berlin to Venice, with the notices written in Italian to show how far south we were getting, things changed. The valley of the Saale was highly pictureskew and medaevial (to use the perversion of two famous ladies), and the train took me without a stop to Jena. I was met by Jonathan at Jena, who was very kind. He reminded me most forcibly of Kenneth's friend ——, with a dash of the person of whom a Sparrow said that nobody would mind if he passed away. He was most immensely kind etc., etc., but I foresee the time when I shall be running round corners and hiding under barrows to avoid Jonathan. The room he got for me is very satisfactory—small, but nicely done up, without too many texts, and comfortable. The same may be said of the bed. It is a little higher up than the rest of the town, shady, and looks out on to trees of sorts. The landlady is at present a puzzle..., and, when asked for her name, said Frau *Dr* Glänze. She certainly speaks decent German, but *Dr* is rather a mouthful. And where is the Herr Dr? Is she a widow? and if so, why does she dress in pink? Or does Herr Dr (perhaps a dentist!) live a double life? She has two children and an arm-chair containing a pale thin woman who only smiles. There is certainly an infinite field for research here.

As soon as I walked through Jena, the impression of mediaevalism, which I got from the train as soon as it entered Thuringia, was greatly increased. It lies somewhat like Ballater, and there are, or ought to be, castles on all the surrounding hills. The streets are narrow and gaily-coloured and almost roofed with flags. Then these absurd people with bright ribbons and caps and wounded faces make it look eighteenth century. Unfortunately it has rained almost all to-day, so I have not been able to get up into the hills. What with the passport and seeing about lectures etc., there was plenty to do.

I hope to see Kenneth at Berlin during the Whitsun recess, where he will go, and I too, at the A. K.'s invitation. The A. K.'s second visit was even more of a success. He stayed over Monday, when we had a general break-up evening, reading fairy stories in the dark round an open stove. He has six rooms in Berlin, and is inviting the whole jing-bang lot for a Whitsun jollification. Isn't it kind?

To A. E. Hutchinson

From Herrn stud. phil. C. H. Sorley,
Jena, 4 May 1914

Notice the above address and mind you put it all on the envelope if, after seeing all my titles, you feel exalted enough to write to me again. Isn't it delightful? I am simply beaming at the thought of getting an envelope addressed like that. And it only cost twenty marks. For a mere twenty marks, I received a long list of injunctions, among others that all correspondence to me should be addressed thus. And so I am and remain until the 5th of August a stud. phil.—one, I believe

I am right in saying, among the very few English stud. phils. in existence. How it happened was this :

Last Wednesday I saw a twin-brother installed in my place at the B.s and went off irrevocably, hoping they wouldn't discover the change. So I travelled slowly southward, from where the land is flat and the accent is good, into Thuringia, where the accent is vile and the whole land preserves an air of determined mediaevalism as if dressed up for a fancy dress ball—my parents having decided that I must go to a German university and Jena was the very one to suit Charlie (no explanation given why). I was met at the station by a medical student (a friend of a friend of an old friend of the B.s), who had kindly hired a room for me, who—by way of being friendly—asked me to go for a walk with him that evening. The walk was this : at 8 o'clock I was introduced to eight other medical students at once—and medical students in Germany seem to be about as bloody as medical students in England (with apologies to Jerram)—and taken for a joy-ride in a broken motor-car to a distant inn where they all went mad. They certainly drank plenty, but not enough to justify the amount of kissing that went on—kissing themselves and each other, I mean, not their young women, which would have been understandable : but when they began to throw beer at each other, and exchange coats, I began to see that one must be kind to Germany, for it is very young and getting on nicely with its lessons and so pleased with itself and just got into its private school cricket eleven—that stage. So since then I have been running round lamp-posts and diving into milliners' shops to avoid these gentlemen.

I am now giving full play to my nasty Scotch (sorry, Scots) instincts. I have a bed-sit., the size of that dejected bathroom where the one new boy in house may be found washing at any hour of the day—which costs me with breakfast, 25 mks. a month. The landlady insists on being addressed as Frau Doktor, so I suppose her husband (now either in heaven or deserted her) was a dentist. The only objection to my bed-sit. is that it leads off a room which at different hours of the day plays the rôle of dining-room, sitting-room, nursery and bath-room—a most versatile room—let us call it "parlour." Whenever I pass through it, as I must pretty frequently, there are always five to eight children in it who spring to their feet and remain in an attitude of "attention" till, murmuring hurried words of praise, I at last escape. The only other way out of my room is a daring leap through the window on to the roof of an out-house. So now I see why the price of the room is so inordinately cheap.

On Saturday—having no lectures (or shall I call them "lekkers"? I always used to judge the characters of O. M.s by the time it took them to talk about "lekkers," "brekkers," etc.)—I got my pilgrimage to Weimar over. I was frightfully put off by reading a book about it which described it as "the intellectual capital of Germany," but I had to go there some day as it's only twenty miles from here. Of course I was at once caught and spent most of a sunny afternoon inspecting Schiller's discarded pyjamas. I don't think anything is more miserable than a "joy-day" all alone—except of course a "joy-day" in the company of other people. However, I "did" Weimar thoroughly, but got into such a state of desperation that I began sending picture post-cards broadcast over England—a thing *you know* I would never do when in my right mind. However, it is really the most beautiful town I have ever seen, and it wasn't its fault that Goethe lived there. But I was cheered up in the evening by going to a performance of *The Merchant of Venice*, which I had always thought before was a most commonplace thing. Now I see it is far the biggest tragedy that Shakespeare ever wrote. The audience (especially a German audience) took part in the tragedy, because they laughed at Shylock and considered him a comic character throughout. As a glance at the life and methods of ordinary Christians it is simply superb. And the way the last act drivels out in a silly practical joke—while you know Shylock is lying in the same town deliberately robbed of all that he cared for—is a lovely comment on the Christian life. I saw *Faust*, by the way, before I left Schwerin. It is worth going to Germany to see that alone—my God! it is witty, besides, of course, being far the greatest drama in the world.

Thanks awfully for your letter. I followed your advice *in re* my cousin, regarding [her] as 4th witted. I am sorry that you take such a pessimistic view of your chances of being alive at the end of the summer. I had certainly been counting on it. But even now, from my $2\frac{1}{2} \times 3$ ft. bed-sit., I can contemplate with more than Christian complacency the thought of a cold late afternoon (called by courtesy "summer"), bright slippery grass, nasty brown spiked shoes, white sopping flannel trousers (I think wet flannel trousers are the most heartbreaking things in the world), and a ball somewhere over in Sanny and a crowd aimlessly treading down the grass, among them you—O that is worse than death! Last Summer term was rather a nice one, I remember—indeed a particularly nice one.

Your German handwriting filled me with admiration and not a little jealousy. Of all the useless things to learn!

I wrote to the Master begging him to appoint a successor to F. S. P. who would be guaranteed not to join the Corps. He wrote back by return of post (he writes perfectly delightful letters) that "anticipating my imperious wish he had already appointed an entirely non-combative gentleman," but dashed my hopes to the ground by saying "he was a refined scholar who could yet make many runs." One of those unfortunate persons who not content with being good athletes are good scholars as well—ah me, my heart is wae for Marlborough. But you can tell me whether he is really so startling.

Look here, I must stop and write a twinny letter giving my brother "tips" as to how to deal with the Herr Doktor. In my dealings with him I always thought of Footman's epigram over his dealings with ——, "having no subject in common, we both talk down to each other."

Good luck to Third if you are humble enough to play cricket. In spite of my intense desire to hate it, I always liked cricket. It was only school-matches and watching them that ate my heart out and made me think of Francis Thompson's lines of ghastly genius[1]:

It is little I repair to the matches of the Southron folk,
Though my own red roses there may blow;
It is little I repair to the matches of the Southron folk,
Though the red roses crest the caps, I know.

[1] *Works*, vol. i, p. 174 ('At Lord's').

For the field is full of shades as I near the shadowy coast,
And a ghostly batsman plays to the bowling of a ghost,
And I look through my tears on a soundless-clapping host
  As the run-stealers flicker to and fro, to and fro :
  O my Hornby and my Barlow long ago !

Francis T. was only a watcher of cricket and a player on Third like me. I remember when in A House I used to love watching school matches and keep the averages of now-forgotten Shaws. So ist es in der Welt.

To Professor and Mrs Sorley

8 *May* 1914

Thanks very much for the papers—especially the Giffords. I like being addressed "stud. phil." very much and have given orders to all my correspondents to do the same. I am very pleased to be able to read the Giffords.

The English lecturer was very kind and even went to the extent of concocting a "pleasant lie" on my behalf to satisfy the abominable clerk, who at last matriculated me. I have since been visiting all sorts of lectures, rejecting some and accepting others, as is the way here for the first week. I am shocked to say that I am going to no lectures on classical literature (as such) at all. The professor of that put up a convenient notice to say he postponed his lectures till the winter semester ; the other men on the subject are quite impossible—quarrelsome and dry and lecture over post-classical people. Almost all the lecturers speak slowly and distinctly, which is a blessing. After some hesitation, I have decided to go to as many lectures as possible, in spite of Poynton's threatening letter, and let Classics take their chance. Nohl, the man who lectures on Ethik, is far the most attractive and alive. I was surprised to hear someone here say that he represented the thorough school here, as opposed to Eucken "who swam about in large ideas." Eucken is a wonderfully beautiful old man to look at, and comparatively mild. But I do not yet feel equal to accosting him with the magic word Sorley.

I have been a bit about the place here by now. The impression of mediaevalism is soon dispelled. The whole surrounding is like a saucer whose rim and centre-piece are mediaeval—all between is of the rankest suburban villa type. The tops of the hills are fine: and so is the little mediaeval island in the middle of the town, where many of the older streets are flanked by chestnut trees. But lilac is the prevailing smell here. There are many clumps of it in the town, it hangs from every garden, and it grows wild on the hills. But I should not call the town healthy, though it suits me all right.

I made my pilgrimage on Saturday, when, though I had to get up with the lark to hear the energetic old Eucken lecture at 7 a.m., I had no lecture after 10, and went straight off to Weimar. I spent the rest of the morning (actually) in the museum, inspecting chiefly Preller's wall-paintings of the *Odyssey*. They are the best criticism of the book I have seen and gave me a new and more pleasant idea of Odysseus. Weimar does not give the same impression of musty age as parts of Jena. It seems a flourishing well-watered town, and I should like very much to live there, chiefly for the sake of the park. The name "Park" puts one off, but it is really a beautiful place, like a college garden on an extensive scale. After I had wandered about there very pleasantly for an hour or so, I noticed a statue in a prominent position above me. "Another Goethe," thought I; but I looked at it again, and it had not that look of self-confident self-conscious greatness that all the Goethes have. So I went up to it and recognised a countryman—looking down from this height on Weimar, with one eye half-closed and an attitude of head expressing amused and tolerant but penetrating interest. It was certainly the first satisfactory representation of Shakespeare I have ever seen. It appears quite new, but I could not discover the sculptor's name[1]. The one-eye-half-closed trick was most effective. For, as you looked at it from the right, you thought "this is a very humorous kindly human gentleman"—then you went round to the other side and saw the open eye!

The blot in Weimar is the Schiller-Goethe statue in front of the theatre. They are both embracing rather stupidly—and O so fat!

At 7.30 was *The Merchant of Venice*. The acting on the whole, with the exception of Shylock, was commonplace. But, whether intended or not, this produced the required effect of showing me for the first time the play as one of the most tremendous of Shakespeare's tragedies. The audience (especially a German audience) took part in the tragedy, because they saw in Shylock only a comic character and the villain rightly wronged. The acting of all the Christians was splendidly commonplace. What a perfectly intolerable young woman is Portia! I never

[1] The sculptor was Otto Lessing; the statue was unveiled on 23 April 1904.

realized before that the real worth of her speech in praise of mercy lay in the fact that, three minutes later, so far from exhibiting any herself, she actually and gratuitously called back the despairing Shylock to hunt up a law which robbed him of all his goods—such a further decision being of no use whatever to the already delivered Antonio and just an act of malice. Shylock is no sooner out of the door in a state of collapse, which the quality of mercy need not be strained to appreciate, than she can think of nothing more than devising a practical joke for her young man. And the farce of the fifth act crowns the tragedy. It was a most effective use of anti-climax. Besides Shylock, the only other person who acted with distinction was Jessica. She said the one line "I am never merry when I hear sweet music" with a regret that suggested that the real reason why she was not merry was that she alone of all that happy party thought of her papa's overthrow by which her and the others' merriness was bought. During the rest of the scene while the ring farce was in progress she stood apart a little, and I think she thought of Shylock. It was a remarkable and original performance. Ibsen's key "Es war wohl mehr die Kälte die ihn tötete—Ja, die Herzenskälte" seems to unlock the reason of the tragedy, as it does of most tragedies.

I have abonniert at an inn at a price working out at 75 pf. a day—good food and plenty of it, but badly served. For Abend, I have discovered a wonderful Kaffeestube, where one gets poached eggs, potatoes, cutlets, soup, cocoa, etc., at a wonderfully low price. The cook is a delightful man. There is another strange frequenter who always comes and sits next to me and talks in a vile Thuringian accent about the days when he was in London. It is quite obvious, from cross-examination, that he was never there at all, but is only being polite. I cannot make out his circumstances—

Weiss nicht woher er kommen sei,
  Weiss nicht wohin er geh',
Ob er ein Waldvöglein sei
  Oder eine Fee—

but he has a magnificent imagination and thinks he has travelled all over the world. His accent and ignorance show that physically at least he has never left Thuringia.

I am so glad you are coming over here later on: and I hope you'll come south here. It is really worth seeing.

To Professor and Mrs Sorley

16 *May* 1914

I joined ten days ago a body called the Freie Studentenschaft. This body (containing thirty members) has boldly written a book about its objects; but the only one that really matters is that it is set up in opposition to the silly old-fashioned but still flourishing Vereinigungen. Its objects are altogether so excellent that perhaps it may be excused for being appallingly priggish. I went to the first Hauptversammlung last Wednesday, but unfortunately strayed into the wrong room where a mutual-consolation meeting of future clergymen was going on. So at last, after wondering whether the best way to escape was to clasp my handkerchief to my nose and walk out quickly as if the latter was bleeding, or just to "make a bolt for it" (it was quite late before it dawned on me that I had got into the wrong room), an opportunity was presented to me. A curly-haired young man got up and said it gave him pleasure to think that there was not one person in the room who would not be a shepherd of the church in two years' time. So I ergreift the Augenblick[1], as Mephistopheles says is the mark of a rechter Mann, and said I wouldn't, appending a short autobiography. There was a dead silence, till a voice said "Lead him out." So I was led out and deposited a safe distance from the door and found my way up to the Freie Studentenschaft and got much stared at for coming so late. They were still discussing their purpose, the awful difficulty being that, being "frei," they admitted any one who chose to come, with the result that there were Roman Catholics and Agnoggers among them, and Pegfurth Bannatyne could not bear Pirbright Smith[2]. Then they talked about comradeship, and went on like any ——s. I do not expect to get much from them, though they only cost two marks, and I would be the last to deny the excellence of their purpose.

However, the English lector kindly introduced me to a gentleman who runs a "Freischar" (whatever that is), who has invited me to take part therein once a fortnight. I think they discuss Byron, Bulwer Lytton and Carlyle and other such discarded Englishmen who have found a home in Germany. Further, he has introduced me to one or two other "Füchse,"[3] including a von Wissmann, son of the late African explorer of that name, with whom I have been a walk; but he seems very

[1] Seized the moment.

[2] See R. L. Stevenson's *Letters*, 1st ed., vol. i, p. 244.

[3] The word in the manuscript looks like "finches," but it is probably a mistake for Füchse (foxes), the usual name for freshmen at a German university.

childish. I thought also of joining the Jena Sports-Verein, but found that, with the usual German thoroughness, they concentrate on sport to the exclusion of all other activities.

We are having a real Aberdeen May, with frost at night and rain all day. However, I think it is clearing now and we shall be let in for a real Thuringian summer soon.

I was in Weimar again on Wednesday. The arrangements for that are excellent. A lecture from 5 to 6 leaves time to catch a train at 6.20, arriving at Weimar at a quarter to seven. Then we can have Abendessen comfortably before the theatre which is at 7.30. Also, for certain pieces students get tickets for the stalls for a mark: and as the same is the price of a return to Weimar, we get in altogether considerably cheaper than the inhabitants of Weimar. The piece was Goethe's *Iphigenie auf Tauris*. It has the overwhelming advantage over Goethe's other pieces of having only five characters. It is really a corrected edition of Euripides's play of that name: for while Euripides gets them all into a muddle and gets Athene or Diana or some such supernatural to untie the knot, Goethe lets Iphigenia untie it. The whole play was acted with perfect Greek reticence, and no calls were taken till the very end. I must say I think we have it over the Germans in ten syllable blank verse—it doesn't seem to suit their long vowels, which need rhymes; but there are some fine bits of poetry when Iphigenia bursts away from blank verse and speaks in a wild chorus metre; and she was very finely acted. The play did not impress me on reading—but seeing it made all the difference. In fact

Iphigenia was one of the best pieces of female (sorry, it's a horrid word) acting I have seen. After the play I had time for a wander in the Schlossgarten in complete darkness, and then a visit to Goethe's house, before the train back. I relent, by the way, towards the Goethe-Schiller group before the theatre. It's a nice idea having it there, and they look very nice in the night when it's too dark to notice their corpulence or Schiller's aggressive star-gazing expression.

To K. W. Sorley

19 *May* 1914

Thanks very much indeed for the letter. You will understand why I didn't write to you for our common birthday; because, after all, days are quite meaningless divisions: and expecting a letter from you I did not wish ours to cross, so waited.

You can correct your impression about the weight of Jena. Several things have happened which incline to make things brisk. First, I have been pushed into a small society called Freischar i (I don't know why) which meets twice a week evenings—there are only eight people—one night for literary discussion rather in the manner of Ludwig and you, and the other time for general conversation. And they are really a very nice lot. Again, Father sent me an introduction to the wonderful Eucken. And he asked me to tea on Sunday. It was extraordinarily interesting. There were thirty to forty people there, and one walked about the garden eating éclairs and talking. And I found two other people who wanted to play tennis: so we have already found a fourth and begun. One stays there from about five to eight. Most of the students there—apart from a natural tendency to cross-examine about "what England thought" about this and that, and a trusting confidence in all my opinions as the opinions of England—were really very nice. It was amusing to see this side of German life....Eucken is a wonderfully beautiful old man with an astounding gift of utterly *im*personal heartiness.

I quite see what you mean about Frau B. When one has lived so utterly alone as she has, one must, I suppose, have some artistic outlet for one's feelings. Having (as you say) little sense of humour where she is regarded—which is little wonder, considering one must have a recipient of sorts who can appreciate one's humour, or else I should think it goes—I suppose she has to let out steam in living very "intensely." I know those little contretemps. But I always found that, if "fought out" and brought to a logical conclusion, they were apt to clear the air and lead to a better understanding in future. She always demands complete openness, and detects and dislikes reserve. At first this is a nuisance, I admit, and appears sentimental and leads to "quarrels": but if the demand is met (however hard it is to meet, and perhaps it should only be met half way), things go better. And I think it's worth it. I suppose novelists or psychologists would say that "the unsatisfied maternal instinct" had to do with it. Her judgments are often founded on appearances, and she probably made the accusation not in a spirit of wrath, but as a means to help in the "progress of getting to know you." As you say, she has acquired the merciless habit of brooding: being too fine for her surroundings and having—I should say—no friends in Schwerin, she has to find the answer to all questions in herself. Quite naturally she is thus unbalanced. I always have the feeling about her that she is like Hans Andersen's fir-tree planted in the cellar, so that it missed opportunities of full growth and was thus warped in many places; but was none the less a fir and not one of the toadstools that grew and flourished in the cellar floor. The better one gets to know her, the more one sees the potential rather than the warped fir. But one must rub up against the warps in the process: and a good wrench with the warp, though most uncomfortable for both parties, occasionally is necessary, I think.

She likes discussing "deep" earth-probing subjects: and I think the more one talks that, the more is she happy. Besides, I don't see why you should blame yourself for having written this to me. I had long ago noticed these shortcomings; but after a month or so, recognizing them as faults of her circumstances and surroundings and not her nature, could put them down to Mecklenburg and the folly and narrow-mindedness that characterize that corner of Germany in the minds of all people here—and I think in a large degree rightly—and not to her.

My good landlady here, discovering from a paper that I had to fill up that it was my birthday, presented me with heaps of cakes, exuding sweetness, with which I don't quite know what to do, in the utter kindness of her heart.

To Professor and Mrs Sorley

20 *May* 1914

Things are going pretty smartly here. The Erste Freischar from Jena has turned out admirably, and has kindly invited me to take part in their Wissenschaft and Unterhaltungs[1] evenings held every week alternately. They have got a very nice lot of people—about eight who live and eat and work together, and eight others who (like me) are invited as ausserordentliche Mitglieder[2] to attend their intellectual evenings for the term.

I don't think any good could come of joining a classical Seminar now. The two classical Seminars waste their time on doubtful works of Greek and Roman writers of the decadence—works whose charm lies in their doubtful authorship: and altogether pure classics here is attacked from a strictly antiquarian and textual and grammatical point of view, I think. So the classics I am doing, I read alone.

I gave your note to Eucken, and he asked me to tea on the next day, Sunday. I think the Eucken household has the reputation here of being very English. Anyway, I dutifully went and arriving on the stroke of five was there first. Eucken was exceptionally kind to me and spoke very nicely about you. But soon floods of all peoples, nations, and languages arrived—Greeks, Turks, Russians, Americans, and Japs—and it developed into a most exciting crush. I picked up several interesting students there who, apart from a tendency to cross-examine, were very good company; especially one who

[1] Science and amusement. [2] Extraordinary members.

was looking for tennis and, with the help of me and two others, has now found it. Mrs Eucken is a Greek and rather like one of their statues to look at. Miss Eucken, equally tall, and loosely, almost dangerously, clad in an aggressive green dress that went in hoops, sat beneath a tree, smoking loudly and cracking brilliant epigrams with young privat-dozents while others hovered in the neighbourhood and clapped. She smashed chairs, and shouted loudly to her grey Greek mother on the other side of the garden. But a very lively lady, and perhaps I do her injustice with my similes, for she rode the whirlwind and directed the storm quite well. Well, we all walked about the garden and talked, and I answered a thousand leading questions and arranged about tennis, and the crowd did not diminish till a quarter to eight. So it was a most pleasant Sunday afternoon. And Eucken stood by the door good-byeing, assuring all the guests as they departed that they had been the pleasure of the day for him. He asked me to empfehlen ihn herzlich to you, and told me to come back next Sunday, when one Boutroux is the attraction. The opposite camp (before which the first Freischar bows) say that all the freaks of Jena are to be found at Eucken's on Sunday afternoon. But I am most grateful, for I have got to know one or two people thereby, and it was most pleasant: and also I have now tennis.

I and the thirsty soul got the English lector and his protégé von Wissmann to make up four. (I knew they wanted to play.) We play now every morning (except Saturday)—we started on my birthday—from seven to a quarter to nine (I having crossed off a rather daundering set of lectures on Aesthetik to indulge in Athletik).

This is far the best time; for when once it gets into this hollow, the heat remains much longer than the light, while early morning it is fresh and cool and the light is good. It makes all the difference and I feel ever so much better all morning for the exercise. From two till four, I am awfully ashamed to say, I have dropped into the middle-aged habit of "taking ma rest." It is so hot that there's simply nothing else to do: and then one can sit up much later evenings.

The mixed bag of lectures are going quite well. In one or two cases I wish I had not been so quick in entering my name—which once done is irrevocable—but that is bound to be the case. Eucken I find at present not very fruitful, his Einleitung being entirely amateur, and his Metaphysics rather hard to follow. I am very struck by the lack of honour that the prophet gets in one portion of his own University. Though every one is agreed on his personal charm, there seems a tendency to scoff at him as a sugary thinker, which has surprised me very much. Nohl is the name of the man who is hinted at as the really great man of Jena, and his lectures are certainly most stimulating.

A pleasant addition to the attractions of mediaeval Jena, in the way of the yearly market, has been holding up two of the main streets lately. The wares were negligible. (A penny penknife and three pairs of socks for ninepence were all I could find buyable.) But the coming in of all the Thuringian folk with their square empty baskets on their backs, and their goings out with the baskets full of ribbons and saucepans and Turkish delight, was pleasant to see: and bright flags with hearty notices like "Hurrah! Hurrah! Der billige Jakob ist da, ist da[1]!" were a pleasant off-set to the everlasting corps colours. Indeed the old town of Jena, crushed to death between the University on the one side and Karl Zeiss's microscopes on the other, burst into life with the Jahrmarkt for a couple of days. But now the stalls are gone again and the streets opened to traffic.

To A. E. Hutchinson

26 *May* 1914

It's all very well for you to talk about writing a book about my "little club." It's a perfect little devil of a club. They advertised a Hauptversammlung in a certain hotel, so I turned up at the required hour and, seeing a room full of living things, I entered and took a seat. I said that the barometer was going up to the gentleman on my right, but, not having been introduced, he very properly ignored the fact. Then, after half-an-hour's sad silence on my part, a young man got up and called Silence (which there was already) and proceeded to say that it gave him really unbounded joy to think that of all the gentlemen here to-night not one would not in three years (D.V.) be preaching the gospel to his brother Germans. "We theologians," he continued; and after a ten minutes' speech of the same nature I discovered that I must have strayed into a mutual-consolation meeting of future parsons. So I suddenly rose and (a mass of redness) asked to be let down, appending a brief autobiography. There was a moment's silence, and then a voice said "Lead him out." So I was removed

1 "Cheap Jack is there, is there!"

blushingly and deposited a safe distance away. Then I saw windows of another hall near by and thought I'd have another shot. So I stumbled up to the door and met a waiter coming out. You know that I'm a crushed lily in the hands of waiters, tailors, etc. So when he asked me what I would have, I replied a glass of beer and stumbled into the hall. There sat thirty fat-faced youths, consuming lemonade. One of them was on his legs, and enjoying himself immensely talking. I found afterwards that the subject of his address was Youth and Temptation....And then my glass of beer came and cost me twopence-halfpenny. All eyes were turned towards the late-comer. The speaker stopped his discourse. What need had he to continue when Youth and Temptation were there incarnated before him? Dead Silence. A copy of the rules was slowly passed down to Youth. Youth blushed heavily; in fact he almost cried, so naughty did he feel. The waiter was recalled and twopence-halfpenny Temptation was removed. The Jenaer Freistudentenschaft breathed again. The speaker resumed his discourse, and the waiter re-appeared at Youth's elbow asking whether he preferred orangeade, grape-squash or onion-champagne. What a fool I was! Of course I should have known that all cheap clubs are temperance. However, after talking for three hours and a half, they brought off a pretty stroke of satire by drinking to the future of intellectual life in Jena in barley-water and lemonade.

I have cut all further meetings. But I have joined a Carlyle club on invitation, on being discovered to be of the same nationality as Carlyle. It's really very nice and lively and I've met one or two people for whom I entertain great admiration. But these fat sods of the Frei-studentenschaft! As Flurry Knox in a moment of genius rare with him remarked, "I wouldn't borrow half-a-crown to get drunk with one of them."

I am so glad you're going to come out here to this land of unselfconscious people. I am afraid your ideal German counts, though of course frequent, are all bank-rupt these days, and let their Schlosses to Americans and live in the outside laundry. However, I recommend Weimar. I am so delighted by Weimar that I imagine Zion is going to be a rather over-decorated Weimar. But in any case it can do no harm to anticipate the pleasure. And of course Weimar has the advantage over Zion of having a theatre and a very good one too. But if all the nobility of Germany fail, and even the Thuringian bourgeoisie fail, there is always Schwerin to fall back upon: though that is a part of Germany which takes their "Mit Gott für Kaiser und Vaterland" very seriously, and is apt to confuse the three. For learning the language it is first-rate. But when one comes south a bit, one sees the German isn't such a fool after all.

I go to Berlin in a couple of days for the Whitsuntide recess (they take Whitsuntide awfully seriously here) and then back here again to a life of work and cross-examination from eager students about what England thinks—which however I find very tolerable, in fact quite pleasant. And the Germans can write first-rate lyrics which the English can't. So I'm not offended of it, and prepared to exist in my bedsit. (where I study (?) philosophy) quite decently till August.

I trust by the way that you have not got mumps. I shouldn't like to be writing to a person with mumps—no.

To A. R. Gidney

June 1914

I hope my last letter didn't annoy you so much that you came to the common editorial conclusion of "this correspondence must now cease!" However, at a risk of boring you a second time, I am determined to again report my progress and give you some impressions of Eucken, in the general foreign admiration for whom you seem to join. I say "foreign," because in Germany (especially in Jena) the idea of calling him a philosopher is laughed to scorn. And the same kind of fury that is aroused in me by their admiration of Byron as our greatest poet, is aroused in them by our opinion of Eucken as their greatest living philosopher. Being an essential compromist, I suppose, he doesn't please the systematic, downright, and uncompromising German nature. But they tell us that, as England has no philosophy of its own, they are quite pleased to give us one of their comfortable half-prophet-half-philosophers to help our amateurishness along!

Here in Jena Eucken is chiefly regarded as a great social force, and I owe to him and his Sunday afternoon teas all the swinging life that I am at present enjoying here. Through the said Sunday afternoons I have got to know quite a crowd of other students—the chief purpose of being here at all. Of course I don't 'sociate with the "corps" students who lead their drinking, fighting, singing, idle, picturesque life quite by themselves. But the "nicht-inkorporierte" German students —such are now in the majority even in Jena, the most tradition-laden of German universities—are a most hospitable lot with extraordinarily alert and broad minds. The amount of their knowledge is of course colossal, and would put any corresponding Briton to shame. The north-German or middle-German, however, I find as a rule too cross-examinative and fond of talking patriotic shop. The south-German is almost sure to be delightful. While one of a thousand discoveries I have made in the last six weeks is that the superior better-blooded type of German Jew have far the finest minds of any people I have ever come across.

I attend lectures on philosophy and political economy in the intervals of tennis and talking: and may sometimes also be found reading in the *Odyssey* in my cheap little bed-sit. I have gladly forgotten all my Latin, and don't ever want to remember it again. I bear it a grudge. It's been the ruin of the English language. Just compare our compound words with the German ones! Ours are two dead dried Latin words soldered together. The German compound words are two or more living current German native words grafted one upon another and blooming together so that their separated and common sense can be grasped at the same time whenever one uses them. But I keep up my Homer, Aeschylus, and Euripides and wish I had brought some Plato with me. I read no English, though I miss our prose. German prose is non-existent. They have colossally beautiful words, I find, but their constructions are hopeless. So they bloom in poetry. I am getting down to the modern lyric writers now. There isn't a trick of the trade they don't know. I made a lengthy experiment one night when I was feeling silly:

which resulted in the discovery that German has probably nearly twice as many rhyming words as we (at least beginning with the letter "a," which is as far as my experiment went). This gives them a horribly unfair advantage over us.

I hope the Lit. Soc. is still flourishing. I have not heard anything of its doings since I last heard from you, as my correspondents are not among such high treaders. There seems to be good stuff in the junior one at present, which is hopeful for the future.

Apart from the humanity here, which is delightful, Jena is a loathsome little town, shut in by hills, and thunder every afternoon. So I have the novel experience of hating the land and preferring the human here. At Marlborough for a long time I felt the other way round.

I hear that golf and Ulster are (or have been) dividing the attention of your spare moments. I feel happier, because the accounts in the German papers of Ireland's half-unconscious approaching revenge on England, for the tyranny from 1500 till a few decades ago, are short and cheery.

Excuse this half-sheet. It's not my Scotchness, really, only the fact that it's all the note paper I've left, and Weimar's grand duke has a birthday and the shops are shut.

To the Master of Marlborough

Berlin, 2 *June* 1914

Thanks so much for your letter, and don't be misled by the postmark or above address. I am generally to be found in Jena, not in Berlin at all. But I have been invited here for the Whitsunday (which they take very seriously) holidays, and am at present the only person awake in this blamed building (time 11 a.m.). They strike me as very like Mycerinus in Berlin (I won't swear his name was Mycerinus, but he comes in Herodotus, and the Gods naturally disliked him for rubbing in how much juster he was than his father, and could only stand six years of him)—in that they do manage to cheat the night. The first night my host (a friend of my former host in Mecklenburg, whose kindness in inviting me I cannot overpraise) took me and the other guests mercilessly from café to café in Berlin till early rosy-fingered dawn appeared. All through the night the city was equally alive and humming with happy people. This happened again the night before yesternight, so yesternight I struck and went to bed. Having awoken refreshed at last, I found the rest of the party at last collapsed, huddled up in sofas and rocking-chairs, snoring, very happy. So now I am taking the opportunity of writing letters on my host's notepaper, while my host sleeps.

I do like this town. There are no Westminster Abbeys and such relics of a better-forgotten past to "do." Everything dates from 1871. They take one to see the cafés instead. Dowdiness is the prevailing note, and that's nice. Those gay dogs that stay up all night are all so fat and bourgeois. Outside the army there seems none of that mixture of artificiality and vanity which we call smartness. And they go one better than Mycerinus. They extend the week to seven days, by the inclusion of Sunday. Natural, bourgeois, unaffected Hedonism seems to be the prevailing note : Hedonism of the very best kind, which depends on universality not on contrast for its fulfilment. When Imagination comes, I should think this will be the best of cities. Granted they see Lazarus and his sores, they can no longer be happy in the contrast, but buy him an overcoat which will hide his sores, and give him a good meal which will ensure his being happy as long as they remember his existence. It is in fact rather like a child's idea of Heaven, where every one there is very happy but manages to forget about the misery of others in the less respectable part of the next world. But I'm not complaining, and it's nice that the Germans are so proud of Berlin. When the cafés were finished, I went to see the shops.

Jena is proving very satisfactory. It is a horrid little town and most unhealthily situated. But the University preserves the traditions of Schiller, Fichte, and its other past professors excellently. I have got into many "intellectual" clubs, where we have "knowledge" evenings, "thought" evenings, "religion" evenings, and "joke" evenings, which in spite or on account of their formidable titles are very amusing. Their eager hospitality has ensured my acquiring a large circle of acquaintances: though I keep clear of the "corps" student with beery wounded face. But I dare say he is a very good fellow, and such remind me of our Brad-archers at Marlborough in their love of colour and their simple faith in themselves. I play tennis at 6 *a*.m. every morning and thereafter attend lectures on Philosophy, Literature, Political Economy and such useless subjects. In the evening I am generally to be found avoiding a certain insincere type of German student, who hunts me down ostensibly to "tie a bond of good-comradeship," but really to work up facts about what "England" thinks. Such people of undeveloped individuality tell me in return what "wir Deutschen" think, in a touching national spirit, which would have charmed Plato. But they don't charm me. Indeed I see in them the very worst result of 1871. They have no ideas beyond the "state," and have put me off Socialism for the rest of my life. They are not the kind of people, as George Birmingham[1] puts it, "you could borrow half-a-crown to get drunk with." But such is only a small proportion and come from the north and west; they just show how Sedan has ruined one type of German, for I'm sure the German nature is the nicest in the world, as far as it is not warped by the German Empire. I like their lack of reserve and self-consciousness, our two national virtues. They all write poetry and recite it with gusto to any three hours' old acquaintance. We all write poetry too in England, but we write it on the bedroom wash-stand and lock the bedroom door, and disclaim it vehemently in public. The conclusion of the whole matter is this: send some more Marlburians out here, to unlearn the theatrical-quick-change-double-faced-showing-off-posing habits (this word is getting rather like ὀρθρο-φοιτο etc.[2]) which one learns at a public school.

I am no longer in Berlin, but spending the rest of the Whitsun holidays in Schwerin, where they seem to disapprove of pens. I know it is rude to write to anyone, much more to you, in pencil. But my writing (which you don't seem to like) is at its best in pencil.

[1] Or, rather, the Irish R.M.

[2] Early-prowling, etc.—a word of thirty-nine letters from Aristophanes.

It's very kind of you to ask me to come and stay, and I hope to be able to do so at some later date. I got a tremendous reception here, by the way, as "the appearance in Schwerin of the flying outside right," and all the fat old lawyers came and shook my paw and said they couldn't thank me enough for introducing the laws of offside and sticks into Schwerin. There is talk of a statue to me—in my C I "lower" jersey.

I hope all is well, and best wishes for a successful prize-day and plenty of Lords (I *do* like Lords) on the platform. I hope that golf, tennis, Shackle, fishing and all your other hobbies are continuing to give satisfaction.

P.S. I'm afraid this letter is all very unconnected: the inevitable and promised result of leaving Classics and dissipating my mind over useless modern subjects!

To Professor and Mrs Sorley

Schwerin, 5 *June* 1914

Ken will have told you how he was packed off [from Berlin] on Tuesday morning with Karl: Karl considering that he could no longer stand the strain. It certainly was a tiring time, for that habit of eating out is very restless. And I'm not sure whether K. got quite his money's worth. Sunday was excellent, for we were escorted aimlessly and painlessly through the streets and saw something of "life," even if it was rather more provincial jollificators (like ourselves) than genuine Berliners that we saw. The night before we had been taken to the smartest café in Berlin, a most bourgeois affair, owing probably to the absence of evening dress there, for which I praise Germany. Monday was spent in the Zoological Gardens, where as usual the free human animals outside were far more worth watching than the soured and captive bestial animals inside the cages. In the evening, there being only foolish things on, fit for provincial holiday-makers, we were taken to an unfortunately foolish musical comedy where the prevalent impression of dowdiness was doubled. Kenneth and I went to bed. The others found some friends and went from café to café till 4 a.m. The friends were not to be shaken off and paid them a call from 4 till 7. This seems to be a fashionable hour in Berlin. The morning I spent alone among A. K.'s Chinese curiosities, of which he has innumerable. In the afternoon I visited a "lovely little" friend whom I met originally at Eucken's. He took me round some of the chief shops which, next to the cafés, are the Westminster Abbeys of Berlin. Then I had tea with him and met the others at the Königliches Schauspielhaus.

I wish Ken had got getting staying for that. It was Ibsen's *Peer Gynt* with Grieg's incidental music—the Northern Faust, as it is called: though the mixture of allegory and reality is not carried off so successfully as in the Southern Faust. Peer Gynt has the advantage of being a far more human and amiable creature, and not a cold fish like Faust. I suppose that difference is also to be found in the characters of the respective authors. I always wanted to know why Faust had no relations to make demands on him. *Peer Gynt* is a charmingly light piece, with an irresistible mixture of fantastical poetry and a very racy humour. The scene where Peer returns to his blind and dying mother and, like a practical fellow, instead of sentimentalizing, sits himself on the end of her bed, persuades her it is a chariot and rides her up to heaven, describing the scenes on the way, the surliness of St Peter at the gate, the appearance of God the Father, who "put Peter quite in the shade" and decided to let mother Aasa in, was delightful. The acting was of course perfect.

On Wednesday the Frau and I left by a latish train, having overslept. I am told not to criticize Berlin, as I saw it in holiday time. But, in contrast to the priggish sermon of —— about the Pagan Hedonism in Cannes, I should say that dowdy Christian Hedonism seemed to me the chief note. But that may have been the provincial element. The one thing I never saw was a crooked street. A Regent Street would make it much less efficient-looking. The town seemed all thought out before: built, unlike Rome, in a day. Here of course it is delightful.

Klemm "empfehlt sich." We have both written charming Collinses with suitable invitations to Cambridge.

To Professor and Mrs Sorley

Jena, 12 *June* 1914

I stayed on in Mecklenburg a day longer than I had intended and returned here early on Tuesday, the lectures not recommencing till Tuesday afternoon. You may have already heard of the delightful day we had on Sunday, when we went over to a certain Herr Roggen, a farmer friend of the B.s, whose property is only a mile or two from the sea. Though I didn't get seeing the sea, I smelt it, and the whole country was a great relief after the stiff formalism of the parts round Jena. Wismar, a sea-port, just two kilometres off, was exactly like Southwold from a distance. We were taken over the farm and saw the Russian peasants who work it—the German Bauer[1] being far too lazy or superior for farm-hand work, with the result that there are little Russian colonies dotted all over Mecklenburg wherever a large farm is. The lack of roads and hedges gave the whole country its suitable primitive aspect: and so did the party gathered there—us fashionable fellows from the capital (Schwerin), a few not quite so fashionable from the nearer Wismar, one or two neighbouring land-owners, semi-gentlemen like the farm-inspector and the chief coachman who "left at the pudding," and the parson.

We ate Mittag for just over two hours, a comparatively short time for such feasts: a most kingly Mittag with ice-pudding and a tremendous tub of champagne in the middle of the table. Kenneth was talking a most alarming amount—I don't mean in result of the champagne; but I was relieved because I had feared that my "sojourn," as Cockburn would call it, might have kept him back in his German. The Mecklenburg country is ten times more sympathetic to me than the Thuringian: I saw that clearly for the first time on returning there. I think Jena could only appeal to a southern nature for long. When once one gets accustomed to its quaintness, there's nothing else left. And one is caught in a trap by all those seven (I

[1] Peasant.

suppose they are seven) hills that shut it round on every side; and I am far too lazy to climb them. When one does one only comes to woods with horrid stunted little trees, which are just like the top of the fashionable German's head with all the hair cut down. But this is nothing against the University or the people here. It's only that you must expect a country laid out rather like a garden when you come out here.

To F. A. H. Atkey

June 1914

Very many thanks for your letter which finally found its way to me here. I am writing now to assuage my mind after the horrors of unpacking in a five feet square bed-sit.—having just returned to my present alma mater after the Whitsuntide jollification-week which I spent partly with my old friends in Schwerin who are now educating my twin-brother, and partly with a second-hand acquaintance in Berlin. Unless I regard the whole life here as a holiday, that was my first holiday since January, and I was surprised to find how glad I was to be back in Puritan Mecklenburg for a few days. Both in the country and the people there is something ursprünglich-ly strong and poetical which this Thuringen country, though its soil is rotten with the corpses of great men, can't offer. I find it false here: a precious affectation of mediaevalism seems to have affected the very soil. Not but what we have a kind of chimney on the Mound—Karl Zeiss's microscopic factory, whose recent erection is said to have killed twenty of the older professors within two years. But otherwise the whole surroundings are stamped with insincerity. So I play tennis at 6 a.m. (Things *you* don't do, No. 1), sleep from Mittagstisch till *βουλυτόνδε*[1], disregard the numerous walks which Schiller (I do bar Schiller) used to love, and lead a nice Philistine life. But I go to lectures: on philosophy and political economy chiefly, and one or two raddled dry ones on German literature. The classical professor has got a kranken Magen and Jena in the summer makes him perspire too much (I don't wonder). So he isn't lecturing, and, beyond a book a week of Homer in my bed-sit., I am reserving my classics till August. But besides that, the endless hospitality of these people has got me on to endless (*i.e.*, three) "Freischars" which meet once a week for "thought" evenings, "talk" evenings, "bible" evenings, "joke" evenings etc.—and very nice and interesting fellows they are. What an extraordinarily broad-minded and well-informed fellow the average (nicht-inkorporierte) German student is! But I believe one sees the best of the bag in Jena. Besides that, I am allowed every Sunday to go to Eucken's giant Gesellschafts, and there I meet many more lively people. Eucken is the great joke of Jena. A. R. G. always mentions the word Eucken in the same tone that he reserves for Walter Pater and Ruskin—and you know what that is. And he seems pretty famous in England. In Japan they admire him so that they had him over there in spring to try and form a State Religion—a graduated compound of Christianity and convenience. But even amateurish I can see from his lectures that he is no real big 'un. The idea that he is a philosopher at all is mocked in

[1] Towards evening.

Jena. And I was sent out here with the idea that he was a great one. It's curious. Both Germany and England seem to take each other's commonplace discarded prophets and goddify them. We take their nice old Euckens as great philosophers, and they take our nasty old Lyttons and Carlyles and Dickenses as great writers. But don't think I'm offended of it. I'm pleased with Jena and myself. I get a seat in the stalls in the Weimar theatre for a shilling whenever I like—and it's a first-rate theatre. And I want to stay here another term, and then a term at Berlin, and not go to Oxford at all. A foreigner has the very best of the grapes here. And I find an unfailing gymnastic pleasure in speaking the German language.

I saw by the way your *Peer Gynt* at Berlin, with Grieg's incidental music between the acts, which mercifully prevented applause. The mixture of fact and phantasy, reality and allegory, does not seem to be carried off as well as in *Faust*: and on the stage it fails. But it was very lively and beautiful: magnificently produced. I have no faith in those who say that the last act of the play is the testing-stone. I think the middle is. And *Peer Gynt* begins and ends all right, but that Egyptian middle part is so unconvincing. But the two scenes—(1) where Peer casts off Ingrid (the "ausser einer"—"Die allein!" scene), and (2) especially, Mother Aasa's Himmelfahrt, which has all the humour and much more poetry and less heaviness than Byron's *Vision of Judgment*, I think—were beautiful. I had just seen two days before Gerhart Hauptmann's *Hannele's Himmelfahrt* in Weimar—a weak Wildeian mixture of sentimentality and cynicism. And the fresh bounding witty scene in

Peer Gynt compared so splendidly with it—for the best death-bed scene in the world! The production lasted close on five hours: the staging was infinitely the finest I have ever seen.

Berlin is not one of the cities where I should like to go when I die. I didn't see a crooked street the whole time, nor one the least bent. A merry bourgeois-seeming place, though! No dignity and no idiosyncrasies that I could see.

I am so glad that junior Lit. Soc., now nearing its third birthday, is still running so strong. About X., I knew him only by report, but if he ever scolds you again about the self-conscious Mrs Lewes (I quite agree! She stands cheek by jowl with Tennyson and Schiller and Demosthenes in my Inferno), just tell him this: *we* know that she is dead. X., on the other hand, when requested in a Farrar Prize Paper to write on "Your favourite *living* writer and why," or such Sunday-school topic, wrote on George Eliot. (I know this because, in my impudent way, I read his papers after having in my conceited way finished my papers too early in the said prize to draw attention to myself). And I am horrorstruck that such an one should be cast on a dunghill like the house he was in, and not rather be in a nice quiet house with long intellectual and literary traditions both in housemasters and members like C 1.

But for Matthew Arnold I had always a secret fondness. His lines on Goethe in *Wordsworth's Grave* I like. And him any day rather than Byron or Spenser of the last two years! Do you remember "thē bĕd ŏf Xanthus" and "| rūddȳ | līght ŏf thĕ | fī-re |" for hexameter endings in his Homer essays in the Up. V, three summers back?

I hope you are flourishing and everything round you too. I am probing modern German lyric—Rilke and Hölderlin and sich—do you know them? Their language is colossally beautiful and they are egoists to their finger nails—both of which traits I like. —— always worried me too: something deformed about him, I always thought.

TO A. E. HUTCHINSON

June, 1914

Many thanks for your letter which found me very ill. My illness would be called (in the best circles) "fatigue." Berlin—dowdy, jolly bourgeois Berlin, the city where they don't go to bed—did for me. It is at once the gayest and dullest of cities in the world. The gayest, because they never go to bed, but rush about from café to café all night long: and the dullest, because they are gay on principle, because they think it gay never to go to bed. There is nothing to see in Berlin. It's a mistake to think it's the capital of Germany. It's the capital of Prussia and every Prussian is a bigot or a braggart—except the Prussian Jews: and they alone have humour and independent minds. I like Germany too much to agree that Berlin is its capital. The town has no characteristics except efficiency and conceit and feeble imitation of French artistic vice, where the vice is doubled and the art dropped. It is the "Johnny" among cities. And it has made me very ill—*i.e.*, I stayed in bed for breakfast for the first time in my life. Nasty place. My latest craze is German iced coffee with whipped cream, all in a glass set before you in the ice-can itself and drunk gently through a long tapering straw (length three times that of a vulgar lemonade straw), scented with mild tobacco. I can't afford it ever again; but you could get up a Sorley Shilling Subscription (heading the list yourself with 5), and send me out the presumably huge result, and then I could have as many special German glass iced coffees as I wanted. My idea of Heaven is getting very decadent these days, but I do connect special shilling iced coffee with angels and archangels (or rather it is possible that angels have to put up with ordinary six-penny iced coffee, but you and I will be archangels!). If you knew the heat and the thunder in this Jena of mine, you'd appreciate my thoughts. It's only sheer lack of money that prevents me feeding solely on iced coffee, mushrooms, peaches, and champagne. But having (through a strange mixture of poverty and stinginess) to live on boiled mutton, bad beer, poached eggs and divinely virtuous soup, I have to make up by boring you by accounts of the oysters and the Rhine wine of my dreams.

Under the Greenwood Tree I have read but forgotten. But I seem to remember a very pretty stroke of irony in the last sentence of all which makes the book worth finishing. It was Hardy's first effort, and, if I remember, lacks all the strength and irony and anger of his later books. The whole idyllic setting and simple comic relief is rather like one of Shakespeare's comedies, which act far better than they read. But the "'O, 'tis the nightingale,' murmured she, and thought of a secret she would never tell" (the last sentence, isn't it?) is very pretty and a key to one of Hardy's chief thoughts—that everyone has a skeleton in the cupboard, and that such things as perfect candidness and complete mutual understanding between two people simply don't and shouldn't exist. He always emphasizes the manifold personality.

The Wiltshire people are all poor and stupid, I agree, and those coming from the Pewsey Vale may be also sad. But those living north and north-east are not sad, only philosophical. You know the story of the Aldbourne Bobchick. There was once a Bobchick (whatever a Bobchick is) sailed up to Aldbourne from Ramsbury in one of those temporary rain-streams that abound in Wiltshire. Aldbourne had never seen a Bobchick before, so they caught him and kept him in the Squire's bath (the only one within miles: the Rector hadn't one). Meanwhile they had a meeting of the town council about it. The oldest inhabitant remembered seeing one years before and remembered also some very grand name for it. So they killed it and stuffed it (not knowing it was a mere low Bobchick) and called it this grand name and bought a tripod with a glass case on top and set it up in the village inn for worship and inspection. And it was thought that the great world without of Mildenhall and Marlborough and the Ogbournes each with their Saint —yes, and perhaps the unknown land south of the Kennet, Bedwyn and Grafton and the towns by the great river and the land eastward stretching to the great plain—might hear of this new bird discovered in the (temporary) river at Aldbourne, and the fame of Aldbourne would be exalted. Till one day a town man from Ramsbury on the main road came to Aldbourne, and when they tried to impress the man from the main road with the bird, he said, "Why it's only a Bobchick. They're as common as fleas in Ramsbury." And Aldbourne was put to shame, and Ramsbury mocked Aldbourne. And even now, if you shout "Bobchick" within a mile of Aldbourne, they'll come out and stone you for they'll think you're Ramsbury born. (Dick Richardson[1] told me this.) This by the way. Because I was going to advise you, if ever the dowdy Pewsey road should pall, go through the town, past the green on the road to Mildenhall and Ramsbury, but turn to the left before you cross the railway, where it says "Bridle-track to Aldbourne." And in ten minutes you'll be on the Aldbourne Downs. They're far the best things in the neighbourhood.

A parental visit has livened up last week-end considerably. We "did" western Thuringia, which I recommend for its peculiar strawberry wine, and saw *Midsummer Night's Dream* in a wood, which has put me off theatres for the rest of my life. I laughed like a child and "me to live a hundred years, I should never be tired of praising it." The Germans are so Elizabethan themselves that their productions of Shakespeare are almost perfect. And in this case, the absence of curtains and scenery, and the presence of trees and skies, added the touch of perfection. Shakespeare's humour is primitive but, none the less, perfect.

[1] Henry Richardson (1845–1914), assistant-master at Marlborough, 1870–1905.

To Professor and Mrs Sorley

Early in July 1914

I'm so glad that even Berlin didn't fail to please, and I hope that Kittendorf kept up the high reputation that Germany must have got in the last fortnight. Nevertheless I'm sure that the best thing it gave you was what you ought to have had in England[1]. I wrote a "swarming" letter to the director at "Roda's first," thanking him for a herzlicher Abend and telling him of a berühmter englischer Philosoph and his wife who had been with me and had expressed their satisfaction with the performance—without letting on that the said satisfied people were my parents. I still regret that we weren't able to give them a supper—mayonnaise, champagne, Götterspeise (did you have Götterspeise at Mecklenburg?), iced coffee and Erdbeerenbowle. Nevertheless we have made a friend for life in Bottom: only the supper would have made Bottom make a friend for life in us. The haphazard noticing of that advertisement in Eisenach is just one of these things that makes one believe in a special disposing Providence that sometimes takes the part of master of the revels. I only hope Bottom knows how nice he is.

I am interested about your iced coffee at the Café Bauer: for the first iced coffee of my life I had there. I don't think you missed much by not being able to vet Werthheims: it is only an incarnation of the horrible German way of combining Commerce and Art. It is funny without being in the least vulgar.

[1] An open-air performance of *A Midsummer Night's Dream*, at the Bergtheater, Friedrichroda in Thuringia, 19 June 1914.

The heat here is, as the Germans say, "to shoot." It is just as if the whole of Jena was suffering from extreme central heating. I'm now taking Abendbrot regularly up on the hill, which adds to the expense of life a good deal (as when I began taking mustard); but there's a kind of breeze comes slowly galumphing over there, so it's worth it. Otherwise life is one long perspiration which, I daresay, is very healthy. The Germans are all awfully happy, hanging their hats on their tummies and promenading in the sun. But tennis continues, and I live *in* shorts and an unbuttoned shirt and *on* green salad and cherries. I am also sweatily struggling to the end of *Faust II*, where Goethe's just showing off his knowledge. I am also reading a very interesting book on Goethe and Schiller; very adoring it is, but it lets out quite unconsciously the terrible dryness of their entirely intellectual friendship and (Goethe's at least) entirely intellectual life. If Goethe really died saying "more light," it was very silly of him: what *he* wanted was more warmth. G. and S. apparently made friends, on their own confession, merely because their ideas and artistic ideals were the same, which fact ought to be the very first to make them bore one another.

All this is leading to the following conclusion. The Germans can act Shakespeare, have good beer and poetry, but their prose is cobwebby stuff. Hence I want to read some good prose again. Also it is summer. And for a year or two I had always laid up "The Pageant of Summer" as a treat for a hot July. In spite of all former vows of celibacy in the way of English, now's the time. So, unless the cost of book-postage here is ruinous, could you send me a small volume of Essays by Richard

Jefferies called *The Life of the Fields*, which is bound in green if it isn't bound in red and (unless the drawing-room has suffered another metamorphosis in my absence) is to be found in the little bookcase supposed to contain my books, and bears a hideous production of Marlburian arms stamped on the front, the first essay in the series being "The Pageant of Summer"? No particular hurry, but I should be amazingly grateful if you'll send it (it's quite a little book), especially as I presume the pageant of summer takes place in that part of the country where I should be now had Gidney had a stronger will than you. In the midst of my setting up and smashing of deities—Masefield, Hardy, Goethe—I always fall back on Richard Jefferies wandering about in the background. I have at least the tie of locality with him.

TO THE MASTER OF MARLBOROUGH

July (?) 1914

Thanks very much indeed for your letter. I am awfully sorry to trespass again on your very full time, but just a word in explanation of the Browning incident.

I don't say that I didn't ever make that remark in speech at M. C., for at M. C. I may have said anything. But I'm sorry (1) that I was quoted at all (I hate all posthumous recurrences of O. M.s) and (2) that what is exactly the reverse of my real opinion was quoted. My (intense) objection to Browning is because he seems to me a far too confident and bigoted *theist*—not an atheist at all (this is apart from my objection to the artist who turned himself into trick-jumper and the man who became a society pet). I hope that I never made such a bad criticism, even in joke. I think the writer of the essay (whoever he was, you don't say, but I think I can guess who he was) must have misunderstood me when I was fuming once against B. But when I speak against B., I am never in joke, because the poet is so utterly repulsive to me: and I have often tried to save people from the dusty intellectualism of *Rabbi Ben Ezra* and try and turn them on to the windy elemental strength of *Hard Weather* or other of Meredith's poems. And this bad criticism may have been the result of over-zeal in a good cause! But I wasn't joking, but proselytizing! I admit that I always "corrupted the youth"—but in the same kind of way that Socrates corrupted them!

But I mustn't waste your time any more. Only my hatred of Browning is so great that I could not bear to think that you thought it rested on such unreasonable grounds!

To the Master of Marlborough

July 1914

Very many thanks for your last letter, which provoked an immediate return defending myself against the charge of bad criticism. My sentiments were (as usual) exaggerated therein, for there is much in B. I like. But my feeling towards him has (ever since I read his life) been that of his to the "Lost Leader." I cannot understand him consenting to live a purely literary life in Italy, or (worse still) consenting to be lionised by fashionable London society. And then I always feel that if less people read Browning, more would read Meredith (his poetry, I mean). And I deplore the lack of *earth* in

Browning. So I try to do for others what the—I almost said "the late"!—Mr Bickersteth did for me, i.e., convert them to Meredith, which must necessarily mean a partial throwing over of Browning. Hence my rage.

Another point in your letter leaves me unconvinced. You say that the "corps" aren't bad really. But they are! Black-rotten! The sooner one dispels the libel on German universities that the corps student is the typical student, the better. They comprise only a third of the total number of students at Jena: and Jena is the most traditional of all German universities. They are the froth and the dregs. We, the "nicht-inkorporierten," the other two-thirds, are the good body of the beer. We live in two feet square bedsits., we do a little work (impossible for the first three semesters for the corps students), and pretty soon we can mix with one another without any of the force and disadvantages of the artificially corporate life. A peculiarly offensive form of "fagging" for the six youngest students in each corps: compulsory drunkenness; compulsory development of offensive and aggressive behaviour to the outsider; and a peculiarly sickening anti-Semitism are their chief features. The students with whom I mostly go about are Jews, and so perhaps I see, from their accounts of the insults they've to stand, the worst side of these many-coloured reeling creatures. But they're dying out. Their place is being taken by non-combative and non-disciplinary Verbindungen. One or two will still remain—for they're picturesque enough and their singing is fine: and I like a little froth to my beer. But please don't think they're typical of us. We've most of us outlived that Sedanish spirit here.

Things still go swiftly here. After a great struggle, I have given the Germans Shakespeare! The deciding factor was the witnessing of *Midsummer Night's Dream* in a wood near Weimar. The Elizabethan spirit is not lost. It has only crossed the channel and found a home in Germany. Every Thuringian peasant is a Bottom or a Quince. I am never going into a theatre again, but shall always live on the recollection of that sublime and humorous benignity produced by the Thuringian Shakespeare, the Thuringian forest, and the Thuringian actors in concert. Shakespeare of the comedies *is* German. I am going to keep the histories, also *Lear* and the passionate tragedies, but give them *Hamlet* and the intellectual tragedies: and give them Shakespeare's humour, which does not depend (as the modern English) on malice and slyness. With Mendelssohn's music attached, it was the most harmonious thing I have ever seen.

I've given up German prose altogether. It's like a stale cake compounded of foreign elements. So I have laid in a huge store of Richard Jefferies for the rest of July, and read him none the less voraciously because we are countrymen. (I know it's wrong of me, but I count myself as Wiltshire. So will you when you've been at Marlborough six years. I can still give myself elder-brother airs in that respect, you see[1].) When I die (in sixty years) I am going to leave all my presumably enormous fortune to Marlborough on condition that a thorough knowledge of Richard Jefferies is ensured by the teaching there. I think it is only right considering we are bred upon the self-same hill. It

[1] He forgot apparently that his correspondent was a Wiltshire man.

would also encourage naturalists and discourage cricketers. This as a hint, to add to that long category of "hints"—Japanese, Morris Dancing, etc.—which you related on Prize Day last year. But I'm sure *Wild Life in a Southern County* or *Field and Hedgerow* would make a far healthier extra for the Modern Side than that material blue book they do—"How to become a British citizen" or whatever it is. Only you couldn't examine them on Jefferies. But you ought to try and turn them out Wiltshiremen, and not Britons. I hate Britons with a big big B.

But, in any case, I'm not reading so much German as I did ought to. I dabble in their modern poetry, which is mostly of the morbidly religious kind. The language is massively beautiful, the thought is rich and sleek, the air that of the inside of a church. Magnificent artists they are, with no inspiration, who take religion up as a very responsive subject for art, and mould it in their hands like sticky putty. There are magnificent parts in it, but you can imagine what a relief it was to get back to Jefferies and Liddington Castle.

Yes, I knew Mr Richardson. Once or twice he invited me to take Workers' Education parties out to Aldbourne or Martinsell with him. Then, you could imagine, I saw him at his best. Talk about books in the running brooks and sermons in stones! He had an anecdote peculiar to every square yard on the Aldbourne Downs almost.

I continue to feed on German Philosophy, Staatswissenschaft, and cherries till the end of July: when I hope to meet Hopkinson, who is patronizing some Trippers' Holiday Courses at Marburg, and take him for a walk for a week or so by the Moselle. Then a visit or two, and back. September will find me trying to remember my Latin: which I shouldn't much mind if I forgot. I was never meant for a scholar: but I suppose the farce of making me one will go on for another four years.

I hope all is well with you. And best of holidays in whatever foreign land.

To A. J. Hopkinson[1]

5 *July* 1914

Very many thanks for your letter which had the terrible effect of making me cut an "Eucken," as I got it at breakfast (or what they call breakfast in this breakfastless land) and stayed zu Hause to consider it. You seem to have been living a varied life as cyclist, soldier, dramatic critic, criminal, and finally emigrant: and I hope you're enjoying getting your sleep out with your pastor host. Is, by the way, this "Limeleg[2]" the same as the man who fed you in August and September at Wiesbaden, under a changed address? I'm sure it was a similar name, but as all country pfarrers in Deutschland have similar faces, I dare say they've all got similar names.

But first to business. Your Moselle plan has bucked me tremendously. Would it worry you very much to take a not *quite* final promise to partake? The reason is that I'm not really free for the first week in August,

[1] Of Exeter College, Oxford; formerly of Marlborough; afterwards Captain, Durham L.I.; M.C.

[2] Herr Pf. Lindenbein.

being booked for uninspiring visits. But I'm going to immediately (or immediately to) try and compass my emancipation. I think I'll easily get off, and then let you know for certain. I'm confident it will be yes! Then we can go into details.

About your "culture." You've applied to the wrong door when you asked me to recommend you novels for summer consumption. German novels are indigestible at any time of the year. I wouldn't advise my worst enemy to read one. I believe there is one tolerable one, interesting in its way, called *Der Narr in Christo: Emmanuel Quint* by Gerhart Hauptmann. I haven't read it myself as I can't get it under 6*s.*! But if there's a free library for you wretched Ferien-cursus trippers at Marburg (I've got to keep up the reputation you give me of being "uppish") you can get it there. If you are bent on novel reading, Tolstoi's the thing. You get him well translated in Reclam. Otherwise, I recommend drama, but even then one has to cast one's net for foreign fishes: Ibsen and Strindberg are both in Reclam. Do read Ibsen's last play, *John Gabriel Borkman*, and tell me what you think of it. I think it's the finest thing ever written. But echt German novels—giebt es leider keine. But for Sundays and Saints' days let me recommend very strongly a book called *Goethe und Schiller* by Heinrich von Stein, No. 3090 in Reclam, very well written and interesting, when you've quite done yawning.

Personally I stick to German poetry. I don't think they can write prose. Try Hebbel as a good poetical dramatist: or, if you're getting moderny, Hugo von Hoffmannsthal or Hölderlin (get a catalogue of the

Insel-Bücherei, 50 pf. a volume, nicely bound; little Novellen from Herzog or Rilke are tolerable only if you're still sleepy). Or get Rilke's Stundenbuch (3.50) —that's their best modern poet—or, if you get hold of Storm's—Theodor Storm's—short stories cheaply (I only borrowed them), they're as good as anything.

Here I close the information bureau: but it's open again at any time if you want. But it isn't a good bureau, for I've been busying myself almost entirely with *Faust* and *Egmont* and the better of Goethe's efforts: so I'm not up in modern prose and drama, though I can give you a tip or two in their poetry—Rilke and Hölderlin.

I have been having—if a less ὀρθρο-φοιτο etc. life than you—quite a good average time since I last wrote. I visited Berlin for a few days at Whitsun and met my brother there, and *therefore* (I say *therefore*) enjoyed it: but my advice is, keep clear of Berlin. It is a town of to-day, lives day and night like Mycerinus—and you. (The trams are off duty from 4 to 6 a.m.! It would suit you with your new-won habits of starting for marches at one and doing literary work at 5 a.m.) It has no traditions, not a crooked street in the place, and all the German thoroughness of organization, without any of their artistic fineness. Lately also a visit from my Eltern[1] livened up things considerably. We saw *Midsummer Night's Dream* performed in a wood, and I wished the performance to last for ever.... Jena is at present a swamp of perspiration and Gewitter[2], but the (physically) melting humanity there are still treating me very nicely. I still get up and play tennis with the lark,

[1] Parents. [2] Thunderstorms.

swim, eat, sleep, and walk across mountains, and bathe myself in Abendrot. I live on fresh cherries and wear only a shirt and shorts and sandals like some beast in *Alice through the Looking-glass.* I should be quite happy if only I could sing—were it never so little. Foul as the corps-students mostly are, I love to hear them at "Gaudeamus igitur."

I was awfully interested in your breathless behaviour during June and your short visit to M. C., Wilts. I'm glad all your old house seem to have twenty-twos. About the O. M. dinner and the absurd part put on to poor "new boy" me—the least in the kingdom of heaven—more anon! I shall get down to you when we meet (as I hope) in four weeks' time, and the banks of Moselle shall ring with my angry plaints.

Best of luck in Marburg. You'll probably get much more out of your three weeks than I out of my semester, for Satan tempts me and I cut many lectures to lie by the tennisplätzen and make silly jokes to the scorching German sun. Summer makes me lazy—but I'll buck up the first week in August. I shall at once set the bells tinkling and try and ring my other engagements off. You may take it for practically certain that I will. And details later. And let's hear from your Hochwohlgeborene Hoheit in Marburg.

TO PROFESSOR AND MRS SORLEY

16 *July* 1914

Nothing has been happening here, except that policemen have been worrying me. On the memorable date of my entrance in Jena I had to write two biographies of myself, one for the university and one for the town. The university thought that Charles was a masculine, the town that it was a feminine, name. So when they drew up their statistics, they didn't tally. So they called on me to-day and put the whole matter in my hands. I had also filled up minor details, such as "faith-confession" and "since when educated" differently in both. So that they rather suspected that there were really two of me and I was keeping one of them beneath the washstand: one of them being a Church of England lady who had been educated since September 1908, the other an evangelical gentleman who had begun his education as early as May 1895. But they were soon satisfied.

To A. E. Hutchinson

24 (?) *July* 1914

Many thanks for your letter. I'm awfully sorry to have taken such a time in answering, but Justice has been engaging my attention. You see my landlady keeps a partly tame squirrel: a charming animal whose only fault is a habit of mistaking my bed for its own. Now the landlord of the whole house has accused the landlady of this particular flat that it pestifies the whole house. So it does. But I have spent the last week giving evidence before forty German Beamten[1] that the squirrel in question has the manners of a lamb and smells like eau de Cologne. By the steady honesty of my appearance (for I do look honest, don't I?) I have largely succeeded in getting my landlady off. The reason for my perjury

[1] Officials.

(the first time I have committed perjury—indeed, the first time they've given me a chance to) was this: I should love to have had that squirrel killed and my landlady imprisoned. But I feared. I knew that if I gave evidence against her, she would poison my morning coffee and hide my brushes in my bed. My course has been quite justified, because my landlady has given me a handsome present in the shape of a bunch of sweet-peas. Sweet-peas for Perjurers! Aha!

Yes! I quite agree with you that the Downs like oysters should be reserved for months with an r. But I cannot possibly come down on O. M. Sunday to take you for a walk. (1) I am too poor. (2) It is a peculiarly moth-eaten type of Old Marlburian that leaves the wardrobe on Old Marlburian Day and fills up the back-row of Chapel on Sunday, whimpering over the hymns, and I wouldn't be identified with this type even for all the gold in Araby and the prospect of having to stand you a meal (or possibly two) in the poverty-stricken pubs round Aldbourne. No. I shall come down quietly towards the end of the term, shall take you by the arm, "Now, my boy, you're leaving in a few weeks' time. Well, I left too, ye know. It's a nasty wrench, but there's always work for a soldier of Christ to do," and generally edify you. You'll need edification. I am sure the law is bound to make anyone who adopts it as a profession a hide-bound cynic in a month. So you'ld better not to come to Germany. Cynicism is a vice that doesn't exist here. That's why one's driven into it oneself for pure need of vinegar with the salad. In England there is so much vinegar that it is difficult to find the cucumber at all.

I had always an idea that when you were a fair specimen of the idle rich, and I a journalist and socialist orator campaigning against the same at street corners, you would ask me to stay occasionally and give me oysters and champagne.

——'s little story seemed to me rather silly.... England is seen at its worst when it has to deal with men like Wilde. In Germany Wilde and Byron are appreciated as authors: in England they still go pecking about their love-affairs. Anyone who calls a book "immoral" or "moral" should be caned. A book by itself can be neither. It is only a question of the morality or immorality of the reader. But the English approach all questions of vice with such a curious mixture of curiosity and fear that it's impossible to deal with them.

I'm leaving this place on Tuesday and am at present perfectly miserable at the thought of the imminence of the necessity of packing. On Tuesday I go to Marburg and pick up Hopper who is swimming about in some extraordinary Trippers' Course there: and we are going for a walking tour till one of us dies of heat apoplexy. Supposing I am the survivor, I propose to go to Berlin and then Schwerin. A yearning motherland will receive me again on the 16th of August. At least I hope so.

I am very sad about the death of the Witch of Toller, and sympathize with Emma in her overwhelming sorrow of bereavement. If I had more money I should write an epitaph for her and send it to you. But when one is poor one can't write poetry. One needs to be able to look back on a good meal just behind one, and forward to another good meal just coming. I alas! can do neither. And, with my hopes of Alan becoming quite a rich man thus rudely shattered, I am not happy. Do you think I would ever have associated with you unless I had thought that in time to come you would be constantly lending me fivers without prospect of repayment, and giving me game and a bottle of port for Christmas? The only way out of it is this: when I am had up for forging cheques, your beastly little firm of solicitors shall pull me through gratis.

If the Lord God were to come down from heaven and offer me any gift I liked in reward for the service I had done to him, I should choose to be a Widow. It must be simply grand. Haven't you often prayed—I have—that people you like may die, in order that you may have the luxury of mourning and being wept with and pitied? The dead are after all the supreme aristocrats. And widowhood or any other state involving a close connection with or dependence on Death gives one a magnificent standing. The lady you mention reminds me always of that child in Laurence Housman's[1] poem which ends:

> But in another week they said
> That friendly pinkfaced man was dead.
> "How sad...," they said, "the best of men..."
> So I said too, "How sad"; but then
> Deep in my heart I thought with pride
> "I know a person who has died."

I can depart from Germany with a clear conscience, because I have finished *Faust* at last! I think it's about the best thing ever written. The main idea of the thing —"Er, unbefriedigt jeden Augenblick[2]"—is entirely to my taste. He is really rather a stimulating person,

[1] Or rather Mrs Cornford's.
[2] "He, every moment still unsatisfied."

Goethe. And Germany on the whole is a very good place to get together a kind of amateur Weltanschauung[1] as they call it. The average German does think for himself. He doesn't simply live in the moment like the average Briton (which makes the average Briton pleasanter than the average German, but still!). And he does try to develope his own personality without reference to other people, that is, without making it either absolutely the same or absolutely different from his surroundings, as the Briton always does. They're really quite an admirable lot—and, when they try to be funny, they're like squeaking Teddy Bears.

My address still remains as above till the 12th of August. For, in consideration of my "offices" *in re* the squirrel, my landlady has undertaken to forward my letters. One word more (as Browning says). I have been meaning for ages to write to "the Clever" and tell him to teach "the Good" that one writes letters *an* and not *zu* a person.

I've just received a letter from the Master calling me a "casual heretic," and an "insufferable little cub." The casual, heretic, and insufferable I can stand. But the "little cub" part rankles.

To Professor and Mrs Sorley

26 *July* 1914

The haystack has caught fire. The drunken Verbindungen are parading the streets shouting "Down with the Serbs." Every half-hour, even in secluded Jena, comes a fresh edition of the papers, each time with

[1] View of the world, philosophy.

wilder rumours: so that one can almost hear the firing at Belgrade. But perhaps this is only a German sabbatical liveliness. At any rate, it seems that Russia must to-night settle the question of a continental war, or no. Curious that an Austrian-Servian war—the one ideal of the late Austrian Crown-prince's[1] life—should be attained first by his death. It puts him on a level with the heroes:

> Erst, wenn er sterben muss an diesem Stern,
> Sehen wir dass er an diesem Stern gelebt—

as Rilke says of Christ.

The Euckens send greetings of all sorts. The Schückings, who asked me to supper last Saturday, also send greetings. They *are* nice people.

To Miss M. M. Smith

26 *July* 1914

I'm due to leave Jena in two days. I should now like to spend another term here, for in one Semester one only finds one's bearings: and I'm full of good intentions of what I would do if I could come back for the winter term. However, I shan't be sorry to see an English penny again. There's something so honest and English and unpractical in a big downright English penny—so much nicer than those nasty little ten-pfennig pieces that are for ever making you think they're marks. A good breakfast will be also very welcome, and *Punch*. In these three respects I think we have it over Germany....

[1] Heir to the throne (not Crown-prince).

I'm so glad you're going to visit Germany again after your stay in Sweden. I don't think any one could help it who has been there once. But I hope you'll still like Berlin. I liked it least of what I have seen of Germany. Too much of Prussian officialdom and red tape, I thought. I'll allow it to be called the capital of Prussia —but of Germany, no....

We are having an exciting time with the various Abschied-fests. It is a fine sight to see all the corps dressed up in their old-fashioned costumes, carrying torches, singing through the town at midnight. It almost makes one wish that one was an "inkorporierter" too. To-night, I'm afraid, they are making a war-demonstration and shouting "Down with the Serbs." We are altogether having a thrilling time at present: with new editions of the papers coming out every hour, each time with wilder rumours. It is curious that the one person who would have leapt with joy at this new war is the murdered Crown-prince, whose death has been the means of bringing it about. I hope you'll find a pacified Germany when you come south from Sweden.

So both the sides of the channel we are pretty "angespannt[1]." And the gunpowder seems to have caught fire. The next week should bring exciting things.

[1] Strained.

CHAPTER V

THE ARMY: IN TRAINING

C. H. S. and his friend had been walking for three or four days in the valley of the Moselle (from Coblenz to Trier), and in the evening of Saturday, 1st August, they came down from the hills "somewhat lightheartedly" to the village of Neumagen, thirty kilometres east of Trier. There they learned of the catastrophe which had overtaken the world. The foolish Burgomaster told them to make for home through Luxemburg; and next morning they took train to Trier, gave themselves up to the military guard at the station, and were marched off to prison. Some of his subsequent experiences are recorded in his letters. He also wrote, without signing it, an article which appeared in *The Cambridge Chronicle* of 14th August. This account was written "by request" and lacks the spontaneity of his letters. But one or two passages in it supplement the story as he told it to his correspondents.

The song and guitar were busy in Neumagen all that night. "When you get back to England," said the fatherly policeman to me, "you tell them that Germany doesn't sleep." But what the lights of the street had hid, the light of day next morning showed us. It was "quantum mutatus ab illo Hectore." The children, who seemed to scent disaster, were crying—all of those I saw. The women were mostly snuffling and gulping, which is worse. And the men, the singers of the night before, with drawn faces and forced smiles, were trying to seek comfort from their long drooping pipes and envying those who need not rejoin their barracks till Tuesday. It was Sunday, and the wailing notes of an intercession service on a bad organ were exuded from the church in the background. I have never seen a sight more miserable....

I had just finished reading a German penny novel which I found in the cell, when, attracted by a scraping and whistling, I looked in the direction and saw a small hole in the wall. The next two hours were enlivened by conversation with a most delightful German prisoner whom I never saw: in prison for nine months for remarking in an underbreath on parade that officers were funny fellows! "But thank God this isn't Prussia," said he, "or else it would have been two years." He was now put on shortest rations and not allowed out for prison exercise, because he had smuggled a newspaper in with him and given it thereafter to another prisoner on the sly. That same morning he had been cheering up a citizen of Trier who, in the French pay, had attempted to blow up a bridge, and had been taken away to be shot an hour before I was placed in the cell in which he had spent his last night. He was no malcontent, my friend through the hole, and, whenever I pitied his lot under conscription, "But it's far worse in Prussia," was always his answer. It is very remarkable how much tyranny and arrogance and injustice these fellows can stand, and with what stoutness and easy good humour they stand it....

At the exit of the barracks were much the same crowd of curious people who had longed to see us shot that morning. They regarded our free dismissal with surprise, and crowded up friendlily. "Then you're not the Englishmen who poisoned the water," they said. And when we had said "No," another said "Well you've heard that England has declared war against Russia on Germany's side!" However this extraordinary rumour had started, its effect was to provide us with an almost enthusiastic send-off. It was certainly an expression of the popular belief, shared by many individuals and many of the local papers since the Austrian-Servian war was declared, that the result would be a racial war between Teutons on the one side and Slavs and Romance nations on the other, in which England (whose mixed descent is often not realised by the purer Germans) would be bound to take the side of its cousins across the North Sea. Anyhow, we were prudent enough to fall in with its spirit, and parted with the people on the most friendly terms....

It was now Monday afternoon, but as I passed through Liége I saw nothing to suggest the strength of its defences or the proximity of the Germans. A Belgian soldier or two by the bridges with their helmets like tin top-hats and their uniform resembling that of Waterloo times, alone disturbed the agricultural peace of that tract of country. Many men of military age were still at work in the fields, and the train service was running as quietly and uninterruptedly as ever....

The many inhabitants of Antwerp with whom I spoke seemed to be in a state of philosophic calm and resignation. "The Germans will be here in twelve hours' time," they told me; "there's no doubt of it, they're already over the frontier." So even in Antwerp the lengthy and heroic resistance of their forces at Liége was not anticipated by many of the population.

To A. E. Hutchinson

Cambridge, 10 (?) *August* 1914

I daresay that, after the three years that Lord K. has allotted for the war, they'll forward me from Jena a letter from you written to me about this time. Howbeit, even supposing you sent one loose into that delightful land, I naturally never received it. For, after I had spent three splendid days trying to make Hopper drunk with Mosel wine in the Mosel valley (I never got him further than the state of "not drunk but having drink taken"), they took us up as spies and put us into prison at Trier. To be exact, the "imprisonment" only lasted 8½ hours; but I was feeling a real prisoner by the time they let us out. I had a white cell, a bowl of soup, a pitcher of solidifying water, a hole in the wall through which I talked to the prisoner next door, a prison bed, a prison bible: so altogether they did the thing in style. We had also a hissing crowd shouting "Totschiessen" to accompany us from the barracks to the prison. It couldn't have been arranged more finely: and the man who had occupied the cell before me had just been taken out and shot for being a Frenchman. But the English were in high favour, and I started a rumour that England had declared war on Russia; so they readily gave us a dismissal at our examination, and a free pass calling us unsuspicious. We travelled slowly to Cologne all through Sunday night: but a sad thing happened there, and Paul and Barnabas parted. Barnabas went on in the same train to Amsterdam hoping thereby to reach Hook; while Paul (ravenous for breakfast) "detrained" at Cologne and had a huge meal. I, of course, was Paul.

Meanwhile your post-card has arrived and many thanks. I explain. Your letter probably reached Jena after I had left and was forwarded to the Poste Restante, Trier, as I had directed. But the only three public buildings I was allowed to see were the barracks, the prison, and the station. So, as I have said before, I shall send for the letter and post-cards in three years. They have probably read your letter at Trier and cut out with scissors the words they consider improper.

To proceed, as Sergt-Major Barnes says. I took a train to Brussels, but they turned me out at a deserted village on the Belgian frontier. I walked to the next town and took train sorrowfully to Brussels. At Brussels I had "financial difficulties" and had to call on half the consuls in the place to solve them, and then I travelled sordidly on to Antwerp. The last ship had sailed for Harwich so the English consul chartered an old broken-down sad ship called the "Montrose." It was being embalmed in Antwerp Harbour because Miss le Neve had been taken prisoner on board it four years ago. They gave us Capt. Kendall, who was last seen going down with the "Empress of Ireland," to take command. And after three days' journey with commercial travellers of the most revoltingly John Bullish description, I got home on Thursday and was mistaken for the gardener. He always wears my worn-out clo's, so we are constantly interchanged. But mark. Hopper, who arrived triumphant at Harwich two days before I did, had to pay for his crossing. I got a free passage as far as London, where I borrowed money from my aunt's butler to take me on to Cambridge; and my aunt repaid the debt.

Now, have you ever heard a more commonplace and sordid narrative? At least I found it so in experience—merely dull, after I had left Hopper. The only bright star was a drunken Austrian, with whom we travelled from Trier to Coblenz, who seated himself opposite to us and gazed in our faces and at last said lovingly: "Ihr seid gewiss Hamburger Jungen." The poor man was trying to go from Kiel to Vienna, and, perpetually drunken, had travelled via Brussels, Paris, Marseilles, and Metz, which even you must know is not the shortest way. After he had flung Hopper's cap out of the window, he said that Hopper was a "feiner Mann," but said nothing about me, which just shows how drunk he was. But otherwise it was dull. Now, behold, I cannot stir out of the house, but some lady friend of my mother's, whose mind is upset by the present business, rushes up and says "O, you're the boy that's had such *adventures*. Been in prison too, I hear. You *must* come and tell us all about it." Then there's aunts to be written to. I shall probably be driven into writing a book "Across Germany in an O. M. tie" or "Prison Life in Germany by one who has seen it," followed shortly by another entitled: "Three days on the open sea with Commercial Travellers" or "Britannia Rules the Waves." And so I am simply nauseated by the memory of these five very ordinary and comparatively dull days. The preceding days in the Moselthal were far nicer: only Hopper was so provincial, and, when I entered a Gasthaus with a knowing swagger and said "I wish to sample the local Mosel here; what vintage do you recommend?" Hopper would burst in with "Haben Sie Münchener Bier?" and a huge grin on his face: unwitting what a heinous sin it is to order beer in a wine district. So we generally compromized on hot milk.

Having proved my identity at home as distinct from the gardener's, I investigated my (a-hem!) "papers" and found, among old receipts for college clothes and such like, a lovely piece of paper, which I daresay you have got too, which dismissed me from the corps. Only mine had EXCELLENT written (in the Major's hand) for my General Efficiency. Yours can have had, at most, "very good." I took this down to a man of sorts and said "Mit Gott für Kaiser und Vaterland, I mean, für König und Mutterland: what can I do to have some reasonable answer to give to my acquaintances when they ask me, 'What are *you* doing?'?" He looked me up and down and said, "Send in for a commission in the Territorials. You may get something there. You'll get an answer in a fortnight's time, not before." Compromise as usual. Not heroic enough to do the really straight thing and join the regulars as a Tommy, I have made a stupid compromise [with] my conscience and applied for a commission in the Terriers, where no new officers are wanted. In a month's time I shall probably get the beastly thing: and spend the next twelve months binding the corn, guarding the bridges, frightening the birds away, and otherwise assisting in Home Defence. So I think you were sensible to prefer your last term at Marlborough. Only I wish you could come and join the beastly battalion of Cambridgeshire clerks to which I shall be tacked on: and we could sow the corn and think we were soldiers together.

But isn't all this bloody? I am full of mute and burning rage and annoyance and sulkiness about it.

I could wager that out of twelve million eventual combatants there aren't twelve who really want it. And "serving one's country" is so unpicturesque and unheroic when it comes to the point. Spending a year in a beastly Territorial camp guarding telegraph wires has nothing poetical about it: nor very useful as far as I can see. Besides the Germans are so nice; but I suppose the best thing that could happen to them would be their defeat.

At present I am sitting still here with no clothes (my luggage being all in Germany), swearing mildly under my breath and sulking. There is absolutely nothing to be done, and if I hadn't been a coward I should have joined the Regulars. As it is, I still have decent food and my rubber of bridge every evening; and, as long as I am not supposed to be "telling my adventures" and making sport for the Philistines, things are quite nice and dull. But there's no getting round it, it's a damned nuisance. I shall get off Oxford for a year, however, which is one blessing. Of course I am regarding the whole thing from an egoistic point of view. But, when everyone else is being so splendidly patriotic, that "Wille zu Widerspruch" or cussedness, which is chief among my (few) vices, is making me, since I cannot be actively pro-German, merely sulky.

Having written fifteen pages exclusively about myself, I'd better stop. Yours was the first post-card which has come to this house in the last week which did not say "We are cutting down bacon and *so* amused trying to work out little economies. Now, what are *you* doing?" Therefor thanks. I think at this time of national financial difficulties that, if a fine were put on the use of the word "God" in connection with this catastrophe in private correspondence (such as "Good God," 1*d.*, "Please God," 1*s.*, "Pray God," 1*s.* 6*d.*, these being just interjections; but remarks as "Truly God's ways are inscrutable, he is great," 2 guineas, and "God never meant," £100)—I think we would then raise a large amount of the indemnity which we shall undoubtedly have to pay in a year or two years' time. We have had so many such letters. Also all remarks about the Emperor being mad, 10*s.* 6*d.* I often think that if talking about the war were altogether forbidden it would be good. Our friends and correspondents don't seem to be able to give up physical luxuries without indulging in emotional luxuries as compensation. But I'm thankful to see that Kipling hasn't written a poem yet.

Well, I was very sorry to miss your letter and the subsequent horde of post-cards. But, in spite of your civilian attitude, I hope you are flourishing: unless God (5*s.*) thinks fit to punish your lack of patriotism by sending a murrain among the horses on the Tudhoe acres. I am too helplessly angry still to write coherently. Complete comfort is out of the question, and I like complete comfort.

To A. E. Hutchinson

Churn Camp, August 1914

Very many thanks for your letter, and, in its way, for the photograph. You couldn't have known that I have an elemental and irrational, yet violent, disapproval and abhorrence of photography. Photographs always show up people at their worst. For that reason, I like photographs of my enemies, but dislike photographs of my friends. Why most people—viz. those budding bedroom decorators who used to plaster C I dormitories with views of their relations—think otherwise has always been beyond me. For that reason, there is no photograph of me legally current: my people having during my absence in Germany photographed that portion of a C I House XV group supposed to represent me; but this is a pirated edition whose existence I ignore. I do not want to be sent through the world with a suggestion of football about me.

To pass on. If you read the *Gazette* on Wednesday last, you would have seen that I, even I, had been gazetted as a temporary 2nd Lieut. to the New Army (called Kitchener's Army because it doesn't belong to Kitchener any more than to me). So no Territorials for me! I'm not contented now with anything less than Regulars. I got said commission by applying to Oxford on the first possible day, and as they are taking first come, first served. So I am now a 2nd Lieut. in the Suffolk Regiment till "such time as the war ceases." But, as it would be palpably ridiculous to send me and the people gazetted with me to train recruits at once, an O.T.C. camp has been started to train us how to train recruits. They have chosen for the site the offending Churn, where somewhat over a year ago the corps whose Commander never did and never will command a badly disciplined battalion earned the everlasting Praise and Blame pamphlet and was fed with lemonade and buns. But now I am visiting it under changed conditions, and trying to attach some meaning and purpose to that hideous heap of straight-laced conventionality called drill. But otherwise it's very fairly pleasant. Three in a tent and very good food—but work all day, even on the Lord's. It lasts a month and then, if we've been good, we are to be sent trembling to our regiments for five months' training in this country. Then let us hope that the English will be in Berlin or the Germans in London: either of the two will do. But that's an end, I'm afraid, of the Marlborough Independents, as far as I'm concerned. You and Chappel will be rather a forlorn hope. I saw by the way that your original Guardian and Guide H. P. Clark has got a commission in some London terriers: also de Saumarez's friend Headington. But what care I for terriers? I can now afford to talk of them with scorn. Ridley, by the way, has gone up to Sandhurst, having rashly decided to take a permanent commission in the army. There he will be trained doubtless side by side with Hammond—not but what there are thousands of people I would less rather be trained side by side with than Hammond.

I have made a sad discovery—that I am one of those selfish people who view all problems from a subjective standpoint. While I was in a state of annoyance at not getting a commission, I was a Peace-at-any-Priceist and hated Sir Edward Grey. I still hate Grey (because he has that infernal habit of being *really* always in the right); but since getting that commission I have become a Terror. Hence the dullness of this letter. My mind is taken up with "affairs of national importance." I hope you, whose mind is still doubtless taken up with far more important things than childish and primitive questions of national honour, are still maintaining your equanimity. Mine has gone. I have succumbed. I am almost convinced that war is right and the tales told of German barbarism are true. I have become non-individual and British: dream of quarter-columns and am constantly mistaken for ——. Ichabod!

Well, best of luck in your unequal contest with patriotism. *Remember* that the stud. phil. is now a 2nd Lieut.

I hope to be able to get leave off for a day in three weeks' time to swank in to Marlborough, and rival —— in my heartiness. But meanwhile I bequeath to you (myself being disqualified) the task of realizing that this war is the best joke of the century.

Yours in the King.

To A. E. Hutchinson

Moore Barracks, Shorncliffe,
20 *September* 1914

I partially withdraw my remark about the jocularity of the war. All I meant was that looked at from beyond the standpoint of the individual—in the eyes of the "very young god"—it is a big joke: at least, not the actual killing so much as the mass meetings at the Queen's Hall and both sides' equally ridiculous alliances with I. H. S. You quite misunderstood what I said about Hammond and I must put it right at once. What I meant to say—though I got muddled in the "nots"—was exactly the same as you. Hammond was another of the five or six people with character in House.

Well, here am I (as Samuel put it) with my "unit" on the South Coast. You notice the word "unit." It is supremely characteristic. For the battalion *is* the unit. The component parts of it are merely quarters and fractions of it and are allowed no individuality at all. I am a decimal. Not only that. If (as I on the whole hope) they allow me abroad in three months' time, I may die a decimal. Think of that. With an identification disc stamped with a mythical number and "Church of England" round one's neck. I've resigned all claims to my person, I no longer am my own property. I am not a living creature, but a temporary second lieutenant (but don't put the *temporary* on the envelope or "this correspondence shall cease"): *i.e.*, in the eyes of those with whom I am doomed to live for the next few months, I am a kind of extemporized being called into life a month ago and fading at the end of the war.

I expected at least a drum and three trumpets to meet me as I arrived on Friday, just at the time when you in your horrible north-country habit were bundling into dormitory and awaking all early sleepers from the "special" train. I should have preferred a crowd of jeering jackasses to the reception I got. They all looked at me and passed by on the other side. Arriving six years ago at M. C., I was mocked: here I am ignored. I had to find out everything for myself, and everyone said "Ha! Don't trouble me. Trouble the Ad." I at last discovered the Ad. (the syllables jutant are not *add*ed by the really smart). He refused to be troubled, but told me I wasn't wanted till Monday. Then turning: "Ever been on parade before? Had any training before, ha?" Dignified silence was the only retort, till I heard myself answering in the tones of a Cato, "Sir, I am most efficient" (only Cato didn't tell lies). I suppose this story has gone round the mess by now.

But, to do them justice, they detected my ultra-strong religious instincts and told me to take my platoon to church. I didn't manage to do this through not being able to find my platoon: but took somebody else's. But to-morrow I expect some kind of work will begin. Unless they begin to recognize my existence, I shall tie strings across the door to trip them up and put salt in their tea, until they do. My only present help in trouble is—not, on this occasion, God—but the knowledge that Philpott (J. R.) is arriving next Saturday in the same position as I.

We are living, by the way, like princes. We sleep in beds under roofs. We have five course dinners behind the Bishop of London's back. The comfort is regal.

I arrived at Paddington at 6.10 on Friday; but, knowing you didn't go by it, refused to be so sentimental as to see the special off, but made up a sentimental poem on the way to Shorncliffe instead. I daresay by now you are turned into a regular atrocity-mongering smasher. The scale had gone dangerously near it in your last letter. But—considering you must now be in possession of a dormitory into which you must instil the present un-Christian spirit of *Don't* turn the other cheek but give your adversary as much of your lip as you like—it's just as well. For the joke of seeing an obviously just cause defeated, I hope Germany will win. It would do the world good and show that real faith is not that which says "we *must* win for our cause is just," but that which says "our cause is just: therefore we can disregard defeat." All outlooks are at present material, and the unseen value of justice as justice, independent entirely of results, is forgotten. It is looked upon merely as an agent for winning battles.

The Lord's Day here is still reserved for the Lord, but I hear that for the future it is to be handed over to the King. So I don't know when I shall have a spare moment to write again.

Very best wishes towards a good (I *don't* mean well-behaved) last term. "Sweating" weather will soon be coming on, and I envy you. No coming down to take you across the Aldbourne downs, across the land of Bobchicks to Liddington and home late for Chapel, I'm afraid. For I have bowed the knee to Baal, and Baal is unpleasant to any of his retainers who are restive during their devotions—except through the privacy of the post.

By the way, your idea of trying for the yeomanry is rather a good one, after Christmas. I wish I'd enlisted. I prefer physical discomfort and mental ease to the reverse under which we suffer here.

To A. E. Hutchinson

Shorncliffe, October (?) 1914

I am really quite comparatively happy now. Philpott has come, and he's a great addition and just makes the difference. My platoon are or is quite nice to me—especially the feeble-minded among [them]. Some of the more feeble-minded have been unfortunately sent away: so they aren't so nice now. I still wish I was a Tommy sometimes, since the lower one is in rank the freer one is, and it needs far more self-command to control than to obey. And I hate people with self-command. I am not quite one of those like that man who wrote up to the *Morning Post* Enquiry Bureau (a constant source of joy in these serious times) thus: "Gentleman with cotton umbrella and clean habits feels he can command men. Where will he be useful? Unmarried." The last remark was obvious. We who are critics by nature are somewhat out of our element commanding.

Pretty hopeless outlook isn't it? War certain to last for three years now, and then to end in stalemate. It's really been an admirable tonic. It'll keep you out of your office for three years; it's annoyed me and it's really excellent for one to be annoyed. But I feel the lack of any of my usual interests pretty sharply: nothing to read all day and no time; when one thinks, one does so on the sly; and as for writing poetry in the Officers' Mess—it's almost as bold a thing as that act of God's in writing those naughty words over the wall at Belshazzar's Feast!

But still, it's a great age to live in. Though everything is eclipsed at present except material values, it is something novel. But I don't know that it's really good for the nation. It makes people think too much of the visible virtues—bravery, endurance and the obvious forms of self-sacrifice, which are noticed and given their reward of praise. It's a time of the glorification of the second-best.

I've heard from Atkey by the way. He's a corporal now and very sarcastic about the officers. I think he did right to chuck M. C. He was too much of a free lance in thoughtful matters to come to his own there.

I suppose the tone of Chapel and the preachers therein has been disgraceful and reminiscent of the Book of Kings. I hate those petty attacks on the poor wavering Kaiser. But "such were the Christians in all ages."

Enclosed the poem[1] which eventually came out of the first day of term at Paddington. Not much trace of the origin left: but I think it should get a prize for being the first poem written since August 4th that isn't patriotic.

To A. J. Hopkinson

Shorncliffe, October (?) 1914

I thought the enclosure from [your] Uncle peculiarly interesting and return as you must want to keep it. He put the case for Prussian (as distinct from German) efficiency far more fairly than I had ever thought of it before. I think his transatlantic criticism of England's "imaginative indolence" and consequent social rottenness most stimulating in this time of auto-trumpeting and Old-England-she's-the-same-as-ever-isms. Also I suppose he is to a certain extent right that we have temporarily renounced all our claim to the more articulate and individual parts of our individuality. But in the intervals of doing and dying let's speak to one another as two pro-Germans, or nearly so, who have tramped her roads, bathed in her Moselles, and spent half-a-day in her cells.

The two great sins people impute to Germany are that she says that might is right and bullies the little

[1] See *Marlborough and Other Poems*, 4th ed., p. 66 ("Whom therefore we ignorantly worship").

dogs. But I don't think that she means might *qua* might is right, but that confidence of superiority is right, and by superiority she means spiritual superiority. She said to Belgium, "We enlightened thinkers see that it is necessary to the world that all opposition to Deutsche Kultur should be crushed. As citizens of the world you must assist us in our object and assert those higher ideas of world-citizenship which are not bound by treaties. But if you oppose us, we have only one alternative." That, at least, is what the best of them would have said; only the diplomats put it rather more brusquely. She was going on a missionary voyage with all the zest of Faust—

Er wandle so den Erdentag entlang;
Wenn Geister spuken, geh' er seinen Gang;
Im Weiterschreiten find' er Qual und Glück,
Er, unbefriedigt jeden Augenblick[1]!

—and missionaries know no law. As Uncle Alder says, her Kultur (in its widest sense) is the best in the world: so she must scatter it broadcast through the world perforce, saying like the schoolmaster or the dentist "though it hurts at present, it'll do you no end of good afterwards." (Perhaps she will even have to add at the end of the war "and it's hurt me more than it's hurt you.")

So it seems to me that Germany's only fault (and I think you often commented on it in those you met) is a lack of real insight and sympathy with those who differ from her. We are not fighting a bully, but a bigot. They are a young nation and don't yet see that what they consider is being done for the good of the world may

[1] *Faust*, II, 6820–3, translated in the last four lines of verse on p. 253.

be really being done for self-gratification—like X. who, under pretence of informing the form, dropped into the habit of parading his own knowledge. X. incidentally did the form a service by creating great amusement for it, and so is Germany incidentally doing the world a service (though not in the way it meant) by giving them something to live and die for, which no country but Germany had before. If the bigot conquers he will learn in time his mistaken methods (for it is only of the methods and not of the goal of Germany that one can disapprove)—just as the early Christian bigots conquered by bigotry and grew larger in sympathy and tolerance after conquest. I regard the war as one between sisters, between Martha and Mary, the efficient and intolerant against the casual and sympathetic. Each side has a virtue for which it is fighting, and each that virtue's supplementary vice. And I hope that whatever the material result of the conflict, it will purge these two virtues of their vices, and efficiency and tolerance will no longer be incompatible.

But I think that tolerance is the larger virtue of the two, and efficiency must be her servant. So I am quite glad to fight this rebellious servant. In fact I look at it this way. Suppose my platoon were the world. Then my platoon-sergeant would represent efficiency and I would represent tolerance. And I always take the sternest measures to keep my platoon-sergeant in check! I fully appreciate the wisdom of the War Office when they put inefficient officers to rule sergeants. Adsit omen.

Now you know what Sorley thinks about it. And do excuse all his gassing. I know I already overdosed you on those five splendid days between Coblenz and Neumagen. But I've seen the Fatherland (I like to call it the Fatherland, for in many families Papa represents efficiency and Mamma tolerance—but don't think I'm W.S.P.U.) so horribly misrepresented that I've been burning to put in my case for them to a sympathetic ear. Wir sind gewiss Hamburger Jungen, as that lieber besoffener Österreicher told us[1]. And so we must stand up for them, even while trying to knock them down.

I'm so glad you seem to be flourishing. We are also K1, as it is called, and have a mixed lot of subs—most, sheep in wolves' clothing like us—but amongst them (thank Heaven) J. R. Philpott, who's a delight to have in the mess. I hope that you have by now reported your scheme to General French, or shall I forward your letter—du bayerischer Knödel[2]!

We have had heaps of Belgian soldiers in full flight from Ostend billeted here. They have now returned to the trenches. They told us that the forts around Antwerp were sold to the Germans and many of the Belgian shells were filled with sand only. May the shell that first hits me be thus filled!

Well, here's to a meeting again by the banks of the Mosel 300 yards north of Neumagen where we had our last best bathe! I shan't forget that walking tour. Das war eine feine Tour!

P.S. All I.O.U.s contracted in the old world before the deluge—or contracted in a hostile country—are on no account to be repaid. So beware!

[1] To be sure we are Hamburg lads, as that dear old tipsy Austrian told us.

[2] You Bavarian dumpling.

To the Master of Marlborough

Shorncliffe, October 1914

I was very glad to have the opportunity of seeing you, if only for a few minutes, at Marlborough a month ago. Shortly after that I was removed here, to find my feet amongst my Suffolk fellow-countrymen by adoption. Since then we have been reinforced by that excellent fellow J. R. Philpott, who uses his old gift of apologetic satire to great advantage: so that C1—the most typically Marlburian of all houses at Marlborough, though I says it as shouldn't—is (numerically at any rate) strongly represented. We are sharing an under-sized mess-room, a barrack erected before the days of bathrooms, and one writing table, with the Norfolk Regiment: so that the elegant Tilley is also among my messmates. The rest are mostly sheep in wolves' clothing, like myself, and the fleece is sometimes apt to protrude just now and then, when confronted alone with our platoons: with a fair sprinkling of city merchants, being Special Reservists; discontented Captains left back on depot duty to train "young blood"; and rediscovered regulars of '82 hauled out from the suburbs of Cheltenham or Torquay. The men are sleepy Suffolk fellows with imperturbable good tempers and an intelligent interest rather than an active co-operation in their military duties. We are like the doomed murderer at breakfast, which he has been allowed to choose before being hanged. They're doing us really well.

On return to England, by the way, I renewed my acquaintance with R. B. The last line of *Mr Sludge the*

Medium—"yet there is something in it, tricks and all[1]"—converted me, and since then I have used no other. I wish we could recall him from the stars and get him to write a Dramatic Idyll or something, giving a soliloquy of the feelings and motives and quick changes of heat and cold that must be going through the poor Kaiser's mind at present. He would really show that impartial sympathy for him, which the British press and public so doltishly deny him, when in talk and comment they deny him even the rights of a human being. R. B. could do it perfectly—or Shakespeare. I think the Kaiser not unlike Macbeth, with the military clique in Prussia as his Lady Macbeth, and the court flatterers as the three weird sisters. He'll be a splendid field for dramatists and writers in days to come.

I heard from Atkey (he being a corporal and I an officer, I cannot possibly refer to him now as *Mr* A.) the other day: he'll be a big loss, but I hope only temporary. I hope M. C. hasn't suffered in many other ways. I suppose you have no further news of H. W. R. beyond the bare newspaper announcement of "wounded."

Do you still permit the enemy's language to be taught at Marlborough, or are you substituting Portuguese out of deference to our ally? They are a splendid lot (I don't mean Portugal, but Germany), and I wish the silly papers would realize that they are fighting for a principle just as much as we are. If this war proves

[1] The lines

> This trade of mine—I don't know, can't be sure,
> But there was something in it, tricks and all!

occur nearer the end than the beginning of the poem.

(as I think it will) that you can kill a person and yet remain his greatest friend—or, less preferably, be killed and yet stay friends—it'll have done a splendid thing.

I don't believe I've apologized yet for my terrible brick about Wiltshire[1]. Since I belong to the Suffolks, I'll give you Wilts, till the war's over.

To Mrs Bethune-Baker

Shorncliffe, 10 *November* 1914

I had meant to write to you two days ago on the anniversary of Arthur's death. But we were so busy that up till to-day I had no time to do so.

I had wanted often during the last year to tell you what an increasing influence all my remembrances of Arthur, during the three years that we knew each other well, have had on me. It may seem curious, but now four years since his death I feel at times his loss much stronger than I did at the time: and am getting much more help and stimulus from the example of his memory than a few years ago, when I did not act on my remembrance of his invariably cheerful self-denial half enough. In that pushing race for social power which is the worst side of public school life, now, looking back on it, I can see much more clearly how he was one of those very few I knew at Marlborough who never pushed for his own advancement but always seemed trying to further and rejoicing in that of his friends. I think you ought to know that, since I left, more than one person who was at Marlborough with him told me that he was one of the only people who was unselfish in big things

[1] See above, p. 201.

(or what we used then to consider big things) among the survival-of-the-fittest conditions of a public school. And that he was taken and we others left seems a kind of fulfilment of his cheerful unobtrusive self-denial.

I see now much more clearly that, especially in his last term, he ran the race (as very few of us did) consistently like a gentleman and a Christian. He had disappointments in the football line (this seems a small thing now, but it was one of the biggest then), but yet he always seemed just as pleased with the success of those who had outplaced him. And I never remember him trying to help himself on by depreciation of his weaker contemporaries—which is about the most common vice at public schools. And on the last Sunday before he went to the Sick House, I shall never forget the pains he took not to spoil the afternoon "distant call" walk for De Saumarez and myself—though he could not go with us—by trying to disguise how seedy he was and refusing to let us stay with him.

So I wanted you to know that, especially since I left Marlborough, I have been beginning to remember him not only (as before) as a person it was always very jolly to be with, but now as a kind of example (not realized before, because it was all so natural with him and nobody would have been more astonished than he, if he thought he was being used as an example) whom I can try to imitate: and so for some one else beside you he cannot ever be called dead.

De Saumarez is still at Oxford, seeing a lot of Kenneth. Both are in the same boat of being medically forced to remain civilians. De S. writes very jollily and is carrying it off with his usual good humour.

We are hard at it here, as long as there is daylight to see by. So there is no time for complaints or grumbles, and we shall soon begin wondering when we shall be sent out.

I hope you and Prof. Bethune-Baker are both well. I do not think you will mind me writing like this, but it seemed to me that after our half-finished talk about Arthur three months ago, there was so much more left that I would like to say to you.

To A. E. Hutchinson

Shorncliffe, 14 *November* 1914

Sorry I forgot to mail you my opinion of Israel Zangwill. I admire him enormously and like him about as much. He reminds me often of the author of *Revelation* in his outbursts of revolting sensuousness (he too is fully capable of imagining heaven as inhabited by four beasts and four and twenty elders) varied occasionally by really beautiful passages, but he is far more humorous and witty than St John the Divine. *Dreamers of the Ghetto* is his best. I love Jews—of a type.

I hear that C1 are leaving at the end of term. So you're well out of it. I suppose that, having left, you'll apply for a commission (knowing you won't get one) and then sit tight in your office with the proud consciousness of duty done. After the war, I shall provide you with enough copy to enable you to pretend you were out there. I dread the aftermath of war—what bores the survivors will be!

I'm sorry you were taken to *Drake*, but glad you disapproved of the performance. They should have taken you to *The Great Adventure*, if I could have everything my own way. The Union Jack kettle-holder existed long before my time; probably a presentation to some confirmee in the sixties, when all Marlborough according to its historians was pure and manly and full of zeal, it being Victoria's reign.

I suppose you are starting to leave and already rehearsing the event. This war must be a nuisance because it robs it of much of the importance it would otherwise possess. But you are fortunate in being neither such an egoist, sentimentalist, or poser as yours affectionately. I regarded it (as everything then) from a purely personal standpoint and considered it a great tragedy, having a lamentable lack of perspective. But you have it over me so far that you are the last of the Mohicans, and there's no one worth staying back for, as there was in my case. You may be interested in the following verses I wrote on the last night, while miserably struggling with innumerable packing-cases in the void of an empty, swept and garnished study.

It was spring. And we hoped in the spring
   For a glorious summer.
And the summer came, yes, good old thing!
   But we found the new-comer

Was bright but in days of hope gone,
   But approaching (poor harlot)
Threw us tattered raiment to don
   And gave others the scarlet.

So this is the end of it all!
   Of the sloth and the slumber,
Of the hates that we hated like gall,
   And the loves, few in number.

And no one will now Pity say
Or can back again wish us,
Who have done nothing good in our day,
And (what's worse) nothing vicious.

We have fought for ourselves like black Hell,
But, since we were our standard,
Does it matter we have not fought well
And weak failed where we planned hard?

The time made us Outcast and Dunce,
Though for Kingship intended.
It might have been beautiful—once!
But now it is ended.

The 7th Suffolks are doing nicely, thank you. Philpott is one of the nicest and most amusing fellows in England. England—I am sick of the sound of the word. In training to fight for England, I am training to fight for that deliberate hypocrisy, that terrible middle-class sloth of outlook and appalling "imaginative indolence" that has marked us out from generation to generation. Goliath and Caiaphas—the Philistine and the Pharisee—pound these together and there you have Suburbia and Westminster and Fleet Street. And yet we have the impudence to write down Germany (who with all their bigotry are at least seekers) as "Huns," because they are doing what every brave man ought to do and making experiments in morality. Not that I approve of the experiment in this particular case. Indeed I think that after the war all brave men will renounce their country and confess that they are strangers and pilgrims on the earth. "For they that say such things declare plainly that they seek a country." But all these convictions are useless for me to state since I have not had the courage of them. What a worm one is under the cart-wheels—big clumsy careless lumbering cart-wheels—of public opinion. I might have been giving my mind to fight against Sloth and Stupidity: instead, I am giving my body (by a refinement of cowardice) to fight against the most enterprising nation in the world.

Enough for the present. I thoroughly envy you your Marathon. Do you know that Richard Jefferies, the greatest of English visionaries, felt exactly the same about the high parts of the downs as you? That you climbed great hills that should overlook the sea, but you could see no sea. Only the whole place is like a vast sea-shell where you can hear the echoes of the sea that has once filled it. Du Gott! One can really *live* up there! The earth even more than Christ is the ultimate ideal of what man should strive to be. So I hope you won't find the separation from your first temple as hard as I did.

I hear our Lower are brilliant in spite of your pessimistic forebodings. I too play Rugger—and (as always) talk more than I act. Our regimental colours are the same as C 1. Most affecting!

To Professor and Mrs Sorley

Shorncliffe, 17 *November* 1914

I have been wondering very much about the Bieders lately. Is there any way for me to get a letter through to the Frau? I feel very much that I ought to: one that should arrive before or round about Christmas. Would the best way be to send it to the Pierces of America (Harvard), and ask them to forward it? I suppose Höffding couldn't be troubled again. But I should like very much to do it somehow. I often laugh to myself when I remember Karl's great big doggy smile. I should like to get a letter through.

To Professor and Mrs Sorley

Shorncliffe, 23 *November* 1914

By the way I liked the Armenian article in *The Cambridge Magazine*. It brought back to me that little crooked old fellow that Hopkinson and I met at the fag-end of our hot day's walk as we swung into Neumagen. His little face was lit with a wild uncertain excitement he had not known since 1870, and he advanced towards us waving his stick and yelling at us "Der Krieg ist los, Junge," just as we might be running to watch a football match and he was come to tell us we must hurry up for the game had begun. And then the next night on the platform at Trier, train after train passing crowded with soldiers bound for Metz: varied once or twice by a truck-load of "swarthier alien crews," thin old women like wineskins, with beautiful and piercing faces, and big heavy men and tiny aged-looking children: Italian colonists exiled to their country again. Occasionally one of the men would jump out to fetch a glass of water to relieve their thirst in all that heat and crowding. The heat of the night is worse than the heat of the day, and geistige Getränke were verboten. Then the train would slowly move out into the darkness that led to Metz and an exact reproduction of it would steam in and fill its place: and we watched the signal on the southward side of Trier, till the lights should give a jump and the finger drop and let in the train which was to carry us out of that highly-strung and thrilling land.

At Cologne I saw a herd of some thirty American school-marms whom I had assisted to entertain at Eucken's just a fortnight before. I shouted out to them, but they were far too upset to take any notice, but went bobbing into one compartment and out again and into another like people in a cinematograph. Their haste, anxiety and topsyturviness were caused by thoughts of their own safety and escape, and though perfectly natural contrasted so strangely with all the many other signs of haste, perturbation and distress that I had seen, which were much quieter and stronger and more full-bodied than that of those Americans, because it was the Vaterland and not the individual that was darting about and looking for the way and was in need: and the silent submissive unquestioning faces of the dark uprooted Italians peering from the squeaking trucks formed a fitting background—Cassandra from the backmost car looking steadily down on Agamemnon as he stepped from his triumphal purple chariot and Clytemnestra offered him her hand.

I don't like your Tommy friends sneering at the French courage, when every able-bodied Frenchman is in the field. It is possible that the majority of the French lack that "cauld deidly" courage: but these are the less favourable specimens, I feel sure, whose corresponding types in England are still watching football on Saturdays. I think your Irish friend should see that our own house is in order before making comparison between our "contemptibly little" army (note the emendation) and that of our ally, whose spirit is at any rate willing.

To the Master of Marlborough

Shorncliffe, 28 *November* 1914

Many thanks for your letter. I have just returned from a game of Rugger with that familiar sensation of complete physical subjugation and mental content, formerly procurable any half-holiday at Marlborough, now only to be had on Saturday afternoons. We are leading such a funny life here, one would hardly think it was war-time. There is no longer any strangeness in wearing khaki and being saluted by one's fellow men: there is work, it's true, from 8.30 a.m. till 4, but one has come to regard it, as one regarded work at Marlborough, as a not at all acutely disagreeable necessity, which is sooner or later certain to be over and leave a large interval of freedom before it resumes. As at Marlborough, one goes through the former part passively and unsentiently, and it is only in the latter part that one lives. And as in the latter part one does not read military handbooks nor discuss tactical problems (shockingly enough), it may be said that the war abroad has hardly yet, beyond the loss of some acquaintances and an occasional anxiety for others, affected us here at all.

It is surprising how very little difference a total change of circumstances and prospects makes in the individual. The German (I know from the forty-eight hours of the war that I spent there) is radically changed, and until he is sent to the front, his one dream and thought will be how quickest to die for his country. He is able more clearly to see the tremendous issues, and changes accordingly. I don't know whether it is because the English are more phlegmatic or more shortsighted or more egoistic or what, that makes them inwardly and outwardly so far less shaken by the war than at first seemed probable. The German, I am sure, during the period of training, "dies daily" until he is allowed to die. We go there with our eyes shut.

H. W. R.'s death was a shock. Still, since Achilles's *κάτθανε καὶ Πάτροκλος ὅ περ σέο πολλὸν ἀμείνων*[1], which should be read at the grave of every corpse in addition to the burial service, no saner and splendider comment on death has been made, especially, as here, where it seemed a cruel waste.

You ask me, with a suggestion of triumph, what I and Footman and Edwards think of Nietzsche now? I have only now begun to read the man. I was never one of those more advanced intellectuals who quoted him at debates and in the Sixth coalscuttle: indeed I always went on the childish presumption, while at M. C., that no one was really worth serious attention unless he was in C 1. It is a prejudice I have never been able to give up, though I daresay you can't be expected to share it: but I entered the house while it was still Teucro duce et auspice Teucro (Teucer being G. C. Turner), and that explains it.

Philpott still flourishes here: it is the greatest boon to have him. Tilley is also to be seen among the Norfolks, who share the mess with us: debonair as ever.

A great exodus this term I suppose! Who is to succeed S. C. W. and get the tart on Prize day?

[1] "Died Patroclus too who was a far better man than thou," *Iliad*, xxi, 107. Cp. *Marlborough and Other Poems*, 4th ed., p. 78, line 10.

To Professor and Mrs Sorley

Shorncliffe, 30 *November* 1914

Thanks very much indeed for the letter and *Lit. Sups.*, and especially for *Satires of Circumstance*. I had not got it or ordered it but had often been thinking of doing so. So it came most welcomely.

Needless to say, I do not agree with your criticisms of T. H.'s later work. The actual "Satires of Circumstance" which come in the middle of the book I thought bad poetry. But I think you are too hard on the rest. Hardy explains in the preface to one of his former books of poems that they are expressions of moods and are not to be taken as a whole reading of life, but "the road to a true philosophy of life seems to be in humbly recording divers aspects of its phenomena as they are forced upon us by chance and change." And I don't think he writes these poems [for the reason] you suggest, but with a view to helping people on that "road to a true philosophy of life." Curiously enough, I think that "Men who march away" is the most arid poem in the book, besides being untrue of the sentiments of the ranksman going to war: "Victory crowns the just" is the worst line he ever wrote—filched from a leading article in *The Morning Post*, and unworthy of him who had always previously disdained to insult Justice by offering it a material crown like Victory. I think in looking through it you must have missed a verse like:

> Yes, I accompany him to places
>   Only dreamers know,
> Where the shy hares show their faces,
>   Where the night rooks go;

Into old aisles where the past is all to him,
　Close as his shade can do,
Always lacking the power to call to him,
　Near as I reach thereto!

I have been lately reading a great deal in *The Dynasts*, which I bought three weeks ago. His poetry there is at its very best, especially in the choruses and battle-songs, perhaps because the comprehensiveness of the task did not allow him to introduce himself and his own bitternesses, as he can in his lyrics. It has a realism and true ring which "Men who march away" lacks. I cannot help thinking that Hardy is the greatest artist of the English character since Shakespeare: and much of *The Dynasts* (except its historical fidelity) might be Shakespeare. But I value his lyrics as presenting himself (the self he does not obtrude into the comprehensiveness of his novels and *The Dynasts*) as truly, and with faults as well as strength visible in it, as any character in his novels. His lyrics have not the spontaneity of Shakespeare's or Shelley's: they are rough-hewn and jagged: but I like them, and they stick.

To Professor and Mrs Sorley

Sandgate, 8 *December* 1914

I am still revelling in *The Dynasts*. The amount of historical reading and travelling that must have gone to compose such a work must have been tremendous. The battle descriptions are generally from the general's point of view. The choruses of spirits are the great feature: the Spirit Ironic, who represents the humorist or cynic in Hardy and revels in the absurdity of little men killing each other; the Spirit of the Years, that represents the fatalist in Hardy (his most known side), who refuses to be moved by it this way or that but only sees in the whole melting-pot a sign of the hopeless mechanical methods of the "Immanent Will": they are stern aloof critics with a big dash of fineness in their unsympatheticness:

> Us, ancients, then it ill befits
> To quake, when slaughter's spectre flits
> About the field of Austerlitz;

and lastly the Spirit of the Pities, who represents the man in Hardy and gives utterance to the finest poetry of them all. These are the only characters that appear throughout the epic and on them the whole is strung together. But the characters, especially Napoleon, are finely drawn: and the minor scenes, like the madness of George III and the abdication of Josephine, are as good as Shakespeare. Josephine is made most dignified and moving.

...Don't be put off by too much about the Immanent Will.

To A. E. Hutchinson

C. H. S. had been saving up leave so that he might have a week-end at Marlborough and had planned to be there as the Master's guest from 12th to 14th December, when the Major-General issued an order stopping all further week-end leaves.

Sandgate, 15 *December* 1914

When I asked the Adjutant to ask the Colonel to ask the Brigadier to ask the Garrison-Adjutant to ask the Major-General whether he would make an exception in my case, he told me that when I was in the Army I was in the Army. He made this remark with the air of Solomon when he tried on his trick of bisecting babies, added a qualifying "after all," and I was left lamenting. I don't think I have ever cursed so roundly in my life. I made up three poems and went to bed early on the strength of it, and have been late for parade ever since.

You needn't be over-anxious to see me before I go; if I had come down to M. C., you'd have seen into what a state of degradation I had sunk. I wished to see you then, before you had also started the downward path which comes of having to command men. Never again in my whole life will I exercise any authority over anyone again after this war. It's wrong and results in like evils and wickednesses to the deliberate prevention of my fulfilling a wish I had harboured for months and going on leave to Marlborough last week-end.

I imagine that this letter will find you in the miserable state of trying to compress your terrestrial possessions into boxes. I can stand desertion, desolation, death, but I cannot abear packing.

I should like to wring X.'s neck. I can stand, in fact I can love, all vices except cleanliness and affectation. Man is only himself when he is muddy.

I am not a patriotic O. M.; neither, I imagine, will you be. But if I must have an appellation to go through life with—and I suppose one must be labelled something—it is Marlburian: for Marlborough to me means the "little red-capped town" (sorry for quoting from myself!) and the land that shelters it: not the school which has given it so much and so transient notoriety. It is absurd to say that the school means one's friends there and therefore one should wish to be labelled O. M. The bulk of the people one meets at school are shadowy substances, partially detaching themselves from the huge artificial mass Marlburian and soon disappearing again thereinto. One's (few) friends have a value entirely apart from the accidental circumstances which brought one together with them. I have tried for long to express in words the impression that the land north of Marlborough must leave on all those whose minds' wheels are not clogged and the motive power of their mind not diverted by the artificial machinations that go on within the College Gates. Simplicity, paucity of words, monotony almost, and mystery are necessary. I think I have got it at last here:

Lost

Across my past imaginings
  Has dropped a blindness, silent and slow.
My eye is bent on other things
  Than those it once did see and know.

I may not think on those dear lands
  (O far away and long ago!)
Where the old battered sign-post stands,
  And silently the four roads go

East, west, south and north,
  And the cold winter winds do blow.
And what the evening will bring forth
  Is not for me nor you to know!

The place in question is the junction of the grass tracks on the Aldbourne down—to Ogbourne, Marlborough, Mildenhall and Aldbourne. It stands up quite alone. We could have gone there, had I been able to come down last Sunday.

Best of luck with your regiment. I'm beginning to find that everyone is tolerable, even very nice, if one takes the trouble to cast preconceptions and get to know them—a most lamentable and disappointing discovery! I hope you'll find some kindred spirit in the Durham Yeomanry.

To the Master of Marlborough

Shorncliffe, 27 (?) *December* 1914

I should have written long ago to say what a disappointment it was to me that all leaves were suddenly cancelled and I was forced to ring off at the Lodge. However, such things give one a training—which I always gibbed at and refused properly to submit to at M. C.—in realizing that there are forces able to dock one's seemingly reasonable desires. It just shows one what beastly people the Medes and Persians must have been to live under.

We had a very swinging Christmas—one that makes one realize (in common with other incidents of the war) how near savages we are and how much the stomach (which Nietzsche calls the Father of Melancholy) is also the best procurer of enjoyment. We gave the men a good church (plenty of loud hymns), a good dinner (plenty of beer), and the rest of the day was spent in sleep. I saw then very clearly that, whereas for the upper classes Christmas is a spiritual debauch in which one remembers for a day to be generous and cheerful and open-handed, it is only a more or less physical debauch for the poorer classes, who need no reminder, since they are generous and cheerful and open-handed all the year round. One has fairly good chances of observing the life of the barrack-room, and what a contrast to the life of a house in a public school! The system is roughly the same: the house-master or platoon-commander entrusts the discipline of his charge to prefects or corporals, as the case may be. They never open their mouths in the barrack-room without the introduction of the unprintable swear-words and epithets: they have absolutely no "morality" (in the narrower, generally accepted sense): yet the public school boy should live among them to learn a little Christianity: for they are so extraordinarily nice to one another. They live in and for the present: we in and for the future. So they are cheerful and charitable always: and we often niggardly and unkind and spiteful. In the gymnasium at Marlborough, how the few clumsy specimens are ragged and despised and jeered at by the rest of the squad; in the gymnasium here you should hear the sounding cheer given to the man who has tried for eight weeks to make a long-jump of eight feet and at last by the advice and assistance of others has succeeded. They seem instinctively to regard a man singly, at his own rate, by his own standards and possibilities, not in comparison with themselves or others: that's why they are so far ahead of us in their treatment and sizing up of others.

It's very interesting, what you say about Athens and Sparta, and England and Germany. Curious, isn't it, that in old days a nation fought another for land or money: now we are fighting Germany for her spiritual qualities—thoroughness, and fearlessness of effort, and effacement of the individual. I think that Germany, in spite of her vast bigotry and blindness, is in a kind of way living up to the motto that Goethe left her in the closing words of Faust, before he died.

> Ay, in this thought is my whole life's persistence,
> This is the whole conclusion of the true:
> He only earns his Freedom, owns Existence,
> Who every day must conquer her anew!
> So let him journey through his earthly day,
> Mid hustling spirits, go his self-found way,
> Find torture, bliss, in every forward stride,
> He, every moment still unsatisfied![1]

A very close parallel may be drawn between Faust and present history (with Belgium as Gretchen). And Faust found spiritual salvation in the end!

To K. W. Sorley

Shorncliffe, [*date uncertain*]

The monotony of this existence is alarming, and on the increase. Officers and men are both suffering equally from staleness. We don't look like removing for a long time yet on account of our supposed inefficiency. So the passage of days is swift, and nothing to show for it. Somehow one never lives in the future now, only in the past, which is apt to be morbid and begins to make one like an old man. The war is a chasm in time. I do wish that all journalists etc., who say that war is an ennobling purge etc., etc., could be muzzled. It simply makes people unhappy and uncomfortable, if that is a good thing. All illusions about the splendour of war will, I hope, be gone after the war.

There is not much prospect of coming down to Oxford at present—week-end leaves are still in abeyance. I read that Oriel has the largest percentage of any college in khaki. This must leave you in a very small circle

[1] *Faust*, ii, 6944–7, 6820–3.

with all the advantages and disadvantages of small circles. Still you have the advantage of working with your brain, while mine is stagnant. I have always been meaning to learn French thoroughly here, but have not yet had the will-power; my mind being, I suppose, still shut. Write.

To A. E. Hutchinson

Shorncliffe, 25 *January* 1915

How are you getting on? I can imagine it is not quite heaven. But neither is this. Heaven will have to wait until the war's over. It is the most asphyxiating work after the first fine glow of seeing people twice your age and size obey and salute you has passed off, as it does after a fortnight. The only thing is that the pay is good. The rest, as you are probably finding already, is complete stagnation among a mass of straps and sleeping-bags and water-bottles. War in England only means putting all the men of "military age" in England into a state of routinal coma, preparatory to getting them killed. You are being given six months to become conventional: your peace thus made with God, you will be sent out and killed. At least, if you aren't killed, you'll come back so unfitted for any other job that you'll have to stay in the Army. I should like so much to kill whoever was primarily responsible for the war. The alarming sameness with which day passes day until this unnatural state of affairs is over is worse than any so-called atrocities; for people enjoy grief, the only unbearable thing is dullness.

I have started to read again, having read nothing all the closing months of last year. I have discovered a man called D. H. Lawrence who knows the way to write, and I still stick to Hardy: to whom I never managed to convert you.

We talk of going out in March. I am positively looking forward to that event, not in the brave British drummer-boy spirit, of course, but as a relief from this boredom (part of which, by the way, is caused through Philpott having been away the last three weeks in hospital).

We don't seem to be winning, do we? It looks like an affair of years. If so, pray God for a nice little bullet wound (tidy and clean) in the shoulder. That's the place.

Sorry I haven't more to write—nor had Lot's wife when she was half through being turned into salt; nor will you in three months' time.

To A. R. Gidney

Sandgate, 6 *March* 1915

Our difference about Germany was the difference of people who base their opinions on sentiment and reason. I have always done the former, and let the reason (such as it is) come in afterwards to provide some show of fabric. Nevertheless many thanks for your letter, which I should not have been so long in answering.

I am at present somewhat of a Crusoe. I was going through a musketry course at Hythe (where the victories come from), when suddenly the division ups and marches to Aldershot. I arrive back from Hythe to find myself in charge of an empty barracks, and have been there ever since waiting for the advent of a wild Canadian regiment who shall take them over. The wild Canadian regiment have apparently broken loose en route for Shorncliffe. So while the Suffolks are marching twenty miles per day with packs and full equipment on at Aldershot and firing their Trained Soldiers' Course, the sins of the Canadians are keeping me here idle. And forced idleness is more unpleasant even than forced labour.

I hear viâ Hutchinson that, in spite of a cellar little more than three parts full and then sadly deficient in old wines, House still keeps its head in air. In old days when we lost everything else we used to sometimes win the Gym. That was our Lenten hope and solace. I hope that either in that or in the Sports (poor mutilated Sports, no longer so magnificently all-embracing as in the days when certain Houses used to enter en bloc for the school mile) we will do more than promise well for next year!

Here we play hockey and do cross-country running. The latter, best of all sports, has been established some time. And two Saturdays ago was the culmination with the divisional and garrison cross-country race with 400 starters and 12 teams, including two battalions of the Royal Fusiliers, every one of whom were ex-harriers. A heavy course over the rich Kentish soil, but the win went, as it surely should, to the amateur element, to the team of a county famed for its sluggishness, and in which quoits is the favourite sport. The Suffolks came in an easy first. This has been one of our many triumphs. Indeed agricultural labour in Suffolk fears a crisis in the near future, for it is quite unlikely that more than a few of the farm-labourers who form 60 per cent. of our battalion will return after the war to the earth, in spite of the poetic attractiveness of "returns to the soil" in the eyes of people like me.

I see and appreciate your difficult position in regard to so-called "service." But apart from everything else it has always seemed to me that, magnificent as the prospect of nations in arms may be, the old system of hiring your Wellington and a handful of hundred thousand criminals to bleed for you, that your scholars and students might not let out the torch of learning in its passage from hand to hand, was, from the point of view of civilization and culture, more beneficial to the country. We have to thank Germany for the new system: only she organizes her levy on business lines of selection. Amongst other dearths I imagine there will be an alarming dearth of learning after the long war it's going to be. But every difficulty and doubt about comparative uses of enlistment and "business as usual" points more than ever clearly to the fact that, admirable as the voluntary system may be for punitive raids in the Crimea or Transvaal, it has terrible drawbacks for a knock-out tussle with an equal. Not that I throw it over: I think you must make your Englishman believe he's acting freely before he'll act well. A conscript New Army (*not* to be called Kitchener's army, please) would have lacked that concord during training which will, one hopes, be the foundation of discipline in the field.

I was delighted to think of Gamlen dodging shell-pits and snipers over ruined roads at the helm of a motor transport. May he stick to mechanical things, and may a mechanical department be started at M. C., where such as he may get good outlet for their talents.

I was delighted to see the letters "J. B." appear again in *The Marlburian*. So has he quite recovered, as his two poems would lead you to suppose?

I see quite a lot of Wace here: the Berkshires being in the same brigade as we. He was also at Hythe for the same course as I was. Hythe was a restful time. I learnt and worked voraciously. After months of imperfect leadership and instruction in subjects in which oneself did not feel sure, a fortnight in which one was most magnificently and systematically spoonfed and taught, had to make shorthand notes and write exam.-papers, was a perfect mental rest-cure. The process of sitting and learning and using one's brains for assimilation of plenty (not for production and dissimulation of paucity) of knowledge was delightful to return to: as also the release from responsibility and its attendant falsities.

I apologize for this feminine manner of writing—I mean, in the way of having my last page where you would expect my first, and the consequent difficulties of knowing on which sheet the letter is continued. I imagine you abhor it as much as anyone: but the way the paper is stamped is at fault—not I.

I have heard twice from H. L. R., 2nd R. D. Fusiliers, "in the trenches" (a phrase which has ousted "at the front" in the popularity of the masses). When do we hope to follow him out there? When we are sent, if you want a reliable answer. April the 1st, if you want a rude one.

P.S. And I forgot to ask you a most important question. Comment elle porte-elle, la Lit. Soc.? (I know that's Belgo-French, so you needn't correct me.) Suspended? (don't say it!): or papers confined to Lyra Heroica, William Watson, The Oxford Pamphleteers, and the wickedness of Bernard Shaw? On whom has the mantle of the Secretary descended? And does House (apart from yourself) still keep up its strong representation therein, noticeable since the days when G. C. Turner was first secretary?

To Mrs Sorley

Blenheim Barracks, Aldershot, 9 *March* 1915

I have only just arrived here: the last ten days having been occupied in reading *The Egoist* in the Orderly Room at Moore [Barracks, Shorncliffe]. It was my sad fate to be left in charge of the Details after rejoining from Hythe: to wait on and hand over barracks to the Canadians. The Canadians were a week overdue, when at last they poured in in the small hours of Monday morning. Till then we had been employed in drawing blankets, pillow-slips, coal, candles, etc.—a most extraordinary thing to make one regiment do for another—to make the Canadians feel at home when they arrived! This by order of a motherly War Office. When they did come they impressed me as a smartish lot, of the free and easy description. Their officers are of the kind to dig their C.O. in the ribs and call him "comrade." But their general appearance was far smarter than I had hoped. A cheery lot of officers of the kind that take down one's name and address and are proud to make one's acquaintance: and refer to the Atlantic Ocean as "some pond."

All good luck to your project of meeting in town on Saturday or Sunday. I will do my best. I can tell you nothing now. It is not politic to ask for leave within four hours of rejoining. At present we are doing our Trained Soldiers' Course—a form of amusement sometimes substituted for Church on Sundays. Bewahre! But I'll do my best and let you know the result as soon as possible.

I am going to take a course of Meredith before going out. In a job like this it should act as Eno's Fruit Salt to the constipated brains.

To Professor and Mrs Sorley.

Aldershot, 16 *March* 1915

I have finished and laid by *The Egoist*. I see now that Meredith belongs to that class of novelists with whom I do not usually get on so well (e.g. Dickens), who create and people worlds of their own so that one approaches the characters with amusement, admiration or contempt, not with liking or pity, as with Hardy's people, into whom the author does not inject his own exaggerated characteristics. Brilliant as *The Egoist* is, it is truth in a most fantastic setting. You never meet Mountstuart Jenkinsons or Willoughby Patternes (look at their names!), only momentary suggestions of them. It is as though he saw the world through field-glasses.

To Mrs Sorley

Aldershot, March 1915

We are off for a wild game this week-end under the eyes of Kitchener. But going out still remains an uncertainty as to time, and has become a matter of the indifferent future to most of us. If we had gone out earlier we would have gone out with a thrill in poetic-martial vein: now most of us have become by habit soldiers, at least in so far that we take such things as a matter of course and a part of our day's work that our own anticipations can neither quicken nor delay.

I talked a lot (in her native tongue) to the hostess with whom I was billeted, and her sensible German attitude was like a cold bath. She saw the thing, as German hausfraus would, directly and humanly and righteously. Especially sensible was she in her remarks against the kind ladies who told her she ought to be proud and glad to give her sons to fight. After all, war in this century is inexcusable: and all parties engaged in it must take an equal share in the blame of its occurrence. If only the English from Grey downwards would cease from rubbing in that, in the days that set all the fuel ablaze, they worked for peace honestly and with all their hearts! We know they did; but in the past their lack of openness and trust in their diplomatic relationships helped to pile the fuel to which Germany applied the torch.

I do wish also that people would not deceive themselves by talk of a just war. There is no such thing as a just war. What we are doing is casting out Satan by

Satan. When once war was declared the damage was done: and we, in whom that particular Satan was perhaps less strong than in our foes, had only one course, namely to cast out the far greater Satan by means of him: and he must be fought to the bitter end. But that doesn't alter the fact that long ago there should have been an understanding in Europe that any country that wanted Weltmacht might have it. The Allies may yet score a victory over Germany. But by last August they had thrown away their chances of a true victory. I remember you once on the Ellerby moors telling us the story of Bishop What's-his-name and John-Val-John from *Les Misérables*. And now, although we failed then of the highest, we might have fought, regarding the war—not, as we do regard it, as a candle to shed light upon our unselfishness and love of freedom, but—as a punishment for our past presumptuousness. We had the silver candlesticks and brandished them ever proudly as our own, won by our own valour. Germany must be crushed for her wicked and selfish aspiration to be mistress of the world: but the country that, when mistress of the world, failed to set her an example of unworldliness and renunciation should take to herself half the blame of the blood expended in the crushing.

TO MRS SORLEY

Aldershot, 28 *April* 1915

I saw Rupert Brooke's death in *The Morning Post*. *The Morning Post*, which has always hitherto disapproved of him, is now loud in his praises because he has conformed to their stupid axiom of literary criticism that the only stuff of poetry is violent physical experience, by dying on active service. I think Brooke's earlier poems—especially notably *The Fish* and *Grantchester*, which you can find in *Georgian Poetry*—are his best. That last sonnet-sequence of his, of which you sent me the review in the *Times Lit. Sup.*, and which has been so praised, I find (with the exception of that beginning "These hearts were woven of human joys and cares, Washed marvellously with sorrow" which is not about himself) overpraised. He is far too obsessed with his own sacrifice, regarding the going to war of himself (and others) as a highly intense, remarkable and sacrificial exploit, whereas it is merely the conduct demanded of him (and others) by the turn of circumstances, where non-compliance with this demand would have made life intolerable. It was not that "they" gave up anything of that list he gives in one sonnet: but that the essence of these things had been endangered by circumstances over which he had no control, and he must fight to recapture them. He has clothed his attitude in fine words: but he has taken the sentimental attitude.

Kenneth and I had the most delightful week-end. In spite of the rather dismal atmosphere of an empty Oriel, in which I should not like to remain more than two months at a time, we filled up the time most excellently. The night before, I went to town to see *Macbeth* at the Old Vic.—for they speak their lines clearly at the Vic., and *Macbeth* has more beautiful poetry in it than any other tragedy—and sat next to my anarchist theosophical friend in green, whose acquaintance I made eighteen months ago in the gallery of the Kingsway at

The Great Adventure. I was eating chocolate almonds, of which I had the wit to remember he had expressed himself as very fond.

I enclose my occasional budget[1]. You will notice that most of what I have written is as hurried and angular as the hand-writing: written out at different times and dirty with my pocket: but I have had no time for the final touch nor seem likely to have for some time, and so send them as they are. Nor have I had the time to think out (as I usually do) a rigorous selection, as fit for other eyes. So these are my explanations of the fall in quality. I like "Le Revenant" best, being very interested in the previous and future experience of the character concerned: but it sadly needs the file. You will also find the last of my Marlborough poems called "Lost" written in sideways on the foolscap.

To Professor Sorley

Aldershot, 15 *May* 1915

In London on Wednesday I saw Sara Allgood: not personally, but across the footlights. I went to see the Irish players in *Cathleen Ni Houlihan* and *The Playboy of the Western World.* I had never seen them before and was astonished at the acting, which seemed quite independent of the audience. They are both great plays of their kind: bringing home to me, and making me glad of, my Celtic origin.

[1] Nos. x, xi, xxiii, xxiv, xxvi, xxx, xxxi of *Marlborough and Other Poems*, 4th ed.

I have been utilizing my riding lessons of four years ago—having twice last week had to take up a mounted job at a moment's notice, in our new scheme of casualties. To my surprise I managed to remain in the saddle each time.

To Arthur Watts[1]

Aldershot, 23 *May* 1915

We are in a mass of accounts I do not understand, and sometime next week we shall exchange this bloody "area" for a troop-ship at Southampton, and then a prim little village in France in the middle of some mildly prosperous cultivation—probably. On the other hand we may sit here for weeks, making our wills and looking at our first field dressings and reading our religions on our identity discs. In jedem Falle we know that we are stale to the moulding point and sooner or later must be chucked across to France. We profess no interest in our work; our going has lost all glamour in adjournment; a weary acceptance of the tyranny of discipline, and the undisguised boredom we feel toward one another, mark all our comings and goings: we hate our general, our C.O. and men; we do not hate the Germans: in short we are nearing the attitude of regular soldiers to the army in general.

And so one lives two lives. The other one—appearing very occasionally in London, at the theatre watching the Irish Players; in church, when the band plays and

[1] Second Lieutenant (afterwards Captain) Royal West Kent Regiment; attached Intelligence Department, War Office; formerly Lector in English at the University of Jena.

amazement at the noise and splendour and idolatry shakes one to one's senses—is still as pleasant as ever. So I have no cause to complain, really. I am so convinced that one's profession is bound to be dull, and it is only in by-paths that one finds enjoyment, that I am almost thinking of staying in the army, as a fairly profitable, not too exacting main course.

I imagine you are growing to love Chatham as dearly as I love Aldershot. The latter is a terrible warning of the fate which must swamp every place or thing that is solely given up to one object.

To the Master of Marlborough

Aldershot, May 1915

Wace told me you wanted a report. I am honoured. The reason for my keeping quiet and turning my face from Marlborough is shame. Only two or three days ago I met Turner in the train (the H. F. A. brand from Crescent, not the seraphic from Maltese Cross). We rake up old bones together, till we come to a stinker: namely, that Turner had just met Edwards home on leave from the front, where he had been for some weeks. Edwards already a war-worn veteran: and we (the latchet of whose shoe...) not yet out! Can't you understand my shame?

No! when I next come down to Marlborough it shall be an entry worthy of the place and of the enterer. Not in khaki, with gloves and a little cane, with creased trousers from Aldershot—"dyed garments from Bozrah" —but in grey bags, an old coat and a knapsack, coming over the downland from Chiseldon, putting up at the Sun! Then, after a night there and a tattered stroll through the High Street, feeling perhaps the minor inconveniences of complete communion with Nature, I should put on a gentlemanly suit and crave admittance at your door, talk old scandal, search old Housebooks, swank in Court and sing in Chapel and be a regular O.M.: retaining always the right on Monday afternoon (it always rains on Mondays in Marlborough) to sweat round Barbury and Totterdown, what time you dealt out nasty little oblong unseens to the Upper VI. This would be my Odyssey. At present I am too cornered by my uniform for any such luxuries.

I saw young Woodroffe just after his brother's death. He is now gone to France. Our division follows his, so we all but sleep with puttees on. It has been a dull interval since August, deadly dull: but 'tis nearly over.

I heard from the wounded Ridley, who is greatly elated with himself and his wounds, both clean bullet holes. He deserves luck, and will always be lucky, I think.

Best wishes to Sandford's—I mean, our cricket XI—against Rugby at Lord's: though I rather think the loser will bear the greater palm this year.

CHAPTER VI

THE ARMY: AT THE FRONT

To Professor and Mrs Sorley

7th Suffolks, *12th* Division,
B.E.F., 1 *June* 1915

I have just been censoring letters: which hardly puts one in a mood for writing. Suffice it that we are in a little hamlet, or rather settlement of farms; the men on straw, the officers in old four-posters: within sound of the guns. Nothing disturbs these people. I have never felt so restful. There is cidre and cidre and cidre to drink, which reminds one of Normandy. And over all hangs the smell of never-lifted manure. It is in a valley—a feature which I did not know existed in Northern France.

The reading of a hundred letters has brought home to me one need. Could you send me out some of those filthy Woodbine cigarettes the men smoke—they all ask for them. Pour moi, I am well provided for the present.

So far our company are separated from the rest. It is like a picnic, and the weather is of the best.

To Arthur Watts

1 *June* 1915

Having begun in ink I continue in pencil. Schottische Sparsamkeit. You aren't worth ink. Besides ink hardly gives that impression of strenuous campaigning I am wishful to produce.

"Also," this is a little hamlet, smelling pleasantly of manure. I have never felt more restful. We arrived at dawn: white dawn across the plane trees and coming through the fields of rye. After two hours in an oily ship and ten in a grimy train, the "war area" was a haven of relief. These French trains shriek so: there is no sight more desolating than abandoned engines passing up and down the lines, hooting in their loneliness. There is something eerie in a railway by night.

But this is perfect. The other officers have heard the heavy guns and perhaps I shall soon. They make perfect cider in this valley: still, like them. There are clouds of dust along the roads, and in the leaves: but the dust here is native and caressing and pure, not like the dust of Aldershot, gritted and fouled by motors and thousands of feet. 'Tis a very Limbo lake: set between the tireless railways behind and twenty miles in front the fighting. Drink its cider and paddle in its rushy streams: and see if you care whether you die to-morrow. It brings out a new part of one's self, the loiterer, neither scorning nor desiring delights, gliding listlessly through the minutes from meal-time to meal-time, like the stream through the rushes: or stagnant and smooth like their cider, unfathomably gold: beautiful and calm without mental fear. And in four-score hours we will pull up our braces and fight. These hours will have slipt over me, and I shall march hotly to the firing-line, by turn critic, actor, hero, coward and soldier of fortune: perhaps even for a moment Christian, humble, with "Thy will be done." Then shock, combustion, the emergence of one of these: death or life: and then return to the old rigmarole. I imagine that this, while it may or may not knock about your body, will make very little difference to you otherwise.

A speedy relief from Chatham. There is vibration in the air when you hear "The Battalion will move across the water on......"

The moon won't rise till late, but there is such placid weariness in all the bearing earth, that I must go out to see. I have not been "auf dem Lande" for many years: man muss den Augenblick geniessen[1].

Leb' wohl. I think often of you and Jena: where I was first on my own and found freedom. Leb' wohl.

To Professor Sorley

8 *June* 1915

We have heard no more than the distant rumbling of the guns, but move slowly up in their direction to-morrow. So your plasticine has not been needed yet. Our future movements are very hazy. One is impressed by the immense casualness which seems existent everywhere: France full of troops, marching up and down, but not towards the firing line.

[1] One must enjoy the passing moment.

We live on the fat of the land here: a hamlet of four large farms, inhabited by D Company alone, in magnificent isolation from the rest of the battalion. The women work in the fields: largely aided for the present by our men. Cider is unlimited: one can hardly say the same for water. I should have had to take to washing in the former, had we been here longer. As far as I can see, perspiration will be my chief difficulty.

The dogs still bark at the heavy cannonading: but otherwise the war does not trouble us. We may be sent on soon, i.e., we the officers, for a "course" in the trenches, attached to some other battalion—preferably of the same regiment; but alas! our first and second battalions n'existent plus. My French, by the way, is vigorous, savoured with a dash of German: but the language spoken here is scarcely Parisian: neither, for that, is mine.

It has been said that the soldier's two worst plagues at the front are lice and duchesses. We have suffered from neither as yet. But from a third—Rumour. The Zeppelin raid on the suburbs came to us as having caused two hundred deaths and four hundred wounded: Petticoat Lane on fire; the British retreated twenty miles the other night; and Roumania still keeps joining in.

Nothing could have been smarter than the way we were crossed over. The first battalion of the Brigade left Aldershot at five one evening: the whole Brigade was in France by midnight!

To Professor Sorley

11 *June* 1915

We are billeted in a town of single-line tramways and mean streets: four-foot square vegetable gardens, where plaintive lettuces wither: cobbles, tenements, and cats that walk on tiles. The kindness and Gemüthlichkeit of the Franco-Flemish population—said to be all spies—is in contradiction to their surroundings. We have now seen a stretch of northern France: passed through ruddy villages, where the dark-haired buxom sallow Amazonian beauties stand dumbly on their doorsteps and do not concern themselves much with the current of us aliens, to here where mine hostesses are wizender but chattier and much more wide-awake: always busy if a little "near": but in that and their tousled dress and appearance, their openness, initiative and fussy motherliness, remind me of the Scots peasantry. So far it has been no more than a "Cook's Personally Conducted."

Thanks for *The Sunday Times*, qui est arrivé. (My French by the way is less adulterated with German than formerly and is thriving under the constant pressure of need.) The political crisis is a welcome change from the war—for the reader: perhaps not for the country. I suppose the end of the coalition will be that of all compromises: that in general it will ultimately prove to please both sides or neither, with the odds on it doing the latter. Has England ever been united yet? I don't think it's possible.

To Mrs Sorley

13 *June* 1915

Many thanks for your letter. I'm afraid I think your proposal[1] undesirable for many reasons. The proposal is premature : also I have at present neither the opportunity nor inclination for a careful revision and selection. Besides, this is no time for oliveyards and vineyards ; more especially of the small-holdings type. For three years or the duration of the war, let be.

Nevertheless I send further contributions[2].

I am very sorry to hear of H. C. I think it would be a very nice thing if you could get at Mrs C. I feel that we owe a double debt of gratitude to any Germans who have suffered thus personally on our side.

Could you get me and send out to me Richard Jefferies' *Life of the Fields*: it kept me company at Jena eleven months ago : I used to have it with my supper at the Schweizerhöhe. You can get it in a 2*s*. 6*d*. pocket edition; it is that small portable edition I wish. Before parting with it, I advise you to read the first two : "The Pageant of Summer," and "Field Play." And could you send me my little red copy of *Faust* : some baccy for me and some more Woodbines pour les hommes ?

The Franco-Flems of this district are a nice lot : and wash one's clothes daily : and darn one's socks : and improve one's French.

[1] That a volume of his poems should be printed.

[2] See *Marlborough and Other Poems*, 4th ed., pp. 76, 77 ('Two Sonnets').

To Arthur Watts

16 *June* 1915

The sight of your handwriting was a call back to another world—characters which I first saw (and marked as English) on the blotched and peppered lecture-board in the Jena lecture-rooms: "Im Sommersemester 1914 gedenke ich zu lesen," etc. 'Twas a drenching day—a soaked sack of tweeds on my back and luggage lost—so I went in search of the writer, ploughing through the marshes of Heidenstrasse. But I disliked the look of the house—pictured an elderly Englishman and fat, accustomed to extension lecturing, sitting over weak tea and sponge-cakes with a German wife—and turned back. I returned however in half-an-hour.

But this is scarcely current. Only, in a job like this, one lives in times a year ago—and a year hence, alternately. Keine Nachricht[1]. A large amount of organized disorderliness, killing the spirit. A vagueness and a dullness everywhere: an unromantic sitting still 100 yards from Brother Bosch. There's something rotten in the state of something. One feels it but cannot be definite of what. Not even is there the premonition of something big impending: gathering and ready to burst. None of that feeling of confidence, offensiveness, "personal ascendancy," with which the reports so delight our people at home. Mutual helplessness and lassitude, as when two boxers who have battered each other crouch dancing two paces from each other, waiting for the other to hit. Improvised organization, with its red hat, has

[1] No news.

muddled out romance. It is not the strong god of the Germans—that makes their Prussian Beamter[1] so bloody and their fight against fearful odds so successful. Our organization is like a nasty fat old frowsy cook dressed up in her mistress's clothes: fussy, unpopular, and upstart: trailing the scent of the scullery behind her. In periods of rest we are billeted in a town of sewage farms, mean streets, and starving cats: delightful population: but an air of late June weariness. For Spring again! This is not Hell as I hoped, but Limbo Lake with green growths on the water, full of minnows.

So one lives in a year ago—and a year hence. What are your feet doing a year hence? (For that feeling of stoniness, "too-old-at-fortyness," and late afternoon of which you speak, is only you among strangers, you in Babylon: you were forty when I first saw you: thirty, donnish, and well-mannered when you first asked me to tea: but later, at tennis, you were any age: you will be always forty to strangers perhaps: and youthen as you get to know them, be they knowable. And after all, friends are the same age.) All this in a bracket: but where, while riding in your Kentish lanes, are you riding twelve months hence? I am sometimes in Mexico, selling cloth: or in Russia, doing Lord knows what: in Serbia or the Balkans: in England, never. England remains the dream, the background: at once the memory and the ideal. Sorley is the Gaelic for wanderer. I have had a conventional education: Oxford would have corked it. But this has freed the spirit, glory be. Give me *The Odyssey*, and I return the New Testament to store. Physically as well as spiritually, give me the road.

[1] Official.

Only sometimes the horrible question of bread and butter shadows the dream: it has shadowed many, I should think. It must be tackled. But I always seek to avoid the awkward, by postponing it.

You figure in these dreams as the pioneer-sergeant. Perhaps *you* are the Odysseus, I am but one of the dog-like ἑταῖροι[1]....But however that may be, our lives will be πολύπλαγκτοι[2], though our paths may be different. And we will be buried by the sea—

> Timon will make his everlasting mansion
> Upon the beachèd verge of a salt flood,
> Which twice a day with his embossèd froth
> The turbulent surge shall cover[3].

Details can wait—perhaps for ever. These are the plans. I sometimes almost forgive Tennyson his other enormities for having written *Ulysses*.

I will write later—when the drains are not so close: and let me hear from you meanwhile. Since starting this letter I begin to scent romance in night-patrolling.

To Arthur Watts

17 *June* 1915

The steel to the striker sends greeting. And many thanks for your two letters. I have only time now for a word.

We are busy, pleasantly busy: though riveted with small and senseless orders. Everything is done on a small scale here. You—at the telescope—see the road to the star in its vastness, without the encumbering

[1] Comrades. [2] Far-roaming.

[3] *Timon of Athens*, act v, scene 2—slightly altered.

atoms which blow in the eyes and fill up the living pores of us—half-way to the star—at every turn.

Your news—of yourself—is good. You will now pull through alive—a great advantage, after all! But so shall I, I think. And so to our next meeting!

To Miss Jean Sorley

17 *June* 1915

This is not like our last visit to France: among other things in that I have to speak more French. But it has this in common—mosquitoes: though we are not otherwise plagued by small living things. Indeed the mosquitoes trouble us far more than brother Bosch. It is difficult to get any real news through. But what I have seen of War so far is this. A cornfield: you think it an ordinary cornfield till you see a long narrow trench at either end: in front of each trench is barbed wire among the corn. You might watch that field all day: and if you were deaf, you would never guess that both of these trenches were filled with foes: you would wonder how those queer underground inhabitants spent their time, and why they dared not show their heads above ground. Only, during the night, troops are constantly shifted: back and forward: north and south. The staff know that a sense of humour won't allow of this sitting face to face in a cornfield for long, without both parties coming out and fraternizing, as happened so constantly a few months ago.

To A. E. Hutchinson

20 June 1915

I imagine you expect me to begin this letter by apologizing for having not written for such months. I'm not going to. 'Twas devilishly lazy of me, but this healthy out-door life softens the brain. I daresay you have found that. So, scarcely responsible for my actions, I write at random and then illegibly.

We have been in this ruddy place for more than a fortnight. In the first thrill of crossing I nearly sent you one of those I-am-quite-well-I-have-been-admitted-into-hospital postcards, thinking it would puff you with pride to have such a thing from a real soldier: only another sign of my incipient softening of the brain. I discovered in time that it was a poisonous insult to send anyone such a postcard: besides being a blatant and peculiarly inartistic way of advertising one's presence at the front.

Since writing last I have seen [several O.M.s, also] Kitchener who wasn't looking when I gave him "eyes right." I have also:

(*a*) Killed a horse. I had to ride a horse one field-day, the Adjutant being a malingerer. I had only ridden two previously in my life, and they both donkeys. I couldn't trot but I could canter, so I went at a hack canter up and down the cobble-stones on various errands, the horse casting shoes by way of protest. I am sorry now, as I know how shocked you will be and I must have caused it pain. It reported sick next morning and has since joined its fathers—in a heavenly cab-stand, I imagine.

(*b*) Discovered by a little practical experience that the Germans are going to win this war.

(*c*) Cropped my head close like a criminal or a poodle's bottom.

I have not been down to Marlborough. There is something so vulgar to my mind in going down in uniform. It looks so like an advertisement. Besides, what people to advertise before are the remnant?

But 'tis not so bad here. I have the merciful deliverance to be in a company whose skipper sees things in proportion. So we stand this by laughing at it. You once said that every regular officer had the brains of a kitten (in our Q [dormitory] days). You were wrong.

Do not do to me as I did to you in the way of correspondence!

To Professor Sorley

24 *June* 1915

The war is at present apparently held over until visits from Cabinet Ministers and Labour Leaders shall have ceased. As it is hot there is no objection to this. We lead a mole-like existence: above ground only at night, and even then blind. But neither side shows a great disposition to leave its comparatively comfortable quarters.

To K. W. Sorley

24 *June* 1915

Many thanks for your letter. I have contracted the mistake of always trying to write my letters in the early afternoon—after lunch, when my intelligence has temporarily stopped.

I have absolutely nothing to tell you. There is a very great desultoriness everywhere. I believe I meant to say sultriness, but desultoriness will do just as well. I was expected to say something. The sense of wasting one's time that haunted one at Aldershot is absolutely nothing to the certainty that oppresses one here. One day a man will invent automatic entrenching tools and automatic mowing machines, which will take the place of infantry in war. For the present one would have thought a spiked wall might have been erected along the British front, with several spiked walls behind in case the first got shattered, and these would do our job as efficiently as we: and would probably stand a bombardment better. I noticed in yesterday's *Times* a cheerful statement that we mustn't mind if the great advance, now overdue, had to be postponed till next spring. I suppose we mustn't. Meanwhile we have taken root like trees, and like trees we vegetate. In short, I imagine that the life out here is like nothing so much as your existence in that cheerful nursing-home fifteen months ago: lethargic, restful, fattening to the body, but dulling everything else. Those in need of a Fresh Air Rest Cure should be sent out here.

Just let all concerned know this: that from now onwards my sole address is to be—rank, name, number of battalion and regiment, B. E. F.: that is, no nonsense about Brigade or Division. As one of the men said in a letter home, "a futile order in my opinion, which, as a private soldier's, is worthless."

TO THE MASTER OF MARLBOROUGH

25 *June* 1915

Many thanks for your letter. If I had attempted to obey its command and come and stay with you the next week-end, I should have been shot at dawn. That, I submit, is just about as cogent an excuse for not having come, as those old excuses for not having done any prep.

If you have any friends who want an Open Air Rest Cure: if they want sunshine and quiet and good fattening influences: send them out here. 'Tis a place to rust in, surely. It is duller even than watching a cricket match, duller even than the Crow's circus (with which is incorporated Pop's Panto)—as you were, 2nd Lieut. Atkey's English Literature lessons. So I read Richard Jefferies to remind me of Liddington Castle and the light green and dark green of the Aldbourne Downs in summer: and I learn by heart those epitaphs on my forerunners, signed with the mystic sign J. B., which are "violets by a mossy stone" in the pages of the monthly *Marlburian*.

We have seen as yet neither horrors, nor heroism, nor suffering. The test still lies ahead. To keep our lamps trimmed against that test is our present lot: most damnable.

I saw your letter to *The Times* at the beginning of this month. In the event of Compulsory Service after the war, I wonder how far the Public School system (if at all) will be able to modify and enlarge the army system, with which (in the matter of N.C.O.s) it has half of the principle in common: the N.C.O.s being the prefects of the system, though with little powers of individual action outside stereotyped lines.

The French in this part are for the great part wonderfully kind: I should like to have said, almost German in their hospitality.

This writing will probably be to you unintelligible. 'Tis a pity that we both have difficulty in reading each other's writing.

To Mrs Sorley

29 *June* 1915

We have now been out a month. Our time has been spent in a tedious preparation for possibilities which will never occur. All our behaviour is precautionary and defensive: from the universal silence one would guess that the Germans are similarly engaged behind that mysterious "pie-belt" which divides the two armies that are both incapable of fight. One day, I suppose, six hours' bombardment will knock six months' work to pieces.

I am beginning to "open my mind" to French. Besides being the soul of kindness, the French here are so merry and "gleg at the uptak." The Flemish here are even more untiringly kind—expecting no reward and genuinely insulted if one is offered—but somewhat German in their thoroughness: thoroughness which is after all a sort of stupidity, that is unable to tell a flower without digging to inspect its roots. I can carry on a conversation on most subjects with little difficulty in French—a thing which I could never have done in German when I knew as little German as I know French now—just owing to that quality of keenness: a double-edged wit as keen in perception as in repartee. They catch your drift at once, and give you all the time [the impression] that you are speaking intelligible French.

To Mrs Sorley

10 *July* 1915

We have taken over a new lot of trenches and have been having a busy time this past week: our exertions have been those of the navvy rather than those of the soldier. And—without at all "fraternizing"—we refrain from interfering with Brother Bosch seventy yards away, as long as he is kind to us. So all day there is trench duty broken by feverish letter censoring. No amount of work will break the men's epistolary spirit: I am qualifying for the position of either navvy or post-office clerk after the war. During the night a little excitement is provided by patrolling the enemy's wire. Our chief enemy is nettles and mosquitoes. All patrols—English and German—are much averse to the death and glory principle; so, on running up against one another in the long wet rustling clover, both pretend that they are Levites and the other is a Good Samaritan—and pass by on the other side, no word spoken. For either side to bomb the other would be a useless violation of the unwritten laws that govern the relations of combatants permanently within a hundred yards of distance of each other, who have found out that to provide discomfort for the other is but a roundabout way of providing it for themselves: until they have their heads banged forcibly together by the red-capped powers behind them, whom neither attempts to understand. Meanwhile weather is "no bon": food, "plenty bon": temper, fair: sleep, jamais.

Such is "attrition," that last resort of paralysed strategy of which we hear so much.

I hate the growing tendency to think that every man drops overboard his individuality between Folkestone and Boulogne, and becomes on landing either "Tommy" with a character like a nice big fighting pet bear and an incurable yearning and whining for mouth-organs and cheap cigarettes: or the Young Officer with a face like a hero and a silly habit of giggling in the face of death. The kind of man who writes leading articles in *The Morning Post*, and fills the sadly huge gaps in his arguments by stating that the men at the front either all want conscription or think that Haldane should be hanged, is one step worse than [the people] who think that our letters concern our profession and not our interests. "I hate a fool."

I should think that that swarm of alliterative busybodies, who see no reason why everyone they meet, and do not take the trouble to "kennen lernen," should not be Girl Guides or Women Workers or Lady Lamplighters or whatever the latest craze is, must be almost as annoying to J. as the mother-of-sixteen flies are out here. A pity that she cannot adopt the same method with them as I can with my flies. Still "kill that fly" would be a crushing retort.

To Arthur Watts

July 1915

Mein lieber Vernachlässiger[1].—Did you get my last letter, in answer to yours (undated) of about three weeks ago? If so, has that stupor of an ordered life so clogged your pen—as it has clogged mine—that you can stare at the paper and ruminate gently, but write you cannot. I have been suffering in this way lately. I have either no thoughts or cannot express those I have: or because it is July. From the time that the May blossom is scattered till the first frosts of September, one is always at one's worst. Summer is stagnating: there is no more spring (in both senses) anywhere. When the corn is grown and the autumn seed not yet sown, it has only to bask in the sun, to fatten and ripen: a damnable time for man; heaven for the vegetables. And so I am sunk deep in "Denkfaulheit,"[2] trying to catch in the distant but incessant upper thunder of the air promise of October rainstorms: long runs clad only in jersey and shorts over the Marlborough downs, cloked in rain, as of yore: likewise, in the aimless toothless grumbling of the guns, promise of a great advance to come: hailstones and coals of fire. So I confine my correspondence to Field Service Postcards during the period of glutting fullness, having half the day to write in. Only because I want a letter from you do I manage a letter for once.

[1] My dear Neglector.

[2] Mental lethargy.

To Professor Sorley

14 *July* 1915

I suppose the old Lawyer-Liberal party has now definitely split from the new, one might almost call it, Journalist-Liberal party, Lloyd George's rude contradiction of Haldane marking the schism. You don't read *The Daily Mail*, I suppose; but reading it out here opens one's eyes to the dangerous influence the press is beginning to arrogate and may ultimately attain. That paper makes one sick, not because what it says is untrue (for the most part) or unsound or insincere: but because of its colossal egoism ("What we have ventured to call the *Daily Mail* policy"—"The government acting on the advice given in yesterday's *Daily Mail* has etc."), and its power of anticipating public opinion by twenty-four hours and giving it just the turn in the direction *The Daily Mail* wishes.

To Professor Sorley

15 *July* 1915

Your letter, dated 13th, has just arrived. We are now at the end of a few days' rest, a kilometre behind the lines. Except for the farmyard noises (new style) it might almost be the little village that first took us to its arms six weeks ago. It has been a fine day, following on a day's rain, so that the earth smells like spring. I have just managed to break off a long conversation with the farmer in charge, a tall thin stooping man with sad eyes, in trouble about his land: les Anglais stole his peas, trod down his corn and robbed his young potatoes: he told it as a father telling of infanticide. There may have been fifteen francs' worth of damage done; he will never get compensation out of those shifty Belgian burgomasters; but it was not exactly the fifteen francs but the invasion of the soil that had been his for forty years, in which the weather was his only enemy, that gave him a kind of Niobe's dignity to his complaint.

Meanwhile there is the usual evening sluggishness. Close by, a quickfirer is pounding away its allowance of a dozen shells a day. It is like a cow coughing. Eastward there begins a sound (all sounds begin at sundown and continue intermittently till midnight, reaching their zenith at about 9 p.m. and then dying away as sleepiness claims their makers)—a sound like a motor-cycle race—thousands of motor-cycles tearing round and round a track, with cut-outs out: it is really a pair of machine guns firing. And now one sound awakens another. The old cow coughing has started the motor-bikes: and now at intervals of a few minutes come express trains in our direction: you can hear them rushing toward us; they pass going straight for the town behind us: and you hear them begin to slow down as they reach the town: they will soon stop: but no, every time, just before they reach it, is a tremendous railway accident. At least, it must be a railway accident, there is so much noise, and you can see the dust that the wreckage scatters. Sometimes the train behind comes very close, but it too smashes on the wreckage of its forerunners. A tremendous cloud of dust, and then the groans. So many trains and accidents start the cow coughing again: only another cow this time, somewhere behind us, a tremendous-sized cow, θαυμάσιον ὅσον[1], with awful whooping-cough. It must be a buffalo: this cough must burst its sides. And now someone starts sliding down the stairs on a tin tray, to soften the heart of the cow, make it laugh and cure its cough. The din he makes is appalling. He is beating the tray with a broom now, every two minutes a stroke: he has certainly stopped the cow by this time, probably killed it. He will leave off soon (thanks to the "shell tragedy"): we know he can't last.

It is now almost dark: come out and see the fireworks. While waiting for them to begin you can notice how pale and white the corn is in the summer twilight: no wonder with all this whooping-cough about. And the motor-cycles: notice how all these races have at least a hundred entries: there is never a single cycle going. And why are there no birds coming back to roost? Where is the lark? I haven't heard him all today. He must have got whooping-cough as well, or be staying at home through fear of the cow. I think it will rain to-morrow, but there have been no swallows circling low, stroking their breasts on the full ears of corn. Anyhow, it is night now, but the circus does not close till twelve. Look! there is the first of them! The fireworks are beginning. Red flares shooting up high into the night, or skimming low over the ground, like the swallows that are not: and rockets bursting into stars. See how they illumine that patch of ground a mile in front. See it, it is deadly pale in their searching light: ghastly, I think, and featureless except for two big lines of eyebrows ashy white, parallel along it, raised

[1] Wonderfully great.

a little from its surface. Eyebrows. Where are the eyes? Hush, there are no eyes. What those shooting flares illumine is a mole. A long thin mole. Burrowing by day, and shoving a timorous enquiring snout above the ground by night. Look, did you see it? No, you cannot see it from here. But were you a good deal nearer, you would see behind that snout a long and endless row of sharp shining teeth. The rockets catch the light from these teeth and the teeth glitter: they are silently removed from the poison-spitting gums of the mole. For the mole's gums spit fire and, they say, send something more concrete than fire darting into the night. Even when its teeth are off. But you cannot see all this from here: you can only see the rockets and then for a moment the pale ground beneath. But it is quite dark now.

And now for the fun of the fair! You will hear soon the riding-master crack his whip—why, there it is. Listen, a thousand whips are cracking, whipping the horses round the ring. At last! The fun of the circus is begun. For the motor-cycle team race has started off again: and the whips are cracking all: and the wares-man starts again, beating his loud tin tray to attract the customers: and the cows in the cattle-show start coughing, coughing: and the firework display is at its best: and the circus specials come one after another bearing the merry-makers back to town, all to the inevitable crash, the inevitable accident. It can't last long: these accidents are so frequent, they'll all get soon killed off, I hope. Yes, it is diminishing. The train service is cancelled (and time too): the cows have stopped coughing: and the cycle race is done. Only the kids who have bought new whips at the fair continue to crack them: and unused rockets that lie about the ground are still sent up occasionally. But now the children are being driven off to bed : only an occasional whip-crack now (perhaps the child is now the sufferer): and the tired showmen going over the ground pick up the rocket-sticks and dead flares. At least I suppose this is what must be happening: for occasionally they still find one that has not yet gone off and send it up out of mere perversity. Else what silence!

It must be midnight now. Yes, it is midnight. But before you go to bed, bend down, put your ear against the ground. What do you hear? "I hear an endless tapping and a tramping to and fro: both are muffled: but they come from everywhere. Tap, tap, tap: pick, pick, pick: tra-mp, tra-mp, tra-mp." So you see the circus-goers are not all gone to sleep. There is noise coming from the womb of earth, noise of men who tap and mine and dig and pass to and fro on their watch. What you have seen is the foam and froth of war: but underground is labour and throbbing and long watch. Which will one day bear their fruit. They will set the circus on fire. Then what pandemonium! Let us hope it will not be to-morrow!

To Arthur Watts

End of July 1915

Herewith a jingle or two. I think you said "Send me anything you write." Without obeying that to the letter, I send the enclosed[1]—the harvest of an unquiet

[1] See *Marlborough and Other Poems*, 4th ed., pp. 59, 76, and 79–80.

and not deep-seeing eye. If it variegates your work with a suggestion of our open-airiness here, well.

We visit and return from the trenches with an almost monotonous regularity: we eat the fresh bread of the land and tramp over waste acres of tangled corn, self-seeded from last year's ungathered harvest. The existence is incredibly peaceful: till suddenly some officer whom one had known and not disliked—dies: one wonders; and forgets about him in a week.

A year ago I and a not too English friend were footing it from Coblenz to Trier, full of the delights of Germany. You had already fled to Munich.

Do the Generals whom you no doubt associate daily with know what bloody fools they are all considered when they visit us with six pink-faced A.D.C.s, one Staff Officer to do their thinking and another to act as their megaphone? Being human, I suppose they do. The British private has this virtue: he will never be impressed.

A p.c. if you have time—for you are really doing the work now—and why the term "slackers" should be applied to those who have not enlisted, God knows. Plenty of slackers here, thank you. I never was so idle in my life.

To the Master of Marlborough

4 *August* 1915

Many thanks for your last letter. You'll excuse a two months' silence.

There is really very little to say about the life here. Change of circumstance, I find, means little compared to change of company. And as one has gone out and is still with the same officers with whom one had rubbed shoulders unceasingly for the last nine months, and of whom one had acquired that extraordinarily intimate knowledge which comes of constant συνουσία[1], one does not notice the change: until one or two or three drop off. And one wonders why.

They are extraordinarily close, really, these friendships of circumstance, distinct as they remain from friendships of choice. If one looks back to early September and sees what one thought of these others then: how one would never, while not disliking them, have wished to see any of them again: but that incorrigible circumstance kept us penned together, rubbed off our odd and awkward corners where we grated: developing in each a part of himself that might have remained always unsuspected, which could tread on common ground with another. Only, I think, once or twice does one stumble across that person into whom one fits at once: to whom one can stand naked, all disclosed. But circumstance provides the second best: and I'm sure that any gathering of men will in time lead to a very very close half-friendship between them all (I only say half-friendship because I wish to distinguish it from the other). So there has really been no change in coming over here: the change is to come when half of this improvised "band of brothers" are wiped away in a day. We are learning to be soldiers slowly—that is to say, adopting the soldierly attitude of complete disconnection with our job during odd hours. No shop. So when I think I should tell you

[1] Companionship.

"something about the trenches," I find I have neither the inclination nor the power.

This however. On our weekly march from the trenches back to our old farmhouse a mile or two behind, we leave the communication-trench for a road, hedged on one side only, with open ploughland to the right. It runs a little down hill till the road branches. Then half left up over open country goes our track, with the ground shelving away to right of us. Can you see it? The Toll House to the First Post on Trainers Down (old finishing point of A House sweats) on a small scale. There is something in the way that at the end of the hedge the road leaps up to the left into the beyond that puts me in mind of Trainers Down (as C House called it). It is what that turn into unhedged country and that leap promises, not what it achieves, that makes the likeness. It is nothing when you get up, no wildness, no openness. But there it remains to cheer me on each relief.

I hear Wace's wound is not serious. Though he is in the same Brigade I saw him only occasionally out here.

Is it true that Hammond has been killed? One of the cheeriest pieces of vitality I think I ever knew at Marlborough.

Examns—your curse—will now be over, "Lists" read, and the "Toun o' Touns" sung. I hear that a *very* select group of public schools will by this time be enjoying the Camp "somewhere in England." May they not take it too seriously! Seein' as 'ow all training is washed out as soon as you turn that narrow street corner at Boulogne, where some watcher with a lantern is always up for the English troops arriving, with a "Bon courage" for every man.

A year ago to-day—but that way madness lies.

A reference in the letter that follows is explained by an account, written by a brother-officer, of a bombing expedition made on one of the last nights of July:

"We were holding trenches just to the south of Ploegsteert wood. D Coy were on the left of the Battalion, about 100 yards from the Germans. That opposite C.'s platoon was, I think, the most interesting part of our line, as the Germans were working on it from the day we took over till the day we left. They seemed to be making a redoubt of some kind, and, as those were the days when shells were scarce, we couldn't ask the gunners to blow it up....C. knew the ground in front of this better than anyone in the company: where the ditches and disused saps ran; where the different shell-holes lay; where the beetroot met the clover, and where the clover ended in a strip of long thin grass up to the enemy's wire. C. had been out crawling often before, just for the fun of the thing....It was all planned out cleverly beforehand: C. and three other bombers to crawl up to within bombing distance, he leading and directing the show; four riflemen were to come up on the flank and cover their retirement....It was a dark night and everything went off splendidly up to the point when the bombs were to be thrown....The pins had all been taken out and the second signal was just being passed when the third bomber dropped his infernal machine. I think the others heard it thud and tried to get clear; at any rate he was stupid enough to fumble about in the long wet grass in an attempt to find it. There was a dreadful five seconds' suspense: then the thing exploded right under him. In the confusion C. and one of the other men managed to throw their bombs, and that and the fire of the riflemen, who opened up a steady burst immediately, saved the party somewhat. C. crawled to the man who had dropped his bomb and dragged him into the shell-hole....The shell-hole was his salvation. They had only just got into it when the Germans swept the ground with an absolute hail of rifle and machine-gun fire and lit up all around with Véry lights....When the Germans had quieted down a bit, some more men came out and helped to get the wounded in. The one with C. was in a very bad way and died soon after. C. said every bone in the upper part of his body must have been broken—it was like carrying a piece of living pulp—and he never forgot the curious inarticulate cry of the man as he picked him up....

"Next morning, a brilliant July day, I went round to pick up Intelligence and met C. on trench patrol. He had just come from breakfasting and was dressed in summer get-up; gum boots, breeches, shirt-sleeves, sambrown belt and pistol. He had a bandage round his head, but only a very slight scratch from a fragment of bomb. He was walking along, reading from his German pocket edition of *Faust*. He told me the whole story of the raid: rather sorry that his plans had been let down just when they might have been so successful; but he took it all in his happy careless fashion."

To Mrs Sorley

7 *August* 1915

We are busy, very busy, with the pruning-hook however more than with the sword, as our part of the line is quietish. Our Major-General never sleepeth; and since his Division took over this part of the line, farms have been devastated and harvests ruined, and to be in reserve means work eight hours a day: but I think our piece of ground is now inviolable. Every day almost, one meets this tired, nervous, haggard, incredibly vivacious and sympathetic chief: who knows almost all the (300 odd) officers under him by name, and visits your part of the trench with the same apologetic agreeable air as an insurance agent assessing a private house: never interfering (on the spot) or directing, only apparently anxious to learn—till divisional orders come out!

Hard "spade-work" (as school reports used to say) —"curry" in the form of occasional skirmishes at night between patrols—still keep our days full and our nights unquiet. Armed with bombs and equipped with night one can do much raiding with extraordinary safety: much to the Bosch's annoyance, or to his amusement when with infinite care a bombing party creeps up to his wire and commences with deadly effect to bomb itself. Such has happened more than once. The unfathomable laboriousness of the people opposite, infinite and aloof! Working day and night, nor heeding us. Thorns in their side we are, often pricking ourselves more than them; till we get too close, too harmful, too informed one day—and then a whip of lead! We are the gnat that buzzes, hums and stings without ceasing: they the bee, undisturbable in toil till roused, and then a deep sting which remains. Who does the greater damage none can say. Both do enough to keep alive a spark of considerable mutual irritation which this year or next year must burst into flame.

So I go about collecting odd ends of trades, learning lessons in handiness. Besides of course post-office clerk, I could now earn a wage as a bricklayer: wouldn't do badly as a common or garden sort of navvy: any offers for a job with barbed wire fences would be gratefully received: and I wouldn't do badly as a poacher. I am now fairly at home in the midst of explosives and detonators and can make the simpler sorts of bombs: I could drain the garden path: I could neatly floor the leads: could erect loopholes in my bedroom window (by cunning arrangement of the pillows) for pot-shots at the birds, A. C. B., or anything else that might haunt the Magdalene wilderness. Our nine weeks out here have not been wasted.

Thanks again for the letters, which make better reading than all the books you send—not that I wish to decry the latter.

To Mrs C. H. Turner

15 *August* 1915

Very many thanks for your letter and the white heather and the oatcakes and the other good things. You will now be able to take much of the credit of D Company's magnificent charge (or strategical retreat) when it comes: it will be due to the white heather on the mess table.

Capt. Henty heard from the Major[1]—or is it yet the Colonel?—yesterday: and of the new Dug Out which is the talk of the British front. We all hope very much for a visit: only we shall have to call Solomon in to decide whether we or the Battalion H.Q. have the prior claim to his company.

We are still all flourishing here: fattening on your kind gifts: looking forward to a peaceful winter and trusting to the artillery to win the war in the spring, whence we shall return to civil life all the merrier for the jolly people whom we have met in our invasion into the army. This time last year—but no, I mustn't. What bores all men will be in August twenty years hence!

[1] Captain C. H. Turner, the "skipper" of D Coy, had, some weeks earlier, been promoted Major and given the command of the 2nd Battalion of the Regiment. He was killed in action in front of Ypres early in October 1915.

To Miss Jean Sorley

15 *August* 1915

Many thanks and belated for the parcel you sent about a week ago and your letter. The apples are always a good thing to have and these remained fresh.

I have not answered before because I have spent all my spare moments during the last week reading with avidity *Cranford.* I bought it in how-much-would-you-give-to-know-where: the only English book in the only bookshop left standing there: an English edition published in France, retaining the "loin" for "lion" misprint. That I had not read it before I count as a great gain, as it enabled me to read it now. Now you can never put in my epitaph "He had never read *Cranford*, nor reading it had he failed to enjoy it." You can make the remark about Jane Austen, however.

By the way, Kitchener wants Pipe Cleaners. Young officers at the front are starving for want of Pipe Cleaners. Read *The Daily Mail*, the paper that exposed the Pipe Cleaner Tragedy.

Tell Mother I shall shortly embark on a detailed criticism of the various methods of warfare on flies: such a criticism that she will almost imagine the letter to be from Kenneth.

I hope you are resisting the "this time last year I" epidemic, which is causing havoc out here. August will be henceforward a month to tread delicately in—a month of awful egoism and sentimentalism and inventions, especially when we get old.

To Professor Sorley

17 *August* 1915

We are looking forward to this time next month. By that time we shall have done our "three months' hard" in the trenches and will be starting to think of "leaf," as the sergeants call it. It is not impossible, however, that the Germans will interfere with our arrangements in that sphere.

All goes well. I touch wood (my pencil), but at present we have been twice as lucky as any other battalion in our Division in the way of losses in commissioned ranks. Shakespeare's lie about "the rain it raineth every day" has held good for the last ten days. One somehow feels that the Germans score in rain: their sentries have umbrellas and their trenches are probably better paved; though ours are passable, and only sufficiently uncomfortable in wet to make us feel a well-off far-off sympathy with the sufferings of the troops out here last winter.

Hence to bed! It is 8.30 a.m.—till midday is my night-time.

To Miss M. S. Sorley

17 *August* 1915

Many thanks for your letter which greeted me on our weekly return to our old farmhouse behind the lines. One comes back laden like a mule with all the appurtenances one had taken up eight days before, wherewith to fight rain or heatwaves or flies or "Alleymans"—whichever might turn out to be our most troublesome obstacles: slushing and swearing and tripping through the dark and shell-pitted roads with the vision of a few days' comparative rest before one. So it was pleasant to hear from you and from that fine and windy country over which I roamed just two years ago.

I'm sending herewith—it strikes me it may interest you—a copy of *The Imitation of Christ* in Flemish. Two days ago we blew up an old half-ruined estaminet just in front of our trenches, which would have been a useful point of vantage for brother Bosch in case of him attacking. In consolidating the position and digging it in, I found among other things this book in the cellar (which had escaped the explosive) on the top of a barrel still half-full of beer (what can the Germans have been doing?) with some French recipes inside. Perhaps the phrase-book of which you speak would have enabled me to understand them, though I think that *The Complete French Scholar* price threepence which I already have is sufficient for my present needs—finding the way, billeting troops, saying "C'est la guerre" to all complaints of the natives, and buying up such things as fresh vegetables, fresh bread etc., which the inhabitants are not willing to part with and which have generally to be for "le Général" or "les pauvres, pauvres blessés" before we can get them! Anyhow, there was a—well, decomposed body in that estaminet, who may have written this recipe and read his Thomas à Kempis with diligence daily. Or more likely 'twas a German body; and the canny publican and wife and child had fled at the first approach of Germans, leaving their

Imitation and—much more wonderful—their recipes behind them. In any case it will answer for my contribution to the reigning passion for souvenirs; and your professional opinion may agree that it is quite a nice binding—for Belgium!

I cannot say where we are. But I think it's a little south of where you say you were. I'm feeling very "fit"—sorry, you object to that word—but growing a little fat, though you needn't send out any antipon just yet.

I hope the Duchy (which I believe is a rather knowing way of referring to Cornwall) will continue to treat you well! I do not insist that you should read this book I'm sending.

To Mrs Sorley

24 *August* 1915

Our work and routine is still the same as ever. We are like the fielder who is put at long leg when a good batsman is at the wicket: not because the batsman will ever hit a ball there, but because, if the fielder in question were to be removed, he would.

I have finished *Horace Blake*. It is a great pity that the authoress did not spend more time on it, for except in one or two chapters—notably the Brittany chapters—the style is hardly equal to the theme. I found the book intensely interesting. The novel as schemed and the characters as presented are the work of a great artist. But the only reason that I can find why the novel can not really be called a great novel is that the style is not uniform, is fine in the more intense passages but is apt to sink with the subject, and, for much of the book, is totally undistinguished even by simplicity. I imagine the chief difficulty of novel-writing would be the threading together of the master-ideas and master-incidents which first appear as the whole novel to the brain of the novelist. Now this novel is admirably constructed, but the intermediary passages are not sustained by what one can call a style. Indeed the authoress has no style save where the greatness of the subject begets one. The difficulty of present-day novels is that it is so difficult to describe familiar events among drawing rooms and flats in a style which is not reminiscent of police-court evidence or the introduction to a good salesman's catalogue. There is enough fine and true writing in the book to show that a greater amount of time spent would have saved Mrs Wilfrid Ward from falling, as she often does, into a style like a well-dressed housemaid, which too much reading of newspapers makes a ready pitfall for any writer now-a-days. It is a great pity, for such a book deserves the finest raiment. Horace is convincing because you are left to think, if you want to, that his conversion was due to broken health: the incident is, as it should be, merely recorded. You know that it happened and, because you are left to explain it as you will, you feel that it could have happened. If only the author of *The Acts of the Apostles* (such a dull book!) had adopted the same method, instead of forcing his Parthians, Medes and Elamites down your throat! The restraint and gentle broad-minded assurance of the telling are wonderful, especially in so ardent a propagandist as I had always believed Mrs Wilfrid Ward to be, and win their triumph in the end. And in the background the curé, with his little actions recorded without comment—refusing to admit Trix on impulse into the Church, removing all symbols of his faith from Blake's deathbed before Kate came in—is a fitting incarnation of the spirit of the whole book: that of the Dove, not the rushing mighty wind.

I think I have now sufficient weapons against insects. Of course the evil is already on the decline. The nights are not without a suggestion of frost.

Thanks also for the books. There are now enough to keep our Company Mess going for some time, as time for reading is nearly as limited as time for writing—but by no means quite as much so, because one is often free from duty but in a state in which output is an effort but absorption easy and delightful.

To Arthur Watts

26 *August* 1915

Your letter arrived and awoke the now drifting ME to consciousness. I had understood and acquiesced in your silence. The re-creation of that self which one is to a friend is an effort: repaying if it succeeds, but not to be forced. Wherefore, were it not for the dangers dancing attendance on the adjourning type of mind—which a year's military training has not been able to efface from me—I should not be writing to you now. For it is just after breakfast—and you know what breakfast is: putter to sleep of all mental energy and discontent: charmer, sedative, leveller: maker of Britons. I should wait till after tea when the undiscriminating sun has shown his back—a fine back—on the world, and one's self by the aid of tea has thrown off the mental sleep of heat. But after tea I am on duty. So with bacon in my throat and my brain like a poached egg I will try to do you justice.

On the whole—except for the subtle distinction that I *am* at the front, you not (merely a nominal distinction for the present)—I am disposed to envy you. I am moving smally to and fro over an unblessed stretch of plain—a fly on a bald man's head. You are at least among rich surroundings, like the head of hair of your half-Slav. I wonder how long it takes the King's Pawn, who so proudly initiates the game of chess, to realize that he is a pawn. Same with us. We are finding out that we play the unimportant if necessary part. At present a dam, untested, whose presence not whose action stops the stream from approaching: and then—a mere handle to steel: dealers of death which we are not allowed to plan. But I have complained enough before of the minion state of the "damned foot." It is something to have no responsibility—an inglorious ease of mind.

So half-lit nights with the foam and flotsam of the world—here we have only the little ordered breakers that lap pleasantly merry on the English shores—has its charm to the imagination. Possibly its romance fades by experience and leaves a taste of damp blotting-paper in the mouth—as of one who has slept with his mouth open. But yet these men—and women—whom you meet must by their very needs and isolations be more distinct and living than the very pleasant officers with whom I live. Very pleasant they are: humorous, vivacious and good comrades: but some have never entered, most perhaps have entered and now keep locked and barred,

> The heart's heart whose immurèd plot
> Hath keys yourself keep not[1].

They have stifled their loneliness of spirit till they scarcely know it, seeking new easy unexacting companionships. They are surface wells. Not two hundred feet deep, so that you can see the stars at the bottom.

Health—and I don't know what ill-health is—invites you so much to smooth and shallow ways: where a happiness may only be found by renouncing the other happiness of which one set out in search. Yet here there is enough to stay the bubbling surface stream. Looking into the future one sees a holocaust somewhere: and at present there is—thank God—enough of "experience" to keep the wits edged (a callous way of putting it, perhaps). But out in front at night in that no-man's land and long graveyard there is a freedom and a spur. Rustling of the grasses and grave tap-tapping of distant workers: the tension and silence of encounter, when one struggles in the dark for moral victory over the enemy patrol: the wail of the exploded bomb and the animal cries of wounded men. Then death and the horrible thankfulness when one sees that the next man is dead: "We won't have to *carry* him in under fire, thank God; dragging will do": hauling in of the great resistless body in the dark, the smashed head rattling: the relief, the relief that the thing has ceased to groan: that the bullet or bomb that made the man an animal has now made the animal a corpse. One is hardened by now: purged of all false pity: perhaps more selfish

[1] F. Thompson, *Works*, vol. i, p. 183 ('A Fallen Yew').

than before. The spiritual and the animal get so much more sharply divided in hours of encounter, taking possession of the body by swift turns.

And now I have 200 letters to censor before the post goes....You'll write again, won't you, as soon as the mood comes—after tea? And good health to you.

To Professor Sorley

2 September 1915

Many thanks for your letter and congratulations. Without this promotion, I should have been with you on "leaf" in a fortnight's time: as it is, as junior Captain, no longer as second senior subaltern, I shall have to wait my time till the end of October—supposing the present state of busy deadlock continues, or that a bullet or shell or bomb does not quicken that desired time. I have, of course, left behind my platoon and am now second in command of D Coy. The second in command's job is with the Coy money and business—the pay, rations, records, etc., of the men: also unfortunately their correspondence. In so far as it gives me a training in accounts and business, it will be a very useful move for me. Curiously enough my platoon-sergeant has got a move at the same time: he is now Coy Quartermaster-sergeant, that is, I still have him to work with.

I now run (during our periods in reserve) a large public-house: buying barrels of beer direct from neighbouring brewers and selling it as nearly as possible at cost price to the men, thus saving them from the adulterated and expensive beer at the local estaminets. Selling beer at 10 centimes a pint I still manage to make a slight profit—about 5 francs to 60 gallons—which goes in mouth-organs and suet, the Suffolk's love of suet pudding being as great almost as his love of sleep. The quartermaster-sergeant of course is the publican, myself merely the landlord.

We are still very busy, but more on our protections from weather than from Germans, the latter being about complete. The line can now never be bent backwards where we are: but I wonder if it can or will ever bend forward. Reading the casualty lists each morning I feel thankful our division was not sent to the Dardanelles.

During next week I take on the Adjutant's job, that official going on leave. So you can think of me as hard-worked but absolutely safe in a triple-sandbagged office well removed from the front line.

We are now dealing in our Coy Mess with a very excellent thing "The Field Force Canteen" just set up in France by the W.O. So perhaps Mother could save on her parcels to me to the advantage of —'s brothers and her old hospital friends to whom she sends....A parcel once a fortnight...would be sufficient. You know we are rather spoiled out here at present!

To John Bain

10 *September* 1915

It is a month since I got your verses to the "Voice[1]." I never dreamed that you would know who I was. Somehow my name spoils it. I prefer being the Voice! But very glad and proud I was to get some lines from

[1] See *Marlborough and Other Poems*, 4th ed., p. 131.

you. And thank you for your translation in *The Westminster*, which followed hard on the heels of the other. And yet I held over my thanks for a month: but I had "To the Voice" with me (and have still) all the time.

I have sent up a verse to *The Marlburian* as my poor offering to the memory and praise of Sidney Woodroffe[1]. My one thought when I opened the paper yesterday and read of his V.C. was "of course!" I knew it and had known it somehow all along!

In ten days there will be bare knees and punts[2] bouncing on Common I.

I'm just sending you two verses[3], come lately of this business. I thought you would like perhaps to read them.

So now I can do no more than thank you...and echo in my heart the last verse of yours to the Voice. Next April—yes, it will be next April.

To Professor and Mrs Sorley

10, 16 *September* 1915

Just a line of the I-am-quite-well type. Both parcels received with many thanks. Excellently useful. A wonderful burst of rich September sunshine. I have just been into ——? and had such a lunch! We become such villagers here. A visit to an unbombarded civilized town is a treat which makes one quite excited. I was so set up by that lunch—seven courses, lager beer and coffee. I in my newly-arrived tunic too!...

[1] See *Marlborough and Other Poems*, 4th ed., p. 85.
[2] Footballs.
[3] See *Marlborough and Other Poems*, 4th ed., pp. 29, 76.

Leave seems to be offering itself to me about the middle of October, though heaven knows what we have done to deserve it. However the great advantage of the Army is the freedom from questions of deserts and preferences that it gives. Going where you are sent and taking what you can get makes life very easy.

To MISS JEAN SORLEY

21 *September* 1915

I do hope that your plan of visiting Avebury and Marlborough and the Forest succeeded. Term would not have begun, but the magic name of Sorley should have been sufficient to give you free passage into C House and the Chapel (what a conceited thing to say) now in these piping times of peace when strange lady visitors are no longer suspected of being grenadiers in disguise. A bomb is such a horrid thing when it goes off that I can't conceive even the most ardent suffragette having ever [used one]. They whine like whipped dogs or hungry children at street corners when they explode.

I suppose you are looking forward to an inevitably tedious winter, like us. Tennis I suppose was dormant last summer. I suspect it will be a two years' sleep.

You probably saw that Sidney Woodroffe who was contemporary with me at Marlborough got a posthumous V.C.—the first decoration awarded to "Kitchener's" Army.

To the Master of Marlborough

5 October 1915

I have just time (or rather paper, for that is at present more valuable than time) enough to send a reply to your welcome letter which arrived with the bacon. The chess players are no longer waiting so infernal long between their moves. And the patient pawns are all in movement, hourly expecting further advances—whether to be taken or reach the back lines and be queened. 'Tis sweet, this pawn-being: there are no cares, no doubts: wherefore no regrets. The burden which I am sure is the parent of ill-temper, drunkenness and premature old age—to wit, the making up of one's own mind—is lifted from our shoulders. I can now understand the value of dogma, which is the General Commander-in-Chief of the mind. I am now beginning to think that free thinkers should give their minds into subjection, for we who have given our actions and volitions into subjection gain such marvellous rest thereby. Only of course it is the subjection of their powers of will and deed to a wrong master on the part of a great nation that has led Europe into war. Perhaps afterwards, I and my likes will again become indiscriminate rebels. For the present we find high relief in making ourselves soldiers.

I sent a few lines to *The Marlburian* to the memory and praise of Sidney Woodroffe. Now that one looks back, such an end seemed destined. The Woodroffes were a pair in whom every one of however different temperaments and interests seemed to unite to find a friend.

We no longer know what tomorrow may bring. As I indicated, we no longer worry. Only certain it is that the Bosch has started his long way homeward.

Have heard from Atkey—full of spirits. I think he did right to go even at the risk of leaving a sphere in which he was more useful. Ridley[1], too, recovered from his wound and setting sail on his birthday for the Mediterranean: Ridley with whom I brewed, "worked," and shared a study, and quarrelled absolutely unceasingly for over three years. We have so thoroughly told each other all each other's faults and oddities for so long a time that nothing now could part our friendship. He is to me the best type of Englishman: whose gold lies hid and is never marketed: like one of the heroes of Hardy's earlier novels—the Trumpet Major, or Giles Winterborne in *The Woodlanders*. Hopkinson also writes, full of chuckles and red blood.

Good luck to Capt. Hughes. And many thanks for your two letters. O for a pair of shorts and my long loose coloured jersey—gules and argent—once again! My love to Marlborough.

To Arthur Watts

5 *October* 1915

Just a line—albeit on military ruled paper. It is the eve of our crowning hour.

I am bleached with chalk and grown hairy. And I think exultantly and sweetly of the one or two or three

[1] Captain, Royal Dublin Fusiliers; M.C.; killed in action in France, 15 July 1917.

outstandingly admirable meals of my life. One in Yorkshire, in an inn upon the moors, with a fire of logs and ale and tea and every sort of Yorkshire bakery, especially bears me company. And yet another in Mecklenburg-Schwerin (where they are very English) in a farm-house utterly at peace in broad fields sloping to the sea. I remember a tureen of champagne in the middle of the table, to which we helped ourselves with ladles! I remember my hunger after three hours' ride over the country: and the fishing-town of Wismar lying like an English town on the sea. In that great old farm-house where I dined at 3 p.m. as the May day began to cool, fruit of sea and of land joined hands together, fish fresh caught and ducks fresh killed: it was a wedding of the elements. It was perhaps the greatest meal I have had ever, for everything we ate had been alive that morning—the champagne was alive yet. We feasted like kings till the sun sank, for it was impossible to overeat. 'Twas Homeric and its memory fills many hungry hours.

I was interested in your tale of meeting Wells. Yet a man to whom every private incident is legitimate "copy" I cannot understand.

I can see you amongst your staff of warrior non-combatants: and (with you) both wish you, and wish you not, rid of them. To be able to prove oneself no coward to oneself, will be great, if it comes off: but suppose one finds oneself fail in the test? I dread my own censorious self in the coming conflict—I also have great physical dread of pain. Still, a good edge is given to the sword here. And one learns to be a servant. The soul is disciplined. So much for me. But the good it would do in your case is that it would discipline your liver. The first need of man is health. And I wish it you for your happiness, though somehow I seem to know you more closely when you are fighting a well-fought battle with ill-health.

Adieu! or (chances three to one in favour of the pleasanter alternative) auf wiedersehen! Pray that I ride my frisky nerves with a cool and steady hand when the time arrives. And you don't know how much I long for our next meeting—more even than for the aforementioned meal!

To Professor Sorley

5 *October* 1915

Many thanks for the letters which arrived with the rations this morning. We are now embarked on a very different kind of life; whether one considers it preferable or otherwise to the previous, depending on one's mood. It is going to be a very slow business, but I hope a steady one. There is absolutely no doubt that the Bosch is now on his way home, though it is a long way and he will have many halts by the wayside. That "the war may end any year now" is the latest joke, which sums up the situation....

You will have seen that we have suffered by the loss of our chief: also that our battalion has lost its finest officer—otherwise commissioned ranks have been extraordinarily lucky. For the present, rain and dirt and damp cold. O for a bath! Much love to all.

INDEX

For EU product safety concerns, contact us at Calle de José Abascal, 56–1°,
28003 Madrid, Spain or eugpsr@cambridge.org.

www.ingramcontent.com/pod-product-compliance
Ingram Content Group UK Ltd.
Pitfield, Milton Keynes, MK11 3LW, UK
UKHW042148130625
459647UK00011B/1242

* 9 7 8 1 1 0 7 5 4 4 6 4 2 *